WHEN THE CLYDE RAN RED

Also by Maggie Craig

WHEN THE CLYDE RAN RED

MAGGIE CRAIG

MAINSTREAM
PUBLISHING

EDINBURGH AND LONDON

First published in Great Britain in 2011 by
MAINSTREAM PUBLISHING COMPANY
(EDINBURGH) LTD
7 Albany Street
Edinburgh EH1 3UG

ISBN 9781845967352

A catalogue record for this book is available
from the British Library

Printed and bound by
CPI Group (UK) Ltd, Croydon, CR0 4YY

1 3 5 7 9 10 8 6 4 2

For my father,
Alexander Dewar Craig,
who first sang me the songs,
and first told me the tales of Red Clydeside;

and for the other exceptional human being who is
his beautiful granddaughter & our brilliant daughter.

Acknowledgements

I should like to express my sincere thanks to the following people and institutions for the help they gave me with my research and in supplying illustrations for this book: Audrey Canning, librarian, Gallacher Memorial Library, Glasgow Caledonian University, with special thanks for pointing me in the direction of Helen Crawfurd and Margaret Irwin; Carole McCallum, archivist, Glasgow Caledonian University; all those who contributed to Glasgow Caledonian University's Red Clydeside website; the late Mr James Wotherspoon of Clydebank, still sharp as a tack at the age of 105; Pat Malcolm and her colleagues at Local Studies, Clydebank Library; the librarians and all other staff at the Mitchell Library, Glasgow, with particular thanks to Nerys Tunnicliffe, Patricia Grant, and Martin O'Neill; Claire McKendrick, Special Collections, University of Glasgow Library; the Willow Tea Rooms, Sauchiehall Street, Glasgow; James Higgins and Christine Miller of Bishopbriggs Library; Marie Henderson of Glasgow Digital Library at the University of Strathclyde; Shona Gonnella and Anne Wade at the Scottish Screen Archive, National Library of Scotland; Kevin Turner of the *Herald* and *Evening Times* Photo Library; the Marx Memorial Library for permission to quote from Helen Crawfurd's unpublished memoirs; and, for permission to quote from his poem on the launch of the *Queen Mary*, The Society of Authors as the Literary Representative of the Estate of John Masefield.

I should also like to express my appreciation to all the Bankies, some of whom have now passed on, who have shared with me over the years their memories of the Clydebank Blitz. They have included my parents, Margaret Hamilton, Grace Peace, Grace Howie, Joen McFarlane, Jean

Morrison, Andrew Hamilton and Maisie Nicoll née Swan, with special thanks to Maisie for the pianos. Thanks are due also to Kate McLelland for another great cover, and to everyone at Mainstream, most particularly Ailsa Bathgate, and Eliza Wright.

I'd also like to thank the wonderful Will, Tamise, Alexander and Ria for all their love and support, with special thanks to Ria for coming up with *le mot juste* in the nick of time.

Contents

Preface

This book is about Red Clydeside, those heady decades at the beginning of the twentieth century when passionate people and passionate politics swept like a whirlwind through Glasgow, Clydebank and the west of Scotland. It's also about the world in which those people lived. My aim has been to paint a vivid picture, telling the story by setting them and their politics within the wider context of the place and the times.

These were years of great wealth and appalling poverty, when Glasgow was home to some of Europe's most magnificent public buildings and some of its worst slums. This Glasgow welcomed the world to spectacular open-air exhibitions, chatted with its friends in elegant art nouveau tea rooms, fell in love with the movies in glittering art deco picture palaces and tangoed and foxtrotted the night away in the *palais de danse* which dotted the city.

This Glasgow also lost a thousand young adults each year to tuberculosis. Overcrowded and insanitary tenements where a bed to yourself was an unheard-of luxury provided the perfect breeding ground for the Captain of all the Men of Death. Other spectres stalked the poor. Thousands of Glasgow's children were born to die. Thousands of women had a child each year until it killed them, dying worn out before they were even 40 years old.

Outside the home, men and women worked exhaustingly long hours for low pay in filthy conditions where health and safety had never even been thought of. Horrific workplace accidents were commonplace. Find yourself incapacitated by such an injury and the most you could hope for to help pay the rent and feed your family was a whip-round organized by your workmates. There was no National Insurance, Social Security or National Health Service. Other than the absolute last resort and shame of going on the parish, only the kindness of others caught you when you fell. Small wonder that one Red Clydesider described this Glasgow as 'Earth's nearest suburb to hell'.

Yet poverty, an unequal struggle and lack of opportunity do not always breed despair. Sometimes they breed a special kind of man or woman, one who uses his or her anger and apparent powerlessness to fuel a fight for justice and fair treatment for everyone. The Red Clydesiders belonged to this special breed. So did my father.

Growing up in Old Monkland at Coatbridge during the Depression of the 1930s, he and his family knew real hardship. Yet they knew how to laugh too, as they knew how to tell stories. A railwayman who worked his way up from shunter to stationmaster, my father travelled all over Scotland in his work, and he knew the story behind every stone. A Buchan quine who loved both her native Aberdeenshire and her adopted Glasgow, my mother too had her stories to tell, as did our battalion of aunts and uncles.

Growing up where I did, my earliest memories are of Clydebank and the Clyde and all the stories that went with them. My father, active in Labour politics and a lifelong member of the National Union of Railwaymen, had many tales to tell about the Red Clydesiders. Rebels, reformers and revolutionaries, these radicals, socialists and communists were larger-than-life characters, yet approachable to all. Far beyond their own family and social circles, they were known by the affectionate diminutives of their first names. It was always Jimmy Maxton, Davie Kirkwood, Wee Willie Gallacher, Tom Johnston, Manny Shinwell.

It was during the turbulent years before, during and immediately after the First World War that the sobriquet of Red Clydeside was earned. That history extended to include the General Strike of 1926, the Hungry '30s, the Spanish Civil War of the late 1930s and the Clydebank Blitz of 1941. The great Clydebuilt ships belonged in there too.

Meeting a debt of honour to my family and forebears, I wrote six novels set in Glasgow and Clydebank during the years when the Clyde ran red. This is the history that goes with them.

Enter, stage left, the Red Clydesiders.

1

Rebels, Reformers & Revolutionaries

Distorted and destroyed by poverty.

James Maxton was one of the great personalities of Red Clydeside. Jimmy or Jim to his friends and family, he was a man of enormous warmth, compassion and charisma. An inspiring public speaker, he could hold huge audiences in the palm of his hand, moving them to tears one moment and making them laugh out loud the next. His sense of humour was legendary, sometimes sardonic and cynical but never cruel. Born in 1885, Maxton served for more than 20 years as a Labour MP at Westminster, where he also shone as an orator. Loved by his friends and respected by his political foes, he was described by Sir Winston Churchill as the greatest gentleman in the House of Commons. Former prime minister Gordon Brown wrote an engaging biography of him, entitled simply *Maxton*.

Maxton was born into a family which, while not wealthy, was quite comfortably off. Both his parents were teachers. His mother had to give up her career when she married, as female teachers of that time were obliged to do. Young Jimmy grew up as one of five children in a pleasant villa on a sunny ridge overlooking Barrhead near Paisley, at the back of the Gleniffer Braes. He is remembered there today in the names of surrounding streets and the Maxton Memorial Garden.

Tragedy struck the Maxtons when Jimmy was 17 years old. After a swim during a family holiday at Millport on the Isle of Cumbrae in the Firth of Clyde his father had a heart attack and died. Left in straitened circumstances though she was, Melvina Maxton was determined her two sons and three daughters were going to be educated as far as their brains would take them. Her determination paid off: all five became teachers.

His tongue firmly in his cheek, James Maxton was later to observe that his mother should really have sent him and his older siblings out to work. With typically cheerful sarcasm, he recalled that the family lived during those years after his father's death in 'the poverty that is sometimes called genteel'. It was a real struggle, although it helped that Maxton had at the age of 12 won a scholarship to the highly regarded Hutchesons' Grammar School, known more informally as 'Hutchie'. He did well, though he wore his learning and intelligence lightly, awarding himself some ironic distinctions: honours in tomfoolery, first-class honours for cheek, failure in intellectuality and honours advanced in winching. Unlike 'wench', this word could be applied to both sexes, allowing grinning west of Scotland uncles to thoroughly embarrass both teenage nieces and nephews by asking, 'Are ye winchin' yet?'

Although nobody would have called James Maxton handsome, his dark and saturnine looks were undeniably striking. He was a tall man, and his long, lantern-jawed face was framed by straight black hair which he wore much longer than was then fashionable or even acceptable. Curling onto his collar, it gave him a rather theatrical air. You could easily have taken him for an actor.

When Maxton first went to Glasgow University his long hair was as far as any youthful rebellion went. He met Tom Johnston there. Later a highly respected secretary of state for Scotland and prime mover behind the creation of the hydroelectric dams and power stations of the Highlands, Johnston was a young political firebrand from Kirkintilloch who took great delight in scaring the lieges through the pages of the *Forward*, the weekly socialist newspaper he founded in 1906. When he first got to know James Maxton, Tom Johnston described him as a 'harum scarum' who just wanted to get his MA so he could make his living as a teacher. Maxton himself said the only activities in which he excelled at university were swimming, fencing and PE. He was a good runner too.

As his contemporary at Glasgow University, Johnston's first memory of Maxton was indeed a theatrical one. Johnston had fun telling the story in his *Memories*. A group of students had gone together to the Pavilion Theatre, where the evening grew lively with 'the throwing of light missiles to and fro among the unruly audience' – young gentlemen and scholars indulging in some youthful high jinks. Ejecting the well-educated hooligans failed to dampen their enthusiasm. Maxton and his co-conspirators managed to get back in through the stage door and find their way onto the stage, where they 'appeared from one of the wings, dancing with arms akimbo to the footlights'.

It wasn't long before the light-hearted young Mr Maxton began to think seriously about politics. Tom Johnston was an influence. So was John Maclean, the tragic icon of Scottish socialism. When Maxton was at Glasgow University in the early 1900s Maclean was four years older than him and had already got his MA degree. They often met by chance on the train travelling into Glasgow from Pollokshaws, where they both then lived. A teacher by vocation as well as training, Maclean used these railway journeys to tell Maxton about Karl Marx.

Glasgow taught Maxton about life, especially when he began working as a teacher and saw the effects of poverty on his young pupils and their families. Years later, he spoke about how his experiences had influenced his thinking. The title of his 1935 BBC Radio broadcast was *Our Children's Scotland*:

> As a very young teacher, I discovered how individualism and their individualities were cramped, distorted and destroyed by poverty conditions before the child was able to react to its environment. That was the deciding factor in bringing me into the socialist and Labour movement.

Maxton was 19 when, in 1904, he made the decision to join the Independent Labour Party (ILP). Founded by Keir Hardie and others who saw that the Liberal Party was not going to solve the problems of the poor, the ILP was particularly strong in Glasgow and the west of Scotland, one of the engines which powered Red Clydeside. Although later a component part of what is now the modern Labour Party, it was always a more radical group. As one of the ILP's most influential members, James Maxton devoted the rest of his life to politics, becoming part of the band of Labour MPs who swept to power in the pivotal general election of 1922. Tom Johnston was also in that group.

Only once did a heckler get the better of James Maxton, as Tom Johnston recalled. Not long after he graduated from Glasgow University, Maxton returned to address a meeting at the Students' Union:

> That meeting remains in my memory for an interruption which, for once, left Maxton speechless and retortless. Maxton by that time had grown his long tradition-like actors' hair, and during his speeches he would continually and with dramatic effect weave a lock away from his brow. At this Students' Union gathering he was set agoing at his

most impressive oratory . . . '*Three* millions unemployed (pause).
Three millions *unemployed* (pause). Three *millions* unemployed
(pause).' Amid the tense silence came a voice from the back: 'Aye,
Jimmy, and every second yin a barber!'

James Maxton's friend John Maclean comes across as a more sombre
character. He was only eight when his father died, the catastrophe
plunging his widow and their four surviving children into a poverty which
was not at all genteel. Like Melvina Maxton, however, Anne Maclean was
a woman determined that her children should be educated.

Both John Maclean and James Maxton lost their jobs as schoolteachers
because of their political activities. Controversially, they spoke out against
the First World War and conscription. This led to even more serious
consequences: trial, conviction and imprisonment on charges of sedition
and spreading disaffection. Maclean remained a teacher but outside the
system, devoting himself to public speaking, writing articles, running the
Scottish Labour College, which he founded, and imparting the theory of
Marxist economics in night and weekend classes. He advocated revolution
rather than reform, his self-appointed mission to convince the working
classes the only solution to their ills was socialism, the only way to get
that by seizing power. The ruling classes were never going to give it
away.

Tom Johnston was a rebel rather than a revolutionary. Passionate,
romantic and idealistic, he too could be cheerfully sarcastic, as when he
described the decisions taken at the start-up of the *Forward*: 'We would
have no alcoholic advertisements: no gambling news, and my own
stipulation after a month's experience, no amateur poetry; every second
reader at that time appearing to be bursting into *vers libre*.'

Johnston's sarcasm grew savage when he researched and wrote *The
History of the Working Classes in Scotland* and *Our Scots Noble Families*.
Often referred to more simply as *Our Noble Families*, this was published
in 1909, when Johnston was 28 years old. One of his targets was the
Sutherland family, notorious for the role they played in the Highland
Clearances. He fired his first shot at one of their forebears:

> I began to be interested in this Hugo. He floats about in the dawn of
> the land history of Scotland, murdering, massacring, laying waste
> and settling the conquered lands on his offspring.
>
> Rooted in theft (for as every legal authority admits, the clan, or

children of the soil, were the only proprietors), casting every canon of morality to the winds, this family has waxed fat on misery, and, finally, less than 100 years ago, perpetrated such abominable cruelties on the tenantry as aroused the disgust and anger of the whole civilised world.

Forward soon attracted an impressive array of writers. H.G. Wells allowed the paper to carry one of his novels as a serial. Ramsay MacDonald wrote for it, as did suffragette leader Mrs Pankhurst. James Connolly was also a contributor. Born in Edinburgh of Irish parents, Connolly was a revolutionary socialist and Irish nationalist, shot by firing squad after the 1916 Easter Rising in Dublin. The socialist newspaper also benefited from the skill of artist Robins Millar, who drew many cartoons for it. A man of many talents, Millar went on to become a playwright and the doyen of Glasgow's theatre critics.

Trying to cover all bases, the young editor was sincere in his views but very astute. One of the contributors he commissioned to write articles for the *Forward* was John Wheatley, a committed socialist and devout Catholic. Wheatley attracted readers with the same deep religious faith as himself, helping many of them realize it was possible to be both a Catholic and a socialist. That took some doing. When Wheatley first declared himself to be a socialist his local priest and some members of the congregation were so horrified that they made an effigy of him and burned it at his front gate. Wheatley opened the door of his house, stood there with his wife and smiled at them. The next Sunday morning, he went to Mass, as he usually did, and the fuss soon died down.

The eldest of ten children, John Wheatley was born in County Waterford, in Ireland, in 1869. Taking the path of many with Irish roots who feature in the story of Red Clydeside, his family came to Scotland when John was eight or nine years old. The Wheatleys settled in Bargeddie, then known as Braehead, at Coatbridge. At 14, John followed in his father's footsteps and started working as a coalminer in a pit in Baillieston.

Wheatley was a miner for well over 20 years, during which time he educated himself and became involved in politics, another path many Red Clydesiders followed. In his late 30s Wheatley set up a printing firm and joined the ILP. Two years later he was elected a county councillor. He was in his early 50s when he too became one of the 1922 intake of Labour MPs, sitting for Shettleston.

Wheatley was much respected by his younger colleagues, especially James Maxton, who admired his intellect and organizational abilities. Ramsay MacDonald, Britain's first Labour prime minister, saw Wheatley's abilities too, appointing him minister for health in the first Labour government of 1924.

Another writer in the *Forward* stable was a coalminer from Baillieston who, under a pseudonym, specialized in laying into the coal owners and the vast profits they made at the expense of the miners who worked for them. Patrick Joseph Dollan later became lord provost of Glasgow.

The Red Clydesiders were always passionate about children, education, health and housing. Look at the Glasgow of the early 1900s and it's not hard to see why.

Yet this was a city which presented many different faces to the world.

2

The Tokio of Tea Rooms

Very Kate Cranstonish.

In the early years of the twentieth century, Glasgow was the Second City of the Empire and the Workshop of the World. Scotland's largest city and its surrounding towns of Clydebank, Motherwell, Paisley and Greenock blazed with foundries and factories, locomotive works, shipyards, steel mills, textile mills, rope works and sugar refineries. This was the time when the North British Locomotive Works at Springburn produced railway engines which were exported to every continent on Earth and shipbuilding on the Clyde was at its peak. The proud boast was that more than half the world's merchant fleet was Clydebuilt.

In 1907 John Brown's at Clydebank launched the *Lusitania*, a Cunard liner destined for the North Atlantic run. The *Aquitania* was to follow in 1914. Before the Second World War came two of the most famous ocean liners of all, the *Queen Mary* and the *Queen Elizabeth*. The names of these Cunarders are redolent with the elegance of a bygone age.

Glasgow was elegant too. Talented architects such as Alexander 'Greek' Thomson and John Thomas Rochead, who also designed the Wallace Monument at Stirling, had fashioned a cityscape of infinite variety. The Mossmans, a family of sculptors, had adorned a huge number of Glasgow's buildings with beautiful life-size stone figures often inspired by the mythology of Ancient Greece and Rome. These included the caryatids which decorate what is now the entrance to the Mitchell Theatre and Library in Granville Street, formerly the entrance to St Andrew's Halls. When the Halls burned down in 1962 only the façade was saved. So many of the dramas of Red Clydeside were played out here, in what is now the Mitchell Library's café and computer hall.

In 1909 Charles Rennie Mackintosh finished the second phase of the project which gave the city and the world the Glasgow School of Art in Renfrew Street. Five years before that he and his wife and artistic partner, Margaret Macdonald Mackintosh, had created the Willow Tea Rooms in Sauchiehall Street for Mackintosh's patron, highly successful Glasgow businesswoman Miss Kate Cranston.

Along in the West End stood the extravagant red sandstone of the new Kelvingrove Art Gallery and Museum. Completed in 1901, it has been known and loved by generations of Glaswegians ever since simply as 'the Art Galleries', even if the young man about town who wrote it up in a guidebook called *Glasgow in 1901* had fun describing it as 'architecture looking worried in a hundred different ways'. In 1911 the builders were once again busy at Kelvingrove. Glasgow was looking forward to the third great exhibition to be held there: the Scottish Exhibition of National History, Art and Industry was scheduled to open at the beginning of May.

The gorgeously Italianate City Chambers dominated George Square, a physical manifestation of Glasgow's good conceit of itself. In his studio on the corner of North Frederick Street and Cathedral Street John Mossman created some of the figures which decorate it. On the other side of the square rose the dignified and rather more subtly ornamented Merchants' House. Designed by John Burnet senior, it had additions by his son and namesake. John Burnet junior crowned the highest point of the building with a model of the globe, on top of which a sailing ship still rides the waves.

The *Bonny Nancy* belonged to Mr Glassford, one of Glasgow's powerful eighteenth-century tobacco lords. She's a reminder that the city's fortunes were founded on trade and the enterprise of her traders. Those convivial gentlemen used to raise their glasses of Glasgow Punch – take about a dozen lemons, add sugar, Jamaica rum, ice-cold spring water and the juice of a few cut limes – in a confident and cheerful toast: 'The trade of Glasgow and the outward bound!'

Work had to be done on Glasgow's route to the sea before that trade could develop. People had first settled by the Clyde because the shallow river gave them fresh water and abundant fish and was easy to ford. As ships grew larger, the lack of depth became a problem. Goods had to be brought overland from Port Glasgow, causing delays and extra expense. Early civil engineering works such as the Lang Dyke, off Langbank, forced the Clyde into a narrower channel. Routine dredging also began, rendering the river navigable all the way up from Port Glasgow and the Tail of the Bank to the heart of Glasgow.

The 'cleanest and beautifullest and best built city in Britain, London excepted,' which Daniel Defoe had so admired in the eighteenth century could now grow into one of the world's busiest ports. The deepened river also made shipbuilding possible. The Clyde made Glasgow and Glasgow made the Clyde.

The Anchor Line was one of many shipping companies operating out of Glasgow in the early 1900s. Its impressive headquarters in St Vincent Place just west of George Square was faced with white tiles from which the grime of an industrial city could more easily be cleaned. And Glasgow was dirty. Soot-blackened. Buildings of honey-coloured sandstone took only a few years to become as black as the Earl of Hell's waistcoat. Anyone who lived in Glasgow or Clydebank before the Clean Air Act of the early 1960s will remember the choking yellow fogs of winter. They owed as much to what was streaming out of factory chimneys as they did to the damp climate of the west of Scotland.

There were few controls on pollution in the early 1900s. Factories, foundries and shipyards were risky places. The people who worked in them took their chances, no other choice being available. In this city of nearly a million and a half souls life for the majority was about economic survival. Over the course of the nineteenth century people in search of work and – just maybe, if the fates allowed – a better life for themselves and their families flooded into Glasgow. Most came from the Highlands and from Ireland, some from further afield. Traditionally a first settling point for new immigrants, the Gorbals became a predominantly Jewish area, many of those Jews fleeing persecution in Poland and Russia.

Meanwhile, as electric trams took over from horse-drawn ones and local rail links improved, comfortably off Glaswegians decamped to developing suburbs like Bearsden and Pollokshields. What they sought and found there were lawned gardens, woods, open spaces and plenty of fresh air. In suburbs north and south of the Clyde laid out with wide avenues and parks filled with trees, boating ponds, tennis courts and putting greens, families enjoyed life. The lucky few lived in spacious, high-ceilinged villas designed by some of those great Glasgow architects, others in solid tenement flats of warm red and honey sandstone. Out in the suburbs the stone had more chance of retaining its light colour.

Tradesmen who had worked their way up also moved out, taking their families to new houses built on old farmland which aimed to achieve a village-by-the-city feel. The dream of living in a country cottage where your children could play in a flower-filled garden with vegetables growing outside the kitchen door is an old and powerful one. It was shared by the socialists of Red Clydeside.

John Wheatley came up with the idea of the £8 cottage, so called because that was what the yearly rent would be. A drawing by Robins Millar in the *Forward* in 1911 shows Father coming home from his work to be greeted by his young son and daughter running eagerly towards him. His wife stands behind the low fence which surrounds the neat, well-tended garden behind them, the baby in her arms. The first development in this style in Scotland was started before the First World War and finished after it by a housing co-operative of working-class families chaired by Sir John Stirling-Maxwell of Pollok. Lying between the modern-day Switchback Road and the Forth and Clyde Canal, the original name, Westerton Garden Suburb, makes the aspiration clear. It's now simply Westerton, but its residents continue to refer to it as 'the Village'.

Westerton had a railway station, a school, a village hall, a post office and shops. With its grocery and drapery, Westerton Garden Suburb Co-operative Society was an offshoot of the larger Clydebank Co-op. If you wanted the bright lights of the city, they were on your doorstep, a short journey away by train, tram or bus. Step off onto Sauchiehall Street or Buchanan Street and you would find wonderfully opulent shops like Treron's, Daly's, Copland & Lye's, Wylie & Lochhead's, Pettigrew & Stephens' and the jewellers of the Argyll Arcade, each offering all manner of delights: glittering gems, bracelets and necklaces, perfume, lace wraps and handkerchiefs, kid gloves, fox furs and the latest fashions from Paris.

The wives and daughters of Glasgow's industrialists, shipowners and businessmen could wander freely through this enchanted forest of gleaming wood and shining glass counters. Department stores were a transatlantic import which proved wildly popular in Glasgow. After the shopping was done, it would be up in the ornate brass lift to the restaurant to sip coffee while a pianist played discreetly in the background. Or you could go to one of the city's fashionable tea rooms. Glasgow made two indispensable contributions to the popularity of the cup that cheers: Sir Thomas Lipton, the man whose name is still synonymous with tea around the world, was born in the Gorbals; Glasgow also invented the tea room.

It was not the famous Miss Cranston who originally came up with the idea but her brother Stuart. A tea merchant who was an evangelist for the quality of his goods, he offered his customers a tasting before they made a purchase. In 1875 he moved to new premises on the corner of Argyle Street and Queen Street, put out a few tables and chairs, offered some fancy baking to go with the tea and started a trend.

Tea rooms were tailor-made for Glasgow's ladies of leisure. Their husbands and sons could go into pubs and chop-houses. In 1875 the department store hadn't quite arrived and there were few places where respectable women could go unchaperoned. Tea rooms allowed them to meet up with their friends for a chat in safe and pleasant surroundings.

Kate Cranston raised the tea room to an art form. She owned and managed four in Glasgow, in Ingram Street, Argyle Street, Buchanan Street and, most famously of all, the Willow Tea Rooms in Sauchiehall Street. In her patronage of Charles Rennie Mackintosh, his artist wife Margaret Macdonald Mackintosh and their equally talented friends, Miss Cranston gave what became known as the Glasgow Style a stage on which it could flourish and grow. She was very much identified with this achingly fashionable and very modern look. Soon everything influenced by it, be that furniture, home decor or the crockery with which you set your table, was described not only as 'artistic' but also as 'very Kate Cranstonish'.

Oddly enough, although she was happy to give young designers such as Mackintosh and George Walton carte blanche to be as modern as they liked, Miss Cranston never updated her own personal style. Born in 1849, she wore the long, full skirts and extravagant flounces of the Victorian era until she died in 1933. Her only bizarre variation was to sport a cloak and sombrero.

Once the Cranstons had thought up the idea, tea rooms sprouted all over Glasgow and beyond. By 1921 the well-known City Bakeries had dozens of branches and was running a profit-sharing scheme with its bakers and waitresses. The 1930s saw the establishment of Wendy's Tea Rooms. They offered the homely atmosphere of the country in the bustle and smoke of the big city: back to the rural idyll.

Reid's in Gordon Street gave men the chance to meet their friends over coffee and a cigarette, in separate smoking rooms, of course. Miss Cranston also provided those to her gentlemen customers at the Willow Tea Rooms, along with billiard rooms. These male preserves occupied the second floor. The Room de Luxe, with its high-backed silver-painted chairs designed by Charles Rennie Mackintosh, was on the first.

In 1915 John Anderson's Royal Polytechnic in Argyle Street, advertising itself, as it was always known to Glaswegians, as 'the Poly', offered 'A Restful Den for Business Men' in its Byzantine Hall. The delights of 'Glasgow's Grandest Smoke Room' encompassed 'fragrant coffees, delicious teas, telephones, magazines and all the leading newspapers'.

In 1916 Stuart Cranston opened a new tea room in Renfield Street which included a cinema. This tea room became a popular gathering place for members of the ILP. During the First World War Renfield Street itself became a focus for regular Sunday-afternoon open-air meetings opposing the war.

Tea rooms appealed to men as well as women, particularly those who supported the temperance movement. This included the majority of the socialists of Red Clydeside, who had too often seen the damage alcohol could do. Willie Gallacher, a key figure in the story of Red Clydeside, grew up in poverty in Paisley in the 1880s and '90s, the son of an Irish father and a Highland mother. He was only 14 when he joined the temperance movement, having very personal reasons to hate alcohol. Gallacher's father was a good husband and an affectionate parent but his dependence on drink blighted family life. As Gallacher later said:

> I was still very young when my father died, but my eldest brother was already a young man. He was my mother's favourite child. She was fond of all of us, but how she adored the oldest boy! When he developed a weakness for alcohol it almost drove her crazy. Her suffering was so acute that I used to clench my boyish fists in rage every time I passed by a pub.

Many men, particularly young ones living what could be a lonely life between work in a Glasgow office and lodgings, went to tea rooms to enjoy the company of the waitresses. The book which poked fun at the architecture of the Art Galleries waxed lyrical on the subject. *Glasgow in 1901* was written by three young men as a kind of guidebook advising visitors who would be in the city for the exhibition of that year on local ways of going about things.

Describing Glasgow as 'a very Tokio for tea rooms', Archibald Charteris found it a great delight that tea room waitresses were Glasgow girls who spoke with a warm Glasgow accent, 'the most accessible well of local English'. Describing what could happen after a young woman started working at a particular tea room, he was at pains to point out that she and her colleagues were highly respectable young ladies:

Once installed, she may discover that a covey of young gentlemen wait daily for her ministrations, and will even have the loyalty to follow her should she change her employer. This is the only point in which she resembles a barmaid, from whom in all others she must be carefully distinguished.

To other people she has a more human interest, and to a young man coming without friends and introductions from the country, she may be a little tender. For it is not impossible that, his landlady apart, she is the only petticoated being with whom he can converse without shame. So the smile which greets him (even if it is readily given to any other) is sweet to the lonely soul, and a friendly word from her seems a message from the blessed damosel.

Kate Cranston did not escape the censure of the Red Clydesiders. An article published in the *Forward* on Saturday, 15 July 1911 was headed 'How Miss Cranston Treats Her Workers', with a subtitle of 'The Limit of Tea Room Generosity'. The piece was based on a set of typewritten 'Rules for Girls', so presumably one of those girls had made a copy of the rules and smuggled it out. Did Miss Cranston investigate afterwards to try to establish who the culprit was?

Hours were long. Six days a week, Miss Cranston's waitresses worked from seven in the morning till eight at night. On Saturdays, they worked until five o'clock, except at the Willow Tea Rooms, which stayed open until eight o'clock on Saturdays too. Hours for girls under 18 were 'not to exceed 74 per week'. Unless you were working the extra hours required at the Willow, you were working 74 hours a week anyway. Maybe the breaks weren't counted, although these were not very generous. The *Forward* drew particular attention to the lunch break of ten minutes, during which each girl was provided with a cup of cocoa or a glass of hot milk and a biscuit.

In 1920 discontent among the waitresses who worked in Kerr's Cafés boiled over into a strike. Their boss was William Kerr, who advertised himself as 'the military caterer'. If his management style followed military lines that may well have been part of the problem. A leaflet was printed to alert the people of Glasgow to the conditions under which the waitresses in his cafés worked:

Sweated Workers in Glasgow

STRIKE OF WAITRESSES AT KERR'S CAFES

Citizens of Glasgow, your attention
is drawn to the conditions which prevail
at above establishments:
<u>12/- per week for 12 hours per day</u>

1/- deducted if girl breaks a plate
9d deducted if girl breaks a cup
6d deducted if girl breaks a saucer
2/- deducted if girl breaks a wineglass
3d deducted for being late in morning

The Girls decided to join the Union, with the result that the Shop
Steward was dismissed, which is quite evidently an attempt to
undermine the Girls' Union.

**Previous to joining the Union, the minimum wage of
restaurant workers was 10/- per week, and they had to
purchase uniform from the firm.**

**We are asking the public to
SUPPORT THE GIRLS**

Some of Kerr's Cafés stayed open till quarter to eleven at night for late
suppers, so presumably being late for work the following morning was a
not uncommon occurrence. The strike lasted less than a month, and
during it most of the waitresses at Kerr's voted with their feet and went
looking for work elsewhere.

Harry McShane, Red Clydesider and Marxist, described the wages
earned by the waitresses at Kerr's as pitiful. Yet away from the clinking
of china cups, cake stands piled high with scones, shortbread and
chocolate eclairs and the stylish decor of Miss Cranston's artistic tea
rooms, there were plenty of Glaswegians who would have leapt at the
chance to earn even those pitiful few shillings.

3

Earth's Nearest Suburb to Hell

A whole world of sacrifice and effort.

Helen Jack, who became better known under her married name of Helen Crawfurd, was born in 1877 in Glasgow's Gorbals, where her father was a master baker. In her unpublished memoirs she neatly summed up the character of her birthplace as a Jewish working-class district.

Her father William Jack had an open-minded attitude not always usual among Gentiles at that time towards his many Jewish neighbours, now and again attending services at his local synagogue. He also had a highly developed social conscience in respect of the poorer families among whom he and his more well-off family lived. He and his wife brought their children up to have a strong religious faith and this Christian family practised what it preached.

When times were especially hard in the Gorbals during a strike, William Jack set up a soup kitchen in his bakery for those struggling to feed themselves and their families. As Helen later remembered, even as a master and a man who voted Conservative, his sympathies were always with the workers. As committed as he was to helping their fellow men and women, Helen's mother and grandmother ran the soup kitchen. Identify the problem, work out what you can do about it and then do it: the example set was to form the pattern for Helen Crawfurd's life.

Mrs Jack, also Helen, helped foster that social conscience in her children by what she read to them. *Uncle Tom's Cabin* was a favourite. Her daughter remembered that she and her brothers and sisters would call to their mother not to start reading until they had fetched their hankies, because they knew they would not be able to hold back the tears when they heard 'this tragic story of negro suffering'.

Helen junior saw suffering in Glasgow too, and with fresh eyes when the Jack family returned to the city after some years living in gentler surroundings near Ipswich in England. By now 16 years old, the maturing young woman was horrified by the Glasgow of the 1890s:

> I was appalled by the dirt, poverty and ugliness I saw all around in Glasgow. I felt that other women along with myself must feel the same resentment and indignation. I watched the faces of the workers in tramcars and buses. They were worn with worry. I do not think any city had more people with bad teeth. In my young days orthopaedic surgery was in its infancy, and a great many people in Glasgow had bandy or bow legs and were undersized. The women carried their children in shawls, and the soft bones became bent. It has been stated that Glasgow's water supply then lacked certain lime essential for bone building. To-day it is unusual to see these deformed people, but in my youth they were very common. The housing conditions and the death rate of infants were appalling.

One statistic in particular struck her. Occupied by large families though they were, forty thousand of Glasgow's tenement flats consisted of only one room and a kitchen. She wrote with feeling of how, when a member of the family died, the living had to share that one room with the body of their loved one till the day of the funeral. That loved one would too often have been a baby. Infant mortality rates in late nineteenth-century Glasgow were indeed appalling, and the grim statistics were to grow even worse. In the years immediately following the First World War 40 per cent more babies died in infancy in Glasgow than in the rest of Britain as a whole. One in every seven children in the city did not reach his or her first birthday.

The difference within Glasgow was also appalling, as statistics from 1911 show. That 29 babies in every 1,000 in middle-class Kelvinside died in infancy might shock and sadden us, but down in the working-class Broomielaw the figure was even worse, standing at an horrific 234. In the Gorbals there were 145 infant deaths per 1,000 births, in Springburn 117.

The Red Clydesider who described Glasgow as 'Earth's nearest suburb to hell' was James Stewart, better known as Jimmy. Another of those Labour MPs who were to triumphantly enter Parliament in 1922, he knew what he was talking about. A hairdresser to trade, he kept the patients at Glasgow Royal Infirmary neat and tidy. Diphtheria, scarlet fever, pneumonia: all these diseases were rife. The great scourge was tuberculosis, also known as consumption or phthisis. TB claimed a thousand lives in Glasgow each year and its favoured victims were young adults. Spreading as it did where people lived on top of one another in overcrowded and unhygienic tenements, it was considered a disease of the poor and the feckless. There was shame attached to contracting TB.

The tenement is a distinctive form of architecture. It provided many Glaswegians with elegant, spacious and comfortable homes, others with less grand but no less substantial and respectable ones – and then there were the slums. As bare of comfort inside as they were rundown outside, many of these grimy grey tenements pressed hard against the city centre, well within walking distance of Glasgow's great public buildings or elegant shopping streets.

That so many well-off Glaswegians made their homes to the west of the city was no accident. That move had begun in Victorian times, when the university, always known as the Old College, left its mediaeval home in the High Street in 1870. This took the students away from the beating heart of the old city but also from dingy closes packed tightly with slums which were breeding grounds for crime, violence and disease.

The Victorian city fathers commissioned photographer Thomas Annan to record the slums of old Glasgow for posterity, the wynds and vennels crammed in behind the High Street and around the Briggait, south of Glasgow Cross. Staring back at the photographer, barefoot children and women in shawls stand under washing dangling from high poles sticking out across the narrow closes and alleyways of these shadowy spaces.

Up on Gilmorehill in the West End the students were now able to breathe clean air. Like the well-off Glaswegians who were lucky enough to live in the gracious Edwardian townhouses of Park Circus, they could trust the prevailing westerly winds of the British Isles to blow any pollution or nasty smells back across to the East End. Over there the cholera and typhus which attacked Glaswegians in their thousands during the epidemics of the nineteenth century might have been swept away with the old slums. Plenty of diseases were left to incubate in the new slums which rose to take their place. Those who did not have to endure such awful living conditions could still manage to turn a blind eye to them.

There were others who found them impossible to ignore, people like James Maxton and Helen Crawfurd. Driven by the same passionate social conscience, another was Margaret Irwin. Among the many achievements of her long life, she was the driving force behind the establishment of the Scottish Trades Union Congress in 1897, a body which has always been completely independent of its English counterpart. Never a member of a trade union herself, Margaret Irwin was the STUC's secretary for the first three years of its existence. Women might not yet have had the vote but that didn't mean they couldn't play an active role in public life.

The daughter of a ship's captain, Margaret Hardinge Irwin was born in 1858 'somewhere in the China Seas' on board a ship called the *Lord Hardinge*, After this romantic start to her life, she grew up in Broughty Ferry, near Dundee. Her father valued education and encouraged and supported his only child while she attended St Andrew's University, from which she graduated in 1880 with a degree in German, French and English Literature.

In her early 30s Margaret Irwin moved to Glasgow, where she took classes at Glasgow School of Art and, in political economy, at Queen Margaret College, newly established for female students within Glasgow University. From then on she dedicated her life to investigating and improving living and working conditions for poor women and their families. She became a recognized and respected authority on the subject. Coming as she did from Broughty Ferry, next door to Dundee and its jute mills where an army of women toiled to 'keep the bairns o' Dundee fed', this may be where her interest in the difficulties facing the working classes started.

For 44 years she was secretary of the Scottish Council for Women's Trades. As an assistant commissioner to the Royal Commission on Labour she compiled many reports on working conditions in laundries, shops, sweatshops and among homeworkers. These housewives struggling to make ends meet had even less protection from unscrupulous employers than women in factories, and earned ludicrously low wages.

Audrey Canning, librarian of the Gallacher Memorial Library at Glasgow Caledonian University, describes Margaret Irwin as being like a modern-day investigative journalist, 'toiling alone up dilapidated tenement stairs to discover the slum housing conditions of women working for a pittance'. Her investigations and reports paint a vivid picture of just how bad those conditions could be.

Shortly before Christmas 1901 she gave a paper on *The Problem of Home Work* at a Saturday conference in Paisley organized by the Renfrewshire Co-operative Association:

Frequently one finds the home worker occupying an attic room at the top of a five-storeyed building, the ascent to which is by a dismal and dilapidated staircase, infested by rats or haunted by that most pitiable of four-footed creatures, the slum cat. The landings are foul with all manner of stale débris; and the atmosphere is merely a congestion of evil odours. At every storey narrow, grimy passages stretch to right and left, on either side, close packed, is a row of 'ticketed houses' . . .

On every landing there is a water tap and sink, both the common property of the tenants, and the latter usually emitting frightful effluvia. Probably the sink represents the entire sanitary system of the landing.

Armed with a box of matches and a taper and battling with the almost solid smells of the place, one finally reaches the top, and on being admitted, finds, perhaps, a room almost destitute of furniture, the work lying in piles on the dirty floor or doing duty as bed clothes for a bed-ridden invalid and the members of the family generally.

Glasgow started ticketing houses in the 1860s in the hope of reducing overcrowding in the city's slums. Every house of fewer than three rooms was measured and it was calculated that each occupant required three hundred cubic feet of living and sleeping space. A metal ticket was then fixed to the front door, stating how many people could legally occupy the house. This was enforced by midnight visits from the sanitary inspectors.

By the 1880s the city had over 23,000 ticketed homes. These housed three-quarters of Glasgow's population, probably rather more than that once the sanitary inspectors had finished their rounds for the night. People were so desperate for a place to lay their heads that the ticketing rules were often flouted. Their unlikely landlords and landladies were in their turn so desperate to make a few extra pence or shillings that they were prepared to squeeze in what Margaret Irwin called 'that unknown and highly elastic quantity, the lodger'. The number of ticketed houses in Glasgow just before the First World War was not much lower than in the 1880s, around 22,000.

While many Glaswegians have fond memories of the camaraderie and warmth of life in the old tenements, and of mothers who kept their homes as neat and clean as a new pin and their children well scrubbed and well turned-out, there is no doubt that thousands who lived in the Second City of the Empire did so in poverty and squalor. The record is there, in photographs and written accounts.

There were always those who managed to rise above their circumstances. After describing the flat 'almost destitute of furniture', Margaret Irwin wrote, 'However, side by side with the worst of these one finds a little room exquisitely neat and clean and representing a whole world of sacrifice and effort.' It must have been heartbreaking, hard to witness, but this woman who could have enjoyed a comfortable middle-class life had set herself a task, and she would not flinch from it. She was well aware that many of the haves saw no reason why they should worry about the have-nots: 'It is often said that one half of the world does not know how the other half lives. It might be said, perhaps with equal truth, that one half does not care to know.'

As Audrey Canning emphasizes, Margaret Irwin did care to know. Determined that everyone else should too, she was prepared to shout her findings from the rooftops. Her voice reached the legislators at Westminster, helping bring about reforms which made a difference to the lives of thousands. Speaking to the second reading of the Seats for Shop Assistants Bill in 1899 the Duke of Westminster quoted from a report Margaret Irwin had made on shop assistants in Glasgow:

> My attention has been directed by several medical men of standing and experience, and also by numerous grave complaints from the women assistants themselves, to two causes which, in addition to long hours and close confinement, operate against the health and comfort of women employed in shops. These are – want of seats, and the absence of, or defective, sanitary provisions.

In other words, they wanted a few seats where they could sit down for a rest now and again, plus a proper toilet. Margaret Irwin recorded a pathetic plea: 'As has been more than once said to me, "If they would only allow us a ledge to rest upon for a minute or two we would be thankful even for that."'

Nor was there any entitlement to meal breaks, shop assistants having to snatch a bite to eat if and when they could. Hours were long, work starting first thing in the morning and lasting until nine or even ten o'clock at night. On average, shop assistants in Glasgow and Scotland's other cities at the turn of the twentieth century worked between 80 and 90 hours in return for wages of 10 shillings per week. So the waitresses at Kerr's Cafés working in excess of 70 hours for 12 shillings per week some 20 years later really were in a pitiful situation, one which had seen no real improvement.

Margaret Irwin was scathing too about how much less women were paid compared with men, firing off a few salvos in what might be described as a hundred-years war:

> Now, it seems reasonable to expect that when there are large discrepancies in the wages of the worker, a corresponding difference would be found in the prices charged to the public for the goods made by the respective sexes. So far as I am aware, however, the difference stops short at the pay-books of the worker, and the vest and cigarette made by the women has the same value put upon it when it goes into the market as that made by the man. If, however, any gentleman present can inform me of a reduction made in his tailor's or tobacconist's bill because of the goods being supplied being the product of women's labour, I shall be glad to note the fact for future reference.

How the shop assistants of the 1890s managed without a toilet is probably best left to the imagination. That Victorian shopkeepers, with that era's outward prudery and respectability, had to be forced by law into supplying this most basic of facilities to their predominantly young female workforce is a telling illustration of their lack of humanity and lack of respect towards the people who made their profits for them. The working classes were there to be worked, and if that took them through humiliation to the brink of exhaustion then so be it.

Working conditions in the many commercial laundries of the period were particularly brutal, employees having to work through the night in stifling temperatures. Margaret Irwin visited one girl of eighteen whose health had broken down under the strain. She earned only six shillings for a working week of ninety hours. Small wonder that her mother described laundry work as 'murderous'.

It might seem ironic to us now that His Grace the Duke of Westminster spoke up for the shop assistants, describing their having to stand all day as 'long hours of enforced sentry duty which would provoke a mutiny if imposed upon soldiers of the Line'. However, there was disquiet at the time that what was also described as the torture of young girls was causing them, when they became mothers, to produce weak and sickly children. There was philanthropy and real concern here, even, across the yawning class divide, an element of chivalry. Essentially though, this was about the future of the race, an obsession of the time.

This brings us uncomfortably close to eugenics, which sought to direct evolution towards a supposed improvement in the human stock. Very much in vogue in the early twentieth century, enthusiasts for eugenics included Marie Stopes, pioneer of birth control, economist John Maynard Keynes, US president Theodore Roosevelt, and Mr Kellogg of cornflakes fame. Eugenics was to be completely discredited after the Nazis took the removal from the human gene pool of what they deemed the degenerate, unfit and racially inferior to the nightmare extreme of the gas chambers. Before that Rubicon was reached, the idea of some intervention to improve humanity was supported by many socialists. The birth control movement was closely bound up with it.

Despite the lack of toilets for shop assistants, an associated preoccupation of the age was hygiene, both moral and physical. In July 1904 Glasgow's Chief Sanitary Inspector, Peter Fyfe, delivered a paper at the Congress of the Sanitary Institute at Glasgow University entitled *What the People Sleep Upon*. His speech was also published by Glasgow Corporation's Committee on Health:

> It has been said that 'there are combinations of evil, against which no human energies can make a stand.' Combinations of evil, at all events in a sanitary sense, seem peculiarly attachable to a certain class of the people. It is this class I had in my mind when I put down the word 'people' in the title of the present paper. The major part of the people in this city are composed of those who nightly sleep in houses of one or two apartments. The most of them dwell in this limited space because they cannot afford to pay for more. Poverty compels them.

Peter Fyfe went on to list some of the medical complaints which dogged the people who lived in these cramped houses: enteric, dysentery, diarrhoea and other 'diseases the origin of which we cannot trace'. Despite giving the city 'an irreproachable water supply', the Victorian engineering marvel of running clean water from Loch Katrine to Glasgow did not seem to have helped. He believed that Glasgow had 'a reasonably perfect sewage system'. Maybe not quite so perfect if people suffering from diarrhoea and dysentery were sharing an outside toilet with every other family who lived up their close, and one tap and one sink with at least three other families on their landing.

Peter Fyfe's diagnosis of what was wrong was that 78 per cent of what he called the lower classes of Glasgow were sleeping on mattresses made out of old rags, 'the offcast of every class of the population, from the wealthy of the West-end to the tramp and vagrant of the East'. Some of these rags were filthy. None was cleaned or disinfected before being processed into the flock with which mattresses were stuffed. Fyfe got the Corporation chemist to carry out experiments on that, comparing it with samples taken from Glasgow's crude sewage. Full of dangerous bacteria, the mattresses were dirtier than the effluent, leading Fyfe to conclude, 'It would be manifestly safer to sleep on a bed filled with sewage than on this material.'

Observing all this, those who wanted to change the lives of the poor for the better took two different approaches. They might meet one another in the middle, working together on specific issues, but there was a profound difference between their respective philosophies. There was philanthropy, and there was politics.

Margaret Irwin spent her life working tirelessly to improve the lot of women workers. Some see her as being very much in the tradition of the middle-class philanthropist, helping the poor from the outside. In contrast, Helen Crawfurd believed in empowering the poor so that they could improve their lot for themselves. Shocked though she was by Glasgow's slum housing and poor health, it took Helen Crawfurd a long time to see socialism as the answer to these ills. Socialism was a radical and a dangerous doctrine. She described her attitude to it when she was younger as being something she would run away from in the street.

Her politics gradually grew more radical, and it was becoming a suffragette which started her on that journey. Clear in her own mind that it was women who held the home and the family together, she came to the unshakeable belief that if only women had the vote and could get themselves organized, they would do their utmost to improve these terrible living conditions.

As a young woman, Helen Crawfurd's religious faith was so strong it persuaded her to marry a man years older than herself because she thought this might be God's plan for her. Alexander Montgomerie Crawfurd was an evangelical minister in the Gorbals, a widower with a daughter and granddaughters. He was 58 when they married in 1898, shortly before Helen's 21st birthday. The marriage lasted 16 years, until Alexander's death in 1914. There were no children.

Although there was affection between Helen and her husband, friction between them grew as she began to challenge what she read in the Bible, especially about the supposedly inferior position of women. The command that women should keep silent in churches infuriated her. When she expressed her criticism of what she saw as the misogyny of the Bible aloud to Alexander Crawfurd, he would thunder his disapproval at his young and passionate wife: 'Woman, that is blasphemy.'

It was the hypocrisy of so many churchgoers which really got to her. As she saw it, religious people were too concerned with the life hereafter and not enough with life on Earth in the present, 'where God's creatures were living in slums, many of them owned by churches, amidst poverty and disease'.

Helen Crawfurd's views crystallized when controversy erupted over the proposed Sunday opening of the People's Palace. Established on Glasgow Green in 1898, this museum with its beautiful winter gardens had been designed as somewhere the working classes could go to enjoy their leisure time in pleasant and uplifting surroundings. A pity then that it didn't open on Sundays, the only full day in the week the working classes could count on having off.

A prominent figure in evangelical Christianity in Glasgow, Lord Overtoun was a vociferous defender of the sanctity of the Sabbath – but Lord Overtoun was a hypocrite. He was exposed by a pamphlet which supporters of the growing Labour movement began to sell on the streets of the city. This pointed out that the chemical works in Rutherglen, which Lord Overtoun owned, just across the Clyde from Glasgow Green and the People's Palace, were open around the clock, seven days a week, including Sundays.

Helen Crawfurd described the pamphlet as showing pictures contrasting the slums in which his workers lived with the well-appointed stables where Lord Overtoun kept the horses which pulled his carriage. There were pictures too of the scabs and sores on the faces and arms of the people who toiled in his chemical works, as well as details of how badly they were paid. She found the pamphlet a powerful response to what she called the hypocrisy and cant of Glasgow's leading evangelists. The opponents of Sunday opening fell silent and the working people for whom the People's Palace had been built were free to visit it on their day off.

The influence of the pamphlet was greater than that. Helen Crawfurd believed the campaign for 'saner Sundays' and the exposure of Lord Overtoun's hypocrisy opened many people's eyes, including her own, to the idea that socialism might have more answers to what was wrong with the world. She herself was to travel even further to the left. In 1920, more than 20 years after the argument over the Sunday opening of the People's Palace, Helen Crawfurd became a founder member of the Communist Party of Great Britain.

The author of the pamphlet which so influenced her was Keir Hardie, self-educated Lanarkshire miner, father of the Labour Party and an inspiration to generations of socialists. In the early 1900s he was joined by a new band of fighters for fairness and justice.

One of the most bitter battles of Red Clydeside was to be fought in Clydebank in 1911.

4

Sewing Machines &
Scientific Management

*It suddenly flashed on him how absurdly stupid
it was to be spending his life like this.*

The Clyde made Clydebank too, arguably even more than it did Glasgow. Surrounded though it is by ancient settlements such as Old Kilpatrick, Dalmuir, Duntocher and Yoker, the town itself is a mere stripling, no more than 150 years old. It was the building of J. & G. Thomson's shipyard in 1871 which called it into being.

In the most literal sense of the term, the forerunners of John Brown's chose a greenfield site. The area between the Forth and Clyde Canal and the river was known as the Barns o' Clyde and it was farmland, dotted here and there with a few cottages. This made it an attractive proposition too for the American Singer Manufacturing Company. Some ten years after Thomson's established their shipyard on the banks of the Clyde, Singer's found the ideal spot on which to build the biggest sewing machine factory in Europe.

Set back a little from the river, Singer's 41 different departments soon spread themselves over a large expanse of ground bounded by the canal and Kilbowie Hill to the north and east and Dalmuir to the south and west. The site is now occupied by Clydebank Business Park. Four strategically placed gates allowed workers to enter and leave the complex at the point closest to where they lived or at the point closest to the railway station. Although the factory has long since disappeared, the station is still called Singer.

Clydebank grew rapidly during the final decades of the nineteenth century and the first years of the twentieth. In 1881 the population was around 3,000. By 1913 it stood at over 43,000. John Brown's, Singer's and

Beardmore's, whose yard lay downriver at Dalmuir, were big employers of labour. In the early 1900s their workforces numbered 5,000, 9,000 and 6,000 respectively.

There was a frenzy of house building to accommodate these economic migrants moving down from Glasgow and over the river to what had so recently been the wide open spaces of the Barns o' Clyde. While many handsome tenements from this era still stand, some were flung up rather too hastily. These included the flat-roofed rows of the 'Holy City', which stood on the edge of Kilbowie Hill overlooking the sewing machine factory and the river and with fine views across the Clyde Valley and to the hills of Renfrewshire. You could almost have waved to James Maxton, over there on the hill above Barrhead.

Local tradition has it that the Holy City acquired its nickname when a sailor on a boat on the river remarked that the flat roofs reminded him of houses he had seen in Jerusalem. The story's a picturesque one, the reality of living in the Holy City less so. Within a year of the houses being built in 1904 tenants were refusing to pay their rent until the landlords carried out repairs needed because corners had been cut during construction.

Despite all the house building, there still weren't enough people in Clydebank to staff the sewing machine factory. Thousands of workers had to be brought in every day by train from Bridgeton and other parts of Glasgow and from the Vale of Leven down at Dumbarton. This continued right up until the factory closed in the 1960s, 'Singer Specials' thundering through intervening stations to get the workers to and from Kilbowie.

At its peak, Singer employed around 14,000 people. In 1911 the workforce numbered well over 10,000, with 4,000 coming in each day on the special trains. A railway clerkess who worked at Singer Station during the Second World War used to reminisce about the difficulties that could pose. Not being an octopus, it was well-nigh impossible for her to collect or check tickets when hundreds of people were piling out of each train and thrusting them towards her.

Singer's 41 different departments, known as 'flats', produced everything required to send a finished sewing machine out of the factory gates. The wood for the cabinets came into the company's own timber yard on the canal, transported there by Clyde puffers, the sturdy little seagoing workhorses of Scotland's west coast. The wrought iron for the beautifully curlicued legs which supported the sewing machines was forged in

Singer's onsite foundry. The Kilbowie plant even had its own power station and railway line to move heavy materials about the complex.

After the opening by Howard Carter of Tutankhamun's tomb in the 1920s the beautiful gold patterns on the shining black enamel of the sewing machines were often motifs inspired by Ancient Egypt. Those were applied in Singer's paintshop. The company's stationery was produced in the printshop, as was the famous 'Wee Green Book'. This neat little instruction manual was sized to fit comfortably into one of the long, narrow drawers of the cabinets which housed the sewing machines. The Wee Green Book was translated into several languages. Singer's exported from Clydebank to the world, one of Kilbowie's biggest markets being pre-revolutionary Russia.

Sadly, the style of Singer's management in 1911 was not to harness the pride all this engendered in those who worked in the town within a town. Like too many employers on Clydeside and elsewhere, they treated their workforce as a potentially volatile assembly of people who had to be kept rigorously under control.

If you were five minutes late for your work you would find the gates shut against you, the gatekeeper under strict instructions not to allow you in until the midday break: half a day's pay lost. If you made it in before the gates closed but arrived late at the flat where you worked – after handing in your brass token or check at the nearest time office – you might be quartered: lose quarter of an hour's pay. You couldn't argue that you hadn't realized what time it was. High up on the tower which rose above the plant, the Singer's clock was a landmark for miles around. This fondly remembered timepiece survived the devastating Clydebank Blitz of the Second World War only to be demolished with the factory in the 1960s.

A large proportion of the workforce at Singer's was female, employed for the sake of their superior manual dexterity when carrying out fine work. In 1911 around 3,000 women and girls worked there. The standard working-class practice was for husbands, sons and daughters to hand over their pay packets to the mother of the family at the end of the week. In return she would give you back some pocket money. However, working outside the home brought more than financial benefits, especially for girls.

You got out into the world, achieved the status of a wage earner and had company of your own age during the day. Although you might have to put up with a strict foreman or supervisor, factories like Singer's bred young women who tended to be more self-confident than their sisters in domestic service. These girls, and most of them were only in their late teens or early 20s, were more likely to speak out if they perceived an injustice being done to them or their workmates. This was to be a significant driver in the trouble brewing at Singer's through 1910 and 1911.

Much of the tension arose out of the practice of Scientific Management, for which the company's American bosses and senior managers were great enthusiasts. This broke work down into small steps, the assembly line concept. The principle could be more crudely expressed – and was. When the inventor of Scientific Management backed up his theories with the example of how to handle pig iron, he wrote:

> This work is so crude and elementary in its nature that the writer firmly believes that it would be possible to train an intelligent gorilla so as to become a more efficient pig-iron handler than any man can be.

So trained gorillas were preferable to men, less likely to ask for a pay rise, shorter hours or better working conditions either. In this modern machine age of the shiny new twentieth century, human intelligence, skill, initiative and experience were not to be valued. Nor did the enthusiasts for Scientific Management take into account the unquantifiable benefits of allowing employees to carry out work in which they could take a pride. In the drive to maximize profits by getting as much work as possible out of people for as little pay as possible, few allowances were made either for the fact that human beings are not machines.

Scientific Management was popular with many companies on Clydeside at the time. Lord Weir of Weir Pumps in Cathcart was another enthusiast. He and the Red Clydesiders were to cross swords on many issues. The bible of the theory was *The Principles of Scientific Management*, published in 1911. Frederick Winslow Taylor was an American whose book was based on a paper he had delivered some years previously to ASME, the American Society of Mechanical Engineers. Perhaps the first-ever management consultant, the man and the theory became so mutually identified that Scientific Management was often referred to as 'Taylorism'.

Taylor was scornful of the claims of 'labor agitators (many of whom are misinformed and misguided)' about '"sweat-shop" work and conditions'. In his view the real problem was that people were intrinsically lazy, most workers naturally inclined, as he put it, to loaf or soldier or "'ca' cannie," as it is called in Scotland'. Although he cites no examples from Scotland in his paper, it's intriguing to speculate how he became familiar with that expression.

Taylor believed that bringing together workers doing similar work and paying them the same standard daily rate of pay only made this problem worse:

> Under this plan the better men gradually but surely slow down their gait to that of the poorest and least efficient. When a naturally energetic man works for a few days beside a lazy one, the logic of the situation is unanswerable. 'Why should I work hard when that lazy fellow gets the same pay that I do and does only half as much work?'

Taylor's solution was not to pay people by the day but by how much they produced each day: piecework. Ironically – or perhaps not, given that Taylorism did tend to view workers as no more than cogs in the machine – after the Russian Revolution of 1917 both Lenin and Stalin tried to introduce the ideas of Scientific Management into Soviet industry.

Taylor did suggest one concession to human biology. At a time when factory and office workers finished at noon on Saturday and thus had weekends which lasted only a day and half, he advised, 'All young women should be given two consecutive days of rest (with pay) each month, to be taken whenever they may choose.'

Taylor argued that Scientific Management would benefit both bosses and workers, allowing the latter to earn higher wages without even having to think for themselves how to do the job. Their manager or supervisor would spell that out to them, each task being broken down into the science of it. He was convinced only managers or supervisors would be capable of making such an analysis.

Knowledge is power. That was a clear undercurrent of Scientific Management. It's also clear that Taylor was reflecting bosses' fears of the intelligent and experienced worker. Knowing their jobs and trades inside out, they had bargaining power that mere cogs in the machine could never have. A telling example of this provides an unintentionally comical vignette in *The Principles of Scientific Management*:

> We have all been used to seeing bricklayers tap each brick after it is placed on its bed of mortar several times with the end of the handle of

the trowel so as to secure the right thickness for the joint. Mr Gilbreth found that by tempering the mortar just right, the bricks could be readily bedded to the proper depth by a downward pressure of the hand with which they are laid. He insisted that his mortar mixers should give special attention to tempering the mortar, and so save the time consumed in tapping the brick.

Whether any of us would have trusted Mr Gilbreth – 'who had himself studied bricklaying in his youth' – to build a wall which wouldn't have come down in the next high wind is another matter entirely.

Scientific Management resulted in work which could be both back-breakingly tiring and mind-numbingly boring. Singer's at Clydebank was producing one million sewing machines every year. Each of these went out with one needle fitted, plus a neat little packet of three spares. Spare needles were also needed for the Singer shops found in high streets all over Britain. So more than four million new needles were required each year.

There were girls at Singer's who spent hours each and every day tapping newly made needles with a light hammer to correct any faults, straightening bends the machining process could put into them. It was quite an art to know where to hit and how strongly: a little harder than you might think so the needle would bend briefly in the opposite direction before coming back to rest perfectly straight. As soon as one batch was finished another box of needles would be delivered to your workbench by a young message boy or girl – a job which gave many people their start at Singer's – so you didn't waste any time by going to fetch it. Nor, of course, did you get the chance to stretch your legs or refocus your eyes.

Arthur McManus, who was to become a significant figure in the story of Red Clydeside, was just 21 years old in 1911 and working at Singer's. His job was to point the needles. Passionate, intelligent and well-read, one day he simply cracked. His friend and workmate Tom Bell told the story in his autobiography, *Pioneering Days*:

> I remember Arthur McManus describing a job he was on, pointing needles. Every morning there were millions of these needles on the table. As fast as he reduced the mountain of needles a fresh load was dumped. Day in, day out, it never grew less. One morning he came in, and found the table empty. He couldn't understand it. He began telling

everyone excitedly that there were no needles on the table. It suddenly
flashed on him how absurdly stupid it was to be spending his life like
this. Without taking his jacket off he turned on his heel and went out,
to go for a ramble over the hills to Balloch.

McManus had to come back, of course. Like everyone else, he needed
the job and he needed the money.

Later generations of Singer's workers were to have fond memories of
their time there, when management encouraged and supported all
manner of clubs, social activities and events. There was a Singer's theatre
and an annual Singer's sports gala. One girl chosen from the factory
would be crowned gala queen, and celebrities were invited to officially
launch the fun and games. In 1950 it was Hollywood star Dorothy Lamour
who did the honours.

With the company filling all their working time and so much of their
leisure time, employees used to joke that they had become 'Singerized'.
It may be that the impetus to create this all-encompassing Singer's culture
had its origins in the troubles of 1911. Perhaps management realized it
would be to their advantage to evoke loyalty rather than hostility from
their employees.

In 1911 that radical thought hadn't yet struck. One man who worked
there at that time described how the morning lasted from seven o'clock
till noon and you weren't even allowed to break off for a cup of tea or a
piece to keep you going. One foreman was notorious for checking on
who was in the toilets. Anyone caught in there smoking and taking an
unofficial break was sacked on the spot.

There was resentment too that, although British industry was
beginning to emerge from the depression which had paralyzed the
economy between 1907 and 1910, pay had not risen with renewed profits.
Wages were still being cut on the basis of timing and testing carried out
by cordially detested 'efficiency engineers' imported from America. Tom
Johnston described the process in the *Forward*. A few months before, in
October 1910, the sensational trial in London of the infamous Dr Crippen
for the murder and dismemberment of his wife had been all over the
newspapers, hence the reference here:

In many of these departments foremen stand with watches in their
hands timing the men and girls so that the maximum amount of
labour can be exacted from the operatives in return for the minimum

wage. In one department especially, a foreman has been nicknamed 'Crippen' because of his timing propensities. The watch is seldom out of this individual's hand. Wages are not reduced collectively. In Singer's the wages of two or three are broken today; a few others tomorrow and so on until all the workers have been reduced, and the game of SCIENTIFIC REDUCTION begins once more.

Singer's in 1911 was a powder keg waiting to explode – and explode it did.

5

An Injury to One is an Injury to All: The Singer Strike of 1911

We've struck work, son. The whole factory's coming out.

O ne chilly March afternoon in 1911 ten-year-old James Wotherspoon was walking home from school in Clydebank. His route took him past Singer's, where his father worked. As he made his way up Kilbowie Road the vast complex lay to the boy's left. To his right, where the Clydebank Shopping Centre now is, coiled the railway lines and sidings of the Singer Lie. During the working day the trains lay here which transported those 4,000 or so Singer employees who didn't live in the town to and from the factory.

As James continued his journey home, he saw a sight he was never to forget. Hours before the end of the working day, people began to stream out of the factory. This was unheard of. In the midst of the crowd he spotted his father, who hurried across to where his young son stood staring in amazement through the railings which surrounded the plant. Till the end of his long life, James Wotherspoon was to remember the exact words his father used that day: 'We've struck work, son. The whole factory's coming out.' What the schoolboy was witnessing was the start of a bitter industrial dispute which began with that mass walkout and carried on with public meetings, rallies and much heady talk only to collapse in acrimony three weeks later.

The spark which ignited the strike was a dispute involving 12 young women who worked as polishers. Their task was to bring the cabinets which housed the sewing machines to a high sheen. When management transferred three polishers out of the department the twelve remaining girls were asked to do their work as well as their own. A change in the way they were paid meant they would also have to accept a reduction of two shillings in their pay packet, a substantial loss when their total weekly wage amounted to around fourteen shillings. Angry at being asked to do more work for less pay, the polishers downed tools and withdrew their labour.

Two thousand other girls immediately came out in sympathy. The men soon followed. By the middle of the following day, Tuesday, 21 March 1911, almost all of the more than 10,000 employees were on strike. Those who remained at their workbenches and desks were largely foremen, managers and skilled men. Pickets at the factory's gates on Second Avenue, Kilbowie Road and Dalmuir did their best to persuade them to come out too.

James Wotherspoon, the schoolboy who witnessed the start of the strike, died in 2005, a few months after his 105th birthday. He spent his own working life at Singer. Almost a century after the events of 1911, he retained a photographic memory of them. He vividly recalled seeing a group of 'girl strikers', as the *Glasgow Herald* quickly dubbed them, trying to get a foreman to join the stoppage. While one contemporary newspaper photograph shows female strikers in elegant large-brimmed hats, James Wotherspoon remembered that many of the younger girls wore brightly coloured berets – red, yellow, blue and green – pulled down over their hair and secured by a hatpin. He described the result as 'not very flattering'.

The attempt to persuade the foreman to join the strike was good-natured but noisy. The girls blew toy paper trumpets, linked hands and danced around the man. Keeping his cool, he repeatedly and politely tipped his bowler hat to them and walked on into the factory.

The initial dispute among the polishers set light to the bonfire of grievances which had been smouldering inside the factory: the imposition of Scientific Management, the continual timing, testing and wage cuts. Union membership was another bone of contention. Singer's management was forced to tolerate those unions to which the relatively small number of time-served men, mainly engineers and printers, belonged. It refused to sanction any union activity in respect of the unskilled workers who made up most of the workforce.

Union activists had, however, been quietly recruiting inside Singer's for about a year before the 1911 strike. Tom Bell, author of *Pioneering Days*, was one of them: 'Factory gate meetings were held, literature was sold, and study classes begun. Soon contacts were extended inside and it was not long before every department had a small group.'

A group to which Bell already belonged changed its name to the

Industrial Workers of Great Britain (IWGB), becoming part of the British branch of the US-based Industrial Workers of the World (IWW). The members of this magnificently named organization, which still exists today, were more familiarly known as 'the Wobblies'.

One of the IWW's brightest lights was Joe Hill, the Swedish–American labour activist. Four years after the Singer's strike, he was executed by firing squad in Utah for a murder that people then and since don't think he committed, believing he was framed to get rid of a troublemaker. His life and story inspired the ballad 'I Dreamed I Saw Joe Hill Last Night'. Most famously sung by Paul Robeson and Joan Baez at Woodstock, it's a song which continues to inspire rebels around the world. Novelist Stephen King and his wife Tabitha named one of their sons Joseph Hillstrom King in honour of Joe Hill.

The Wobblies gave the workers at Singer's a stirring slogan: 'An injury to one is an injury to all'. Tom Bell reported in *Pioneering Days* that it quickly caught on, helping to stiffen the resolve of the new union members.

The organization of the Singer's strike was tight and highly effective. It was masterminded not only by the IWGB but also by the Socialist Labour Party (SLP). Small in membership, the SLP made up for that in dedication to their cause of socialist revolution and the creation of a workers' republic. They would have no truck with those who advocated reform instead. They come across as rather a dour bunch but they seized the opportunity the Singer's dispute presented to them with both hands. Strike headquarters were established at their committee rooms on Second Avenue, part of the Holy City. The flat-roofed houses where many Singer's workers lived now belonged officially to the district of Clydebank known as Radnor Park. This geographically commanding location also had psychological significance, providing a lofty vantage point over Singer's. The Second Avenue gate, one of the factory's main entrances, was nearby. Once through it, a dizzyingly steep flight of stone stairs – they're still there – plunged into the factory grounds.

A strike committee was quickly formed and strike districts established in Bridgeton, Govan, Dumbarton, the Vale of Leven and elsewhere to ensure that the 4,000 workers who did not live in Clydebank were kept in the loop. Accurate information being deemed crucial to morale and the potential success of the strike, each district had a meeting place where the same trusted messenger gave them an update at half past six every evening.

Much stress was laid on good behaviour. Workers at Singer's normally collected their pay packets or had them delivered to their workbenches when they finished work at midday on Saturday. On the first week of the strike, money still being owed to them, they marched en masse into the factory, lifted their pay packets and marched out again. Even the *Glasgow Herald* was impressed by how they did that. No friend to the strikers, the newspaper of Glasgow's Establishment estimated that 10,000 people, not much short of the whole workforce, had taken part in the collection of the pay: 'Although extremely quiet and orderly there was something intensely dramatic about the whole scene.'

Mass meetings, parades and processions were held throughout the strike, in Clydebank and beyond, to gain publicity and support for the strikers' cause. On Thursday, 23 March, four days in, a demonstration estimated to include eight thousand people marched through Clydebank to John Brown's. A meeting was held with the shipyard's workers, requesting their solidarity and support. Headed by Duntocher Brass Band, those marchers must have been a sight to see.

Despite the biting March winds, commented on in contemporary newspaper reports, there's a sense of a carnival atmosphere at the beginning of it all. It must have been quite a novelty to be out and about in normally quiet but now bustling streets during working hours, away from the constant supervision and measuring and testing of the factory.

On Sunday, 26 March, another demonstration was organized on Glasgow Green, time-honoured place of protest. Again, strike leaders emphasized the good behaviour of the strikers. Who those strike leaders were is curiously hard to establish. The records aren't there, either for the strike committee or for Singer's management. Other than the Singer managers, newspapers named no names either. This applies both for the socialist *Forward* and for what its readers called 'the capitalist press'. That the *Forward* was protecting those who might later be blacklisted by Singer's and other employers seems likely, that the capitalist press was doing the same, less so.

Perhaps some newspapers were choosing to diminish the leaders of the dispute by not naming them. After all, many of them were mere 'girl strikers'. Clearly these were females who did not know their place, neither the one allotted to them by class nor by gender. Or perhaps the newspapers were choosing not to give any of the strikers the oxygen of publicity.

The Singer Strike: Clydebank, 1911 is an authoritative account of the strike, published in 1989 by Clydebank District Library and compiled by members of Glasgow Labour History Workshop. It names several names, making educated guesses as to these individuals' involvement. It seems highly likely that Arthur McManus, the 21 year old who decided there had to be more to life than the processing of millions of sewing machine needles, was involved in the strike along with his friend Tom Bell. Bell was not only one of the prime movers behind the establishment of the IWGB union in Singer's; he was also for a time a member of the SLP. Both he and Arthur McManus later became yet more Scottish founder members of the Communist Party of Great Britain, McManus becoming its first chairman.

Neil MacLean, later to become long-standing Labour MP for Govan, may also have been involved, although there is no documentary evidence of this. However, he was doing his apprenticeship as an engineer at Singer's around the time of the strike.

Eighteen-year-old Frances Abbot, later Mrs McBeth, worked as a polisher in the department where the dispute began. Again, there is no documentary evidence of her involvement, but her daughter described her as 'a fighter all her days . . . right into "Red Clydeside"'. Fanny McBeth later came to know James Maxton and Davie Kirkwood, who became MP for the town, and remained throughout her life a dedicated member of the Labour Party.

Jane Rae was in her late 30s at the time of the strike. She worked in the needle flat and was sacked afterwards because of her involvement. She subsequently became a member of the ILP, a suffragette, local councillor, supporter of the temperance movement and Justice of the Peace. In this role she earned a reputation for handing down the toughest penalties she could legally impose on men found guilty of domestic abuse.

It's curious that few references are made to the Singer Strike in the memoirs of the major figures of Red Clydeside. John Maclean certainly wrote at the time about what he called 'this rather romantic effort', but he was not a member of the SLP and there seem to be no accounts of him or his friend and fellow orator James Maxton addressing the strikers at their numerous meetings on Glasgow Green and elsewhere. Admittedly, Maxton was only 26 at the time and still serving his political apprenticeship.

Singer's management met the strike committee on several occasions but insisted there could be no discussion on any grievances until everyone went back to work. Management also emphatically refused to agree to factory-wide union recognition or the principle of collective bargaining, on which the strike had begun to focus.

One of the arguments advanced by strike leaders here was that any individual girl who took a complaint to management was likely to have it ignored. Outspoken and spirited the lassies at Singer's may have been, but nobody paid much attention to what girls had to say.

On Wednesday, 29 March the *Glasgow News* reported the oddly quiet scene in Clydebank at noon, emphasizing how unusual this was:

> It required only a cursory glance at the streets in the Radnor Park district today to discover that there was absolutely no change in the situation in connection with the strike of Singer's workers. There were the usual coteries of men who had come 'out', with numbers of girls who had also left their employment, and the factory itself, except for a few jets of steam issuing from different points, and a few curls of smoke from one of the chimneys, gave no indication of anything like its ordinary busy aspect.
>
> It is estimated that excepting the clerical staff and handymen generally, there are now little over a couple of hundred employees remaining at their posts.
>
> A view of the extensive works from the height of the 'Holy City' gives a picture of almost absolute Desertion and Quietness.

Fewer workers meant fewer trains. Instead of seven from Glasgow, only two had pulled into Singer Railway Station and only one from the Vale of Leven. All three were 'sparsely filled'. The next day, Thursday, 30 March, there was another demonstration on Glasgow Green. About two thousand strikers listened to an unnamed speaker and 'thereafter assembled in military fashion, and headed by three bands, they paraded the principal streets of the city'.

Other than a handful of pickets haranguing 'the few workers who left the factory for dinner', things were much quieter down in Clydebank. Some of the pickets were angry, spitting out accusations of 'blackleg' and 'scab', but there was no violence, as throughout the strike. The *Evening News* told its readers that 'nothing noteworthy transpired'.

The papers were reporting other news too, of course. There was trouble in the Balkans, revolutionary groups seeking independence for Macedonia. The Athens correspondent of the *Manchester Guardian* took 'a grave view of the outlook'. In sport, lots of people were getting excited about the Scotland versus England football international in Liverpool on April Fool's Day. The team travelled down by train on the morning of Friday, 31 March and special trains ran from St Enoch and Glasgow Central to take the fans down on Friday evening and Saturday morning, nine from St Enoch on Friday night alone. The *Glasgow News* promised its readers expert staff reporting from Goodison Park via telephone and telegraph – 'DESCRIPTION OF PLAY, NOTES ON THE GAME . . . FEARLESS AND IMPARTIAL CRITICISM, PHOTOS OF PLAYERS' – and the Scottish fans were buoyant:

> The scenes at the stations last night were of a lively nature. One coterie of about thirty men were loaded with parcels apparently containing 'light' refreshments; while another group, also well loaded with packages, had six of their number as standard bearers of the Scottish flag.
>
> Many others were well provided with melodeons and mouth organs, yielding harmonic discords. Last, but not least, were a couple of pipers, whose skirling appealed to the patriotic heart.

Bless their hearts. Look away now if you don't want to know the score: it was a draw, 1–1. In a busy day for sport, Oxford beat Cambridge in the annual boat race.

Other Scots were embarking on rather more permanent journeys in rather larger boats. Under a headline of 'To The West To-Day: The Rush Continues', the *Evening News* reported that a record 4,000 emigrants were leaving the Clyde that Saturday to start new lives in Canada and the United States. The Anchor Line was taking over 1,100, chartering a special train to Greenock, where the *California* was waiting to carry them across the Atlantic to New York: 'Seldom has such a boom in emigration been experienced as at present.'

Those emigrants were going to miss the Scottish National Exhibition due to open at Kelvingrove in May. Preparations were well in hand, and lots of season tickets had already been sold, although probably not to workers at Singer's. The union had no funds to cover strike pay and money was getting very tight. Half of all women in Clydebank who worked outside the home did so at Singer's. In many households all the wage earners were employed there. That was how it worked: you got a job in the factory because a relative or friend spoke for you. If no money was coming in from Singer's, no money was coming in from anywhere.

Singer's management had not been idle while the strikers had been marching and protesting. As the strike entered its third week, Works Superintendent Hugh MacFarlane, a Glaswegian, and F.A. Park, the American manager of the Kilbowie plant, applied the tried-and-tested strategy of divide and conquer. Questioning the right of the strike committee to speak for all the strikers, they sent letters out to every employee, enclosing a pre-printed postcard which they asked to be completed and returned as soon as possible:

> I wish to resume my work, and agree to do so on the day and hour which may be arranged by you, when you assure me that at least 6,000 persons have signed this agreement.

After signing their agreement to this statement, employees were asked to fill in their names, addresses, check numbers and department numbers. Clerical and management staff at Singer's stayed up till one o'clock in the morning to get those ten thousand letters and postcards ready to send out.

The strike committee tried to persuade people to write 'Refer to Strike Committee' across the postcard and return it unsigned. Not many did. As ever, it came down to economic survival. If you didn't sign and return the postcard but 6,000 of your co-workers did, management could easily work out who those who hadn't signed were. That would be you out of a job at Singer's and very probably blacklisted with other employers too. *Forward* certainly alleged that blacklisting took place after the strike was over, calling for a boycott of Singer sewing machines in response. Singer management expressed their opinion on this via the pages of the *Glasgow Herald*: 'We cannot be expected to retain people in our employ who by word and deed plainly indicate that they are unfriendly to their employers.'

Whether the Singer plebiscite was fairly conducted is a moot point. The strike committee alleged that over 1,000 postcards had gone to employees who no longer worked at Singer's, some of whom were dead. Singer management announced that 6,015 postcards had come back agreeing on a return to work. Several people at the time, on both sides of the dispute, observed that this was a very convenient number.

Three months later, a bitter reflection on the failure of the strike was issued by the Sewing Machine Group of the IWGB:

We make our appeal not only to the Singer Workers, but to the whole working class. The lessons of the Kilbowie Strike are lessons for them too.

We are confronted by a determined and vindictive attack upon the whole principle of organisation . . . The plot aims at reducing the workers to a mass of disorganised serfs, degraded and dehumanised instruments for producing wealth for others, incapable of helping each other or of offering the smallest resistance to the never-ending and ever-increasing robbery of the master class.

The workers might have lost the battle at Singer's but with rhetoric like that the war was still to be won. Some who had tasted the bitterness of defeat at Kilbowie moved on to other battlefields. They took a new and powerful slogan with them: 'An injury to one is an injury to all'. These words were to ring out through the story of Red Clydeside.

6

No Vote, No Census

*If I am intelligent enough to fill in this paper,
I am intelligent enough to put a cross on a voting form.*

The suffragettes have an image problem. The popular perception is of well-off ladies with plenty of time on their hands for smashing windows, pouring acid into pillar boxes, tying themselves to railings and otherwise making mischief. That so many of them fully earned their place within the story of Red Clydeside can come as a surprise.

When asked what he had thought of the suffragettes, Mr James Wotherspoon, schoolboy witness of the start of the Singer Strike, looked a little nervously at his interviewer but stepped manfully up to the mark. He had thought them a bunch of silly middle-class women out to cause trouble.

In *The Hidden History of Glasgow's Women* social historian Elspeth King suggests we may not hear much about working-class suffragettes because their middle-class sisters in arms tried to protect them, believing the police would mete out rougher treatment to mere women than they would to ladies. Considering how brutally some middle-class women were treated in prison, this seems plausible. Descriptions of force-feeding of suffragettes on hunger strike make grim reading.

It's another curiosity that the depiction of suffragettes in popular culture seems always to show them doing what they did only in London. Although the city was an important focal point, suffragettes were active all over Britain, doing whatever they could think of to achieve their goal. The campaign had been a long one.

In Scotland alone there had been women's suffrage committees for 30 years and more in all the major cities and towns, from Lerwick to Dumfries and Inveraray to Dingwall. A large number of Scottish town councils had also declared themselves in favour of extending the franchise to women. In 1870 school boards were created in Scotland, with both men and women eligible to stand for election to them. In 1882 some Scotswomen, essentially those who were householders in their own right, were given the right to vote in local elections. From then on, women not being permitted to vote in parliamentary elections struck many people as illogical as well as unjust.

By 1901 17 per cent of people entitled to vote in local elections in Glasgow were women. They must all have been either single women, widows or divorced, as it was almost always the husband who was the householder in any couple. In his unstinting support for women to get the parliamentary vote Tom Johnston argued sarcastically that no evil results had followed from women being allowed to vote in local elections.

In 1892 the newly formed Scottish Women's Co-operative Guild, a grouping of working-class women, sent a petition to the government calling for votes for women. There had been lots of petitions, literally millions of signatures gathered, but still the prize seemed no closer. Peaceful protests continued. One of the most colourful was held in Edinburgh in October 1909, when hundreds of suffragettes marched along Princes Street watched by thousands of interested onlookers. The female marchers were supported by a sizeable group from the Men's League for Women's Suffrage.

Again according to Elspeth King, this stalwart band had been formed by husbands, brothers and fiancés of suffragettes fed up with being seen as the poor henpecked yes-men of the women in their lives. One of their banners read 'Men's League for Women's Suffrage. Scots wha hae votes – men. Scots wha haena – women.'

The Edinburgh march was also a pageant, with participants portraying famous women from Scottish history: St Margaret; Mary, Queen of Scots; Jenny Geddes; the female Covenanting martyrs. The marchers' banners included the usual simple but effective demand of 'Votes For Women' and the confident claim that 'A Gude Cause Maks A Strong Arm'. The march was re-enacted a century after it happened, on 9 October 2009.

The Scottish suffragettes made a big deal of their Scottishness, as photographs and surviving banners show. It made for great publicity. What newspaper editor could resist a photograph of attractive young women in fashionable clothes well draped in tartan sashes or plaids? In 1908 Mary Phillips of Glasgow served three months in Holloway after being arrested at a demonstration in London. When she was released she was met by a group of her fellow suffragettes dressed exactly like that, Cairngorm plaid brooches and all. They were also carrying a banner with a slogan they had pinched from a long-standing advert for soap: 'Message To Mr Asquith, Ye Mauna Tramp on the Scotch Thistle, Laddie!'

The thistle was an emblem enthusiastically adopted by the suffragettes. Not only was its deep purple eye-catching – the votes-for-women movement had already chosen that as one of their colours – its 'wha daur meddle wi' me' reputation struck a powerful chord. When someone advised Mary Phillips that women who wanted the vote might be more likely to get it if they were 'patient, gentle, womanly and flowerlike', she told them she'd much rather be 'a great big prickly Scots thistle'.

Helen Crawfurd, the young wife of the minister, became a committed suffragette the year after the Gude Cause March. The first person she heard address the subject was Helen Fraser of Glasgow, speaking to an audience of holidaymakers in Rothesay, where the suffragettes of the Women's Freedom League had a summer base. Politics went doon the watter too. Listening attentively, Helen Crawfurd grew indignant at the heckling to which Helen Fraser was being subjected. With magnificent contempt, she described the hecklers as 'undersized bantams'. What they kept yelling at the young and attractive Helen Fraser was, 'It's a man ye want!' You can just hear the shilpit wee nyaffs saying it too.

In 1910, after a meeting in Rutherglen, Helen Crawfurd joined the Women's Social and Political Union (WSPU), which had been founded by Mrs Pankhurst and her daughter Christabel in 1903. The WSPU advocated a militant and increasingly violent approach. Seeking to belittle and diminish these dangerous women, the *Daily Mail* dubbed them 'suffra*gettes*' instead of the correct 'suffra*gists*'. The name the newspaper had come up with eventually stuck for all female supporters of votes for women.

One working-class Glasgow suffragette we do know about who was very much in favour of the militant tactics advocated by the Pankhursts was Agnes Dollan. One of eleven children, she was born Agnes Moir in Springburn. At the age of only 11, she had to leave school and go out to work. She was still a teenager when she began fighting for higher wages and better working conditions for women and soon became involved in the suffragette movement. Her marriage to Patrick Dollan, miner, member of the ILP, *Forward* journalist and future lord provost of Glasgow, became a lifelong personal and political partnership.

Other women were disturbed by the violence perpetrated by the militant suffragettes and by Mrs Pankhurst's dictatorial leadership style. Helen Fraser who had been heckled at Rothesay was one of them, telling her, 'You don't use violence, you use *reason* to get the vote.' Many left the WSPU as a result, joining the Women's Freedom League, which was particularly strong in Scotland.

Some socialists, including many on Clydeside, were ambivalent about extending the vote to women. One argument was that men should come first: by no means did all of them have the vote in parliamentary elections. The figure stood at around 75 per cent, again essentially only householders. During the First World War many contemporary observers made the telling point that thousands of those killed or maimed had no say in the running of the country for which they were being called upon to sacrifice their lives, health and youth. It was not until 1918 that the franchise was extended to all men over 21 and all women over 30.

Ramsay MacDonald, who in 1924 was to become Britain's first Labour prime minister, was a man said to be 'more at ease with women than with men'. He fully supported female suffrage but was dead-set against violence being used to achieve it:

> I have no objection to revolution, if it is necessary, but I have the very strongest objection to childishness masquerading as revolution, and all that one can say of these window-breaking expeditions is that they are simply silly and provocative. I wish the working women of the country who really care for the vote . . . would come to London and tell these pettifogging middle-class damsels who are going out with little hammers in their muffs that if they do not go home they will get their heads broken.

Some socialists thought women would tend to vote cautiously, favouring the political status quo and the established parties. Believing female voters less likely to put their cross against Labour Party candidates, they did not welcome the influx into the electorate of so many who might potentially increase the Liberal or Conservative share of the vote. Yet many suffragettes were themselves socialists. Mrs Pankhurst and her daughters were members of the ILP and personal friends of Labour leader Keir Hardie. He was always a supporter of votes for women. So was Tom Johnston, who gave a regular weekly column in the *Forward* to Glasgow's suffragettes.

Helen Crawfurd contributed many articles to *Suffrage Notes*. So did

Janie Allan. The daughter of Alexander Allan, owner of the shipping company of the same name, she was a wealthy woman who was a committed socialist and member of the ILP. She was generous with her money and resources, on at least one occasion in 1911 loaning her car to fellow suffragettes campaigning during a by-election in North Ayrshire, allowing them to cover a lot more ground in this rural constituency.

Other contributors to *Suffrage Notes* were Frances and Margaret McPhun. These sisters with the great surname had a third sibling, Nessie, who was also a suffragette. Their father was Baillie McPhun, councillor for the East End of Glasgow, prime mover behind the creation of the People's Palace and proud parent to his three clever and politically engaged daughters.

Helen Crawfurd did a speaking tour of Lanarkshire with Frances and Margaret McPhun, on this occasion travelling by train. She was full of admiration for how Frances managed to read the complicated railway timetables and always get the three of them to their destination without any problems.

They always got a sympathetic hearing from the miners, who admired how the suffragettes were fighting to win the vote. Helen Crawfurd thought she probably went down well because her speeches were becoming ever more socialist in tone, peppered with quotes from the Bible so familiar to her and these Lanarkshire colliers. The miners would never take the fee they could have requested for the hire of their halls. They always took up a good collection too. It was usual to do this at political meetings, the money going to the funds of the party or organization the speakers represented. As far as the miners were concerned, class clearly didn't come into it. The suffragettes were fighting to right an injustice, and they understood all about that.

The census of 1911 gave suffragettes throughout Britain another weapon with which to challenge the government and win publicity for their cause. 'If you're not going to give us the vote and consider us full citizens, then you're not going to count us': this was the message they wanted to send. The census was taken on the night of Sunday, 2 April. Presumably all the football supporters who'd been down to Liverpool to see Scotland draw with England were home by then.

All over the country, thousands of women made sure they weren't at home or anywhere else they could be counted. Some wrote comments on the census form before they disappeared for the night in this mass act of civil disobedience. As one English suffragette put it, 'If I am intelligent enough to fill in this paper, I am intelligent enough to put a cross on a voting form.'

Refusing to be counted in the census was against the law, punishable by a fine of £5, but it was a peaceful and non-violent way of expressing strong feelings. So that the protest would have maximum impact, suffragettes made sure the press and the census enumerators knew well in advance what they intended to do. The enumerators were confident they could winkle them out, as the *Glasgow News* reported the day before the count was made:

> The services of the police will be requisitioned in the work. To-morrow night they will make search for the homeless. They will keep an eye on the
> ### Nooks and Crannies
> of the city, where the waifs and strays seek nightly shelter. They must also be accounted for in the Census.

The crews of ships on the Clyde would be counted by officers of HM Customs and the soldiers at Maryhill Barracks would be easy to count, as would visitors staying overnight at Glasgow's hotels. Then came the stern warning:

> It is just possible that some trouble may be occasioned by the
> ### More Militant Members
> of the suffragette movement in the way of withholding information. The officials, however, are prepared for any difficulty that may arise in this way, and arrangements made accordingly.

Bit of an unconvincing threat, that. What were these vague 'arrangements'? If you couldn't find 'em, you couldn't count 'em. How many women did take themselves off to some nook or cranny where even those wily census enumerators wouldn't find them, or concealed themselves at home, is not known.

The official census website for England and Wales, where the 1911 results have been available since 2009, estimates that several thousand women may have boycotted the 1911 count. At the time of writing this book, the 1911 census results for Scotland had not yet been made available, and Helen Crawfurd makes no mention of the 1911 census in her memoirs.

The Glasgow branch of the Women's Freedom League certainly held a wee soirée on the Saturday after the census where war stories were exchanged, as the *Glasgow News* reported: 'A number of ladies gave their Census experiences, which were of an amusing and entertaining character.' Then they don't give any details of those amusing stories. Damn their eyes.

The popular view in Glasgow in 1911 seems to have been that many suffragettes had gone into hiding for the night. A cartoon in the *Glasgow News* shows Mary Ann, a domestic servant of mature years, entertaining a beaming policeman friend in a cosy kitchen while a black cat with a jaunty bow tied around its neck looks on: 'Ye needna hurry. The missis is yin o' them that's no fur fillin' in her census paper. She's below the bed up the stairs. She'll no come oot as lang's ye're here.'

The point had been made, and in Glasgow attention turned to the next big thing.

7

The Picturesque & Historic Past: The Scottish National Exhibition of 1911

Various Highland crafts will be engaged in by native dwellers during their residence.

The bitter March strike at Singer's gave way to the summer of the Scottish Exhibition. This was the third in a line of such events held at Kelvingrove in Glasgow's West End. The first was in 1888 and the second in 1901, when the beautiful red sandstone building we know today as Kelvingrove Art Gallery and Museum was opened, providing a grand new home for Glasgow's civic art collection.

The full title of the 1911 extravaganza was the Scottish Exhibition of National History, Art and Industry. As the *Daily Record* wrote at the time, its purpose was 'to bind Scotland more closely to the glories and victories of its past'. One of the concrete aims of the exhibition was to raise money to fund a chair of Scottish history and literature at nearby Glasgow University, which it successfully did.

Rather unwisely for an Englishman in Scotland, the existing professor of modern history at the university up on Gilmorehill overlooking Kelvingrove had given voice to his opinion that there was no such thing as 'Scottish history'. Perhaps Dudley Medley – inevitably known by the nickname 'Deadley Mudley' – was just trying to provoke debate. Or perhaps, as eminent history professors have been known to do, he set out to cause a stushie in the hope of getting his name in the papers.

The organizers of the 1911 exhibition set out to prove that Scotland had a very rich history indeed. Visiting the exhibition on the press preview day, Monday, 1 May 1911, the *Glasgow Herald*'s reporter had a bit of fun with that. As was usual at the time, there was no byline, so we don't know who he, or maybe she, was. There had been 'lady reporters' for quite some time by then. Allowed almost a full broadsheet page to record first impressions and describe the different exhibits, the reporter begins by quoting Huckleberry Finn, who 'has declared that the world has no need of dead persons'. Or, as Henry Ford, founder of the Ford Motor Company, father of the assembly line and big fan of Scientific Management put it, 'History is bunk.'

Having repeated Huck Finn's uncompromising view on the importance of living in the present, shared by many in the excitingly new twentieth century, the reporter then has his or her cake and eats it. Full credit is given to the Scottish Exhibition for having balanced 'the priceless heritage of Scottish history and art with exhibits demonstrating the achievements of modern Scotland in industry, science and entertainment'.

As the reporter waxes lyrical about the exhibition's *Palace of History*, an interesting contradiction and a cautious rebuke surfaces. Although the Scotland of 1911 feels itself closer to the days of Bruce and Wallace than we, a mere century on, might have thought, perhaps people don't care enough about those stirring times:

> The Scotch [*sic*] War of Independence is not yet remote enough to have become clustered with myth, and the fame of Wallace and Bruce has not yet suffered seriously from the attack of the historic iconoclast. Of the plain hero and the heroic king there are many relics. Save among members of the Scottish Patriotic Association the tragedy of Wallace and the triumph of Bannockburn do not now arouse rage or joy, which perhaps is not as it ought to be. The records here should stimulate a large national memory.

On somewhat safer ground, the *Herald* reporter has absolutely no doubt that 'the romance of the Stuart dynasty retains its glamour', even if Bonnie Prince Charlie is dismissed as his father's 'futile son'. Was a fine line being trod here?

There's a sense at points in this long article of a tension between the political opinions of the journalist and those of the newspaper and its owners for which he or she wrote. Not an uncommon story then or now, but even more of a dilemma back in the days when bosses were all-powerful and would have no compunction about blacklisting you to other potential employers if you stepped over onto the wrong side of that line.

Home Rule for Scotland was a hot topic in 1911, the idea gathering increasing support and momentum. Many of the socialists of Red Clydeside were passionately in favour. Other Scots of all political hues were opposed. Across the board, however, sentimental Scottishness of a type which tends to make modern Scots cringe seems to have been quite acceptable.

The crowds which flocked to Kelvingrove during the fine summer of 1911 loved the historical exhibits, and flock they did. More than nine million visits were made to the exhibition, which spread itself lavishly out over the eastern end of Kelvingrove Park, the part which lies on the other side of Kelvin Way from the Art Galleries.

One of the most popular sections was the 'Auld Toun', with its 'Auld Scotch [*sic*] Street'. Although a few Home Rulers and patriotic Scots had been objecting for a generation and more to the use of the word 'Scotch' rather than 'Scots' other than for broth, shortbread and whisky, the word seems to have raised few hackles in 1911. The *Glasgow Herald* reporter again:

> To step from thoroughfares lined with palaces and pleasure-haunts
> into the quaint courtyard of 'the Auld Toun' is like a piece of travel.
> There is, it is true, an admirable consonancy in the architecture of the
> entire Exhibition, but this quiet, old-world nook, with its towering
> turrets, its crow steps and its toppling chimneys, just so much awry
> as to accentuate the verisimilitude of it all, is a place apart, a spot to
> which one may retire from the din and ecstacy [*sic*] of the coming
> summer nights and recall the picturesque and historic past.

There were living exhibits too. The Highland Clachan spread over three acres along the banks of the Kelvin, stretching back to the Gibson Street entrance to the park:

> ... here and there are sprinkled the thatched cottages which are to be
> inhabited during the summer by native Highlanders. Various Highland
> arts and crafts will be engaged in by native dwellers during their
> residence, and all the attendants will be garbed in the 'Earasaid,' the
> ancient and becoming costume having been presented by the
> Marchioness of Bute.

Well, at least the Clachan was being run on commercial lines and they were hoping to make a profit to be donated to An Comunn Gàidhealach and the Co-operative Council of Highland Home Industries. There was a village hall too, *Talla mhor a' Chlachain* in the Gaelic, where audiences of up to 350 people could enjoy musical events and entertainments in both English and the language of the Garden of Eden.

If the attitude towards the 'native Highlanders' sounds just a wee touch patronizing, they weren't the only people who spent the summer of 1911 being gawped at as quaint aborigines. Close by the Highland Village sat the Equatorial Colony, or West African Village. There were about a hundred adults and children there, kindly requested to demonstrate their traditional way of life in a corner of a Glasgow park. They included musicians and dancers. Lest any visitors to the exhibition had any trepidation about that, reassurance was offered in advance that 'decency is maintained throughout'.

Not far from the West African Village was the Arctic Camp, where a group of Laplanders, complete with reindeer, had been persuaded to spend several months for 'as much milk as they could drink', a statement which raises the art of patronizing people of other cultures to a whole new level. Or lowers it to a whole new depth.

More sophisticated refreshment was available for the exhibition's visitors. As might be expected, the famous Miss Cranston ran two such establishments. One was the White Cockade, whose name fits in perfectly with the historic theme of the exhibition, referring as it does to the symbol adopted by Bonnie Prince Charlie's Jacobite army. Yet Miss Cranston's tea rooms at the Scottish Exhibition were bang up to date too, as she so much liked to be. She commissioned Charles Rennie Mackintosh to design the inside of the White Cockade and Margaret Macdonald to create the menu cards. The Willow Tea Rooms on which they had worked together in 1904 were just a short tram ride away from Kelvingrove.

Examples of Margaret Macdonald Mackintosh's menu cards survive, very dramatic in white on black. Other than a glimpse of a spacious and airy balcony, there are no known photographs of the interiors of the White Cockade or Miss Cranston's other tea room at the exhibition. She gave the commission for that to Frances Macdonald, Margaret's sister.

The blend of old and new was mirrored elsewhere. The *Palace of History* was the main building, designed to look like Falkland Palace in Fife. A modern concert hall could seat 3,000 people and pageants and musical events were staged there, the inaugural concert given by Sir Henry Wood, knighted that same year, and his Queen's Hall Orchestra.

A pageant on the life of Robert Burns caused controversy by pulling no punches on the bard's fondness for a dram.

In the design of its exterior, the *Palace of Industries* followed the unifying historic style. Inside, as befitted Glasgow's proud boast to be both the Second City of the Empire and the Workshop of the World, it was crammed with displays on all types of industrial endeavour. It showcased examples from home and abroad, including what was being produced in Germany, Italy, Japan, Austria, Holland, Denmark and those countries then known as the Colonies.

The *Palace of Industries* had its own spacious quadrangle with 'bandstand, tearooms, verandahs, and promenades – an exhibition in itself'. There was a 500-seat conference hall, plus the exhibition's offices, dedicated post office and telephone exchange.

In the lee of the beautiful Victorian and Edwardian houses up on Park Circus, the Garden Club provided exclusive accommodation for a thousand or so of the more well-heeled visitors to the exhibition. They paid a membership fee for the whole summer of two guineas apiece. The site as a whole being open to all, there had been some concern about the possibility of what was referred to as 'rowdyism'. You never knew what might happen when the working classes set out to enjoy themselves.

Back in 1901 there had been hopes that the Kelvingrove exhibition of that year might leave behind it permanent improvements in both Glasgow and the lives of the working-class people who formed the bulk of the city's population. Bemoaning the fact that the Clyde and the Kelvin were polluted and that 'amid the blankness, uniformity and greyness, exasperated nerves find but one outlet – in drink', the hopeful young authors of *Glasgow in 1901* called for the city to solve the problem of 'how the lives of its workers may be made a little more gracious and tolerable and sweet':

> That the Exhibition will leave behind it a humanising influence we know. It will hasten the coming of our clean rivers, our flowers and trees, and help to rend that intolerable blanket of smoke which, while it keeps out the sun, is not even proof against rain. We want some 'niceness' in the condition of our citizens' lives, and justice done to our city's looks that we may love her in the sight of men as we have loved her shamefacedly and in secret . . .

Ten years on all that was still only a hope. None of the buildings of the

1911 exhibition were permanent, all of them designed to be dismantled after the show was over, although everyone agreed they did look very solid. Given that this was supposed to be a celebration of Scotland's history, it seems a pity that the remains of the old Kelvingrove Mansion, around which the *Palace of History* had been built, were completely swept away after the exhibition closed in November. Then again, as the old saying had it, the greatest vandals in Glasgow were always Glasgow Corporation. Off with the old, on with the new: that's always been the Glasgow way.

The aerial railway was absolutely part of the Modern Age. This thrilling form of transport allowed visitors to fly across the site, over the Highland Village and the Kelvin to the grounds of the university. An artist's impression and a surviving photograph show women in big hats, boys in sailor suits and girls in pinafores looking admiringly up at it. Other visitors to the exhibition are seen riding in the metal, cage-style gondola. This was suspended under a cigar-shaped machinery room running along electric cables fixed to high pylons at either end of the aerial railway's track.

The Scottish Exhibition opened on 2 May 1911, six weeks before the coronation in London of King George V and Queen Mary. Another of the reasons for holding the exhibition had been to celebrate this royal event, London having its Festival of Empire in the same year. In the run-up to the coronation Borwick's Baking Powder took adverts in the Glasgow papers announcing a competition to win 20 free trips to London so their customers could be in the cheering crowds when Their Majesties travelled by coach to Westminster Abbey:

> Each Trip will consist of:
> (1) A return railway ticket to London from any part of Scotland.
> (2) First-rate hotel accommodation and board for 3 clear days.
> (3) A good seat to view the procession.
> Full particulars of the Competitions and Coupons will be found in the 6d., 1s., and 2s. 6d. tins of Borwick's Baking Powder sold in Scotland.

The Bonanza in Argyle Street, 'the largest millinery business in Scotland', was rewarding its customers with free admission to the Scottish Exhibition 'with every pound's worth of goods bought for cash in one day's shopping'. You'd have had to buy at least two of the 'New American Sailors and Mushrooms' to be able to get one of those free tickets. Tragically for fashionistas, the advert shows no pictures of these creations.

Other than requesting its readers visiting Glasgow for the Scottish Exhibition to patronize its advertisers, the *Forward* took little interest in what was going on at Kelvingrove and declared the coronation to be 'neither here nor there'. They were more interested in the suffragettes' protest during the census and in what else was going on in the Scotland of 1911. Keir Hardie said it would be remembered as a year of strikes.

As well as the confrontation at Singer's, 1911 saw a UK-wide railway strike and stoppages in the Welsh coalfields. There were also strikes at the dye works of the United Turkey Red Company in the Vale of Leven, on Glasgow's trams and among the carters, known in local parlance as *cairters*. Forerunners of today's 'White Van Man', this army of men in old tweed suits and flat-cap bunnets worn at a rakish angle drove their horses and carts around Scotland's cities, transporting all manner of goods. Many of them were directly employed by town councils.

Socialists were clear as to why there were so many strikes. The cost of living was rising and wages weren't keeping pace. In its last edition of the year, Saturday, 30 December 1911, the *Forward*'s front-page leading article was entitled 'The Struggle in Scotland during 1911 for a Living Wage'. Their round-up of the year's news included one shocking statistic they had published earlier in the year, that 17,000 women in Glasgow made their living by walking the streets as prostitutes. The socialist newspaper was scathing about how long it had taken the press and the Kirk to wake up to this.

Interestingly, Tom Johnston chose not to mention the National Insurance Act in his overview of 1911. Regarded now as the foundation stone of Britain's Welfare State, this initiative of the Liberal administration in which Asquith was prime minister and David Lloyd George the minister for pensions provided for the first time for health and unemployment insurance for workers. Those who earned less than £160 per annum were to contribute fourpence a week, their employers threepence and the government twopence. Health insurance and the right to consult what became known as the 'panel doctor' did not yet cover workers' families.

Germany had introduced compulsory national insurance as far back as 1884. Lloyd George used this in support of Britain's proposed scheme, arguing that we should be 'putting ourselves in this field on a level with Germany. We should not emulate them only in armaments.' Unfortunately, that race was already being hard run and no one seemed able to stop it, although some people did try.

On the same day as they previewed the Scottish Exhibition, the *Glasgow Herald* published an account of the inaugural meeting at the Mansion House in London of the Anglo–German Friendship Society. This appointed the Duke of Argyll honorary secretary. Lord Aberdeen was also in attendance. The aim of the new society was 'to encourage cordiality and friendly feelings between the British and German peoples'.

Lord Avebury asked, 'What in the world were we to go to war about with Germany or Germany with us?' War, he said, would be disastrous to both countries:

> If European monarchs were to retain their thrones, if peace was to be maintained, statesmen must devise some means of stopping this reckless and ruinous expenditure on armaments, which pressed so heavily on the springs of industry and aggravated so terribly and so unnecessarily the unavoidable anxieties and troubles of life. We were one race, we had a common religion and common interests, we were bound by ties of blood, by centuries of peace, and a thousand years of immemorial friendship.

Keir Hardie agreed with Lord Avebury on this one. In the same edition in which he had written about the struggle to make a living wage, Tom Johnston reported what Hardie had written in *Vorwärts*, the German socialists' counterpart of the *Forward*. Invited by the editor of the German newspaper to contribute, Hardie sent fraternal New Year's greetings in advance of the forthcoming elections to the Reichstag on 12 January 1912:

> It so happens that the Social Democratic Party of Germany is universally admitted in this country to be wholehearted on the side of peace. If therefore the Social Democrats make substantial gains at the polls, every one here – anti-German and pro-German alike – will accept that as indisputable proof that the German people desire peace.
>
> It is for this reason that the result of the elections is being awaited with so much interest and why thousands of people who are not themselves Socialists are praying for the success of the German Social Democratic Party on 12th January.
>
> A great Socialist triumph on that day would not only sweep the clouds of war from off the political horizon but would also make it

easy for an understanding to be reached between Germany and Great Britain concerning future naval policy and thus the taxpayers of both countries would be relieved of the crushing burden which the present rivalry in Dreadnought building imposes.

Meanwhile, back at Kelvingrove, the fine summer of 1911 and the colourful exhibits, pageants and concerts of the Scottish Exhibition were fast becoming a fond memory. The event lives on in a few photographs, postcards and souvenirs. It had been hugely successful, surpassing all expectations.

It's only a pity that the corner of the park in which we're standing allows us to see the Angel of Death, lurking in the shadows under the rustling leaves of the autumn trees as the lights of Kelvingrove's last great exhibition dimmed for the final time.

8

Radicals, Reformers & Martyrs: The Roots of Red Clydeside

George the Third and last, and
damnation to all crowned heads.

The Red Clydesiders had impressive forebears from whom they drew strength and inspiration. Many were driven by their Christian faith. They read their Bible, took its teachings to heart and saw Christ as the first socialist. Protestants looked back to the Covenanters of the seventeenth century and their fight to worship God in the way they thought He wanted them to. Devout Catholics like John Wheatley found their politics and their faith completely compatible. As an advert in the *Forward* in December 1911 had it:

Are you a Socialist and a Christian?
Then for any Sake DO SOMETHING . . .
Get a copy of Brewster's Sermons (cost 6d., or 7d., per post), from
the Reformers' Bookstall. Read it and LEND it!
Brewster was the great Chartist minister of Paisley Abbey, and his
Sermons are the most eloquent Labour Appeals in the English
Language.
MAKE MORE SOCIALISTS:
If you send 7d., we will post you a copy.
BUT DO SOMETHING!

In January 1926 the socialist newspaper carried an extract from a sermon preached by the Reverend John Munro, who was also Labour parliamentary candidate for East Renfrew. He was in absolutely no doubt that 'the ideals of the Labour Party are the ideals of the Old

Testament prophets, thousands of years ago'. The italics which follow are his:

> We come to the founder of our Christian faith, the head of our Church, Jesus, the Carpenter of Nazareth. He fulfilled the sayings of these Old Testament prophets. He went further than any of them. 'Never man spake like this man,' the Bible says.
>
> He was a carpenter to trade, worked in the little Highland village of Nazareth, reading a great deal, and thinking a great deal.
>
> He set out to preach what we now call his gospel. He took with him as comrades a few labouring men, three or four fishermen, a farm labourer, and *one at least (Simon Zelotes) who had lost his job because of his violent political opinions.*

Scotland's history also inspired the Red Clydesiders, although many of them, like communist Harry McShane, would have no truck with a romanticized view of it, especially when it came to kings and queens. In *The History of the Working Classes in Scotland* Tom Johnston took a similar and characteristically robust view. He was particularly scathing about the hero of Bannockburn. Since most ordinary Scots in the Middle Ages lived as vassals to an overlord, for Johnston the battles fought by Robert the Bruce were 'facetiously termed "The War of Independence"'. He quoted Thomas Carlyle's comments on Sir Walter Scott's *Tales of a Grandfather*:

> It is noteworthy that the nobles of the country (Scotland) have maintained a quite despicable behaviour since the days of Wallace downwards – a selfish, ferocious, famishing, unprincipled set of hyenas, from whom at no time, and in no way, has the country derived any benefit whatsoever.

Yet Johnston quotes Wallace too, using words attributed to him when talking of the influence his uncle the Priest of Dunipace had on him. By tradition, this was the man who told his nephew, 'I have brought you to the ring – dance according to your skill.'

Dico tibi verum; Libertas optima rerum,
Nunquam servili sub nexu, vivito fili!

My son, I tell thee soothfastlie
No gift is like to liberty.
Then never live in slaverie!

All these words and more can be read on the dramatic, larger-than-life statue of William Wallace which towers over Union Terrace Gardens in Aberdeen.

Red Clydeside can be viewed as a class and economic struggle, bosses and workers pitted against each other in a never-ending battle. One of the slogans of the Wobblies, the Industrial Workers of the World, neatly sums this up: 'The interests of capital and labour can never be the same.' It may then be somewhat ironic that Clydeside's innate radical bent has roots in Glasgow's long history as a city of merchants and traders. Such entrepreneurs had to be forward-looking, always seeking opportunities, always willing to embrace change. In the eighteenth century Glasgow and the Clyde grew prosperous on the back of such business zeal, most especially through the tobacco trade with America.

By the middle of the 1700s the city was importing half of all the tobacco produced in Virginia and North Carolina. Although some of this was processed in Glasgow, much was sold on, carried across the narrow waist of Scotland, from where it was re-exported to Holland and Belgium. It wasn't only the tobacco lords who profited from this. Glasgow's factories and mills geared up to send the tobacco ships back across the Atlantic with the many different goods the American colonists needed. The Workshop of the World was in business.

There was a trade in ideas too. Scots of the Age of Enlightenment watched with intense interest as Americans sought to free themselves from the British Crown and establish a new kind of government, one in which the people had a say. That the people should even be thought of as being entitled to have their say was a profoundly radical idea. As far as most of Scotland's gentry and aristocracy were concerned, democracy was not something to be aspired to but something to be resisted at all costs. In the same way, reform was also a dirty word.

Decades before the American Revolution, in the Glasgow of the 1740s, merchants and traders were beginning to find the deference demanded by the gentry irksome. It got in the way of business, slowed everything down, put unnecessary checks on commercial and industrial progress. At Glasgow University at the same time, Francis Hutcheson was lecturing during Sunday-evening extramural classes open to townsfolk as well as students, on the need for religious tolerance and political liberty. The Ulster-born son of a Scottish father, he had been preaching this gospel for years before the Jacobite army, led by Bonnie Prince Charlie, occupied Glasgow over Christmas and New Year 1745–6.

Charles Edward Stuart was never a noted fan of democracy. Many of those who rallied to his standard were, seeing in him and the '45 the only focus for their discontent over Scotland's loss of independence a generation before and their desire for change and reform. Indeed, it can be argued that the Jacobites of 1745 forged a political movement ahead of its time. In the days before democracy, how else was change to be brought about other than by fighting for it?

One crucial principle Francis Hutcheson advocated was that people should see themselves as citizens and not subjects of the state. If you lived under a repressive government, it was not only to be expected that you would rebel, it was your duty to rebel. His ideas may well have influenced some of the Jacobites of 1745. Later in the century they certainly had an impact on the Americans who fought for and won the United States' independence from Britain.

Thomas Muir of Huntershill, whose home in Bishopbriggs still stands, was another man who believed tyranny should be challenged wherever it was encountered, a view which got him into trouble when he was a student at Glasgow University in the late eighteenth century. Originally destined for the ministry, he transferred to Edinburgh and studied law instead.

When he graduated and began to practise his trade, 'his rooms were the reform centre in Edinburgh'. Tom Johnston wrote of him, 'Muir was a born rebel, and gathered about him everyone who had sympathies with the French Revolution, as a magnet attracts iron filings.' Muir became a leading light of the Friends of the People, helping found branches throughout central Scotland:

> It was he who organised a meeting of the middle classes in the Star Hotel, Glasgow, on the 30th day of October, 1792, for the purpose of forming a Friends of the People Society in the city which should co-operate with the London Society in demanding 'equal political representation and shorter parliaments'; it was he who conceived and organised the Convention of the Reform Societies for the December following in Edinburgh; it was he who framed the Convention's standing orders; it was he who denounced leaders, and congratulated

the Convention upon paying little attention to leaders; it was he who insisted, despite the frantic pleadings of the milder conventionists, upon reading the treasonable address from the revolutionary society of United Irishmen . . .

Nor did he confine himself to the middle classes. Thomas Muir of Huntershill believed democracy was for everyone:

It was he who toured the weaving districts and addressed the mobs at Kirkintilloch, Kilmarnock, Paisley, Lennoxtown, and innumerable other places; it was he who, though, declaring himself meantime no Republican and setting his face steadily against riot and insurrection as being 'more likely than not to harm the people's cause,' inspired the three hundred delegates of the Edinburgh Convention to conclude the proceedings by standing, and holding up each his right hand, take a solemn oath to live free or die. Suddenly the Government swooped down upon the agitators.

In all this revolutionary fervour three Edinburgh printers drank a toast to 'George the Third and last, and damnation to all crowned heads'. They were sentenced to nine months' hard labour. An excuse to arrest Thomas Muir came when letters intended for him went instead to a different Mr Muir, who handed them over to the authorities.

These letters which so unluckily went astray contained information on the distribution of pamphlets written by Muir of Huntershill. One of the seditious statements he had made in these political tracts was to describe the House of Commons as 'a vile junta of aristocrats'. Those words alone were enough to get him arrested. It was 1793, and he was 28 years old. Released on bail, he travelled to France, where he tried in vain to persuade the revolutionary government not to guillotine Louis XVI and Marie Antoinette because this would damn the cause of reform in other countries. On his return to Scotland, he was arrested when he stepped ashore at Stranraer and taken to Edinburgh for trial. He had the misfortune to come up before the deeply unpleasant Lord Braxfield, notorious as a hanging judge, but remained defiant when he spoke in his own defence:

As for me, I am careless and indifferent to my fate. I can look danger and I can look death in the face, for I am shielded by the consciousness of my own rectitude. I may be condemned to languish in the recesses of a dungeon, I may be doomed to ascend the scaffold; nothing can deprive me of the recollection of the past – nothing can destroy my inward peace of mind arising from the remembrance of having discharged my duty.

Lord Braxfield responded with spluttering distaste for the French and disbelief at the gall of those who dared to demand democracy and universal suffrage. Braxfield spoke the broadest of Scots, reportedly encouraging one of the jury members to 'Come awa', Maister Horner, come awa', and help us to hang ane o' thae damned scoundrels!' His response to Thomas Muir has come down to us translated into Standard English:

> And what kind of folks were they? I never liked the French all the days of my life, and now I hate them . . . Multitudes of ignorant weavers . . . Mr Muir might have known that no attention could be paid to such a rabble. What right had they to representation? I could have told them that Parliament would never listen to their petition. How could they think of it? A Government in every country should be just like a corporation, and in this country it is made up of the landed interest which alone has a right to be represented.

Muir and his fellow defendants were found guilty and sentenced to 14 years of penal servitude in Australia. The French tried unsuccessfully to rescue him on his way there.

Once he was in Botany Bay, Thomas Muir's social status allowed him more freedom than other convicts. Three years into his sentence, he took advantage of this to make good his escape. After an extraordinary series of adventures, which included George Washington sending a ship to rescue him, a shipwreck and a violent clash at sea with a British frigate, he eventually made it back to Europe, where he found refuge in France.

Fighting in the naval skirmish had cost him an eye and left him with a shattered cheekbone. His health never recovered from his injuries or the exertions of his journey halfway across the world. The Radical from Bishopbriggs died at Chantilly in France in 1799, at the age of 34. One hundred years later, Tom Johnston pronounced an angry epitaph:

> He had given his life for political democracy in the land of his birth; perhaps had he known that the Scots people would value their

franchises so lightly that they would hand them over regularly at election times to Braxfield's class – had he foreseen that, perhaps he had spared himself the sacrifice!

Muir was an inspiration to people in his own time, including Robert Burns. The poet might have had to keep his head down for the sake of his job as an exciseman and, more importantly, as he himself wrote, for the sake of 'having a wife and little ones', but his Radicalism was never very far below the surface. It's believed Burns started writing 'Scots Wha Hae' on the first day of Thomas Muir's trial and that the stirring words refer not only to Bruce and Wallace but also to Muir.

The harsh treatment meted out to the Radicals of the 1790s did not stop continuing political protest and agitation for reform. Twenty-one years after Muir of Huntershill died in France came the Radical Rising of 1820. The economic depression which followed the Napoleonic Wars and the increasing pace of the Industrial Revolution helped fuel demands for reform throughout Britain. More and more people had been attracted to Britain's cities with the promise of work in mills and factories. The economic slump which follows all wars led to many of them losing their jobs. An infamous clash came at St Peter's Field in Manchester in 1819, when a meeting calling for parliamentary reform and an extension of the right to vote was attacked by cavalry armed with swords. Eighteen people died in the Peterloo Massacre and five hundred were wounded, including one hundred women.

In the west of Scotland the same discontent came to a head in the spring of 1820. The government played the dirtiest of tricks, employing agents provocateurs to stir genuine Radicals and reformers into actions which would lead to disaster. Spreading rumours that a revolution was planned throughout the British Isles, they chose a sadly appropriate date to post placards all over Glasgow and towns and villages in a wide area around it.

On April Fool's Day 1820, a Sunday, churchgoers found themselves confronted by an 'ADDRESS TO THE INHABITANTS OF GREAT BRITAIN AND IRELAND'. Purporting to be from the 'Committee of Organisation for forming a Provisional Government, Glasgow, April 1, 1820', it was a call to arms: 'Liberty or death is our motto, and we have sworn to *return home* in triumph or return no more!'

Disinformation spread by the government spies makes it hard to get at the truth of the Radical Rising, but the discontent and the desire for change were real and profound. Having provoked the fight, the government readied itself to meet the revolution with lethal force. Tom Johnston again:

> Local eruptions were disregarded; the Government was in no hurry; the troops could bide their time until a Radical army of ill-armed, ill-disciplined rebel weavers had been gathered, and then, in one great carnage, would be taught a lesson that would serve to humiliate two or three generations of the discontented common folk.

One of those rebel weavers was Andrew Hardie, a young Glasgow man. He and about 80 other men rendezvoused on the hill which is now the Necropolis, behind Glasgow Cathedral. There they were met by government spies masquerading as fellow Radicals and persuaded to march to the Carron Iron Works at Falkirk to seize cannons and meet up with a rebel army marching up from England. This army did not exist, an invention of the agents provocateurs.

The Radical army marched via Condorrat and Castlecary. At Condorrat Andrew Hardie met John Baird, the local smith, and the two men found themselves elected leaders of their small force. It grew smaller still as the government spies gradually peeled off. Fear also thinned the ranks, so that only about 50 men reached Bonnymuir, where the next bloody act of the drama was played out. As ever, Tom Johnston tells it beautifully, describing what happened when this ill-equipped army of weavers marched 'straight into the arms of the 10th Hussars':

> What followed is well-known. How the troops dashed upon them, and how they crouched behind a dyke and fought desperately until almost every man of them was wounded and some were killed, and how nineteen weary and wounded men that night lay prisoners of war in Stirling Castle. That was the great battle of Bonnymuir . . . the 'revolution' fell to pieces in a single night.

Blood was shed in Paisley, and in Greenock where six men died when the jail was stormed in a successful attempt to free Radical prisoners.

In Strathaven in Lanarkshire James Wilson, a stocking maker in his 60s, marched with another band which had been filled with false promises of a new dawn by the agents provocateurs. Wilson had carried a banner which read 'Scotland free or a desert! Strathaven Union'. They arrested him and hanged him in Jail Square in Glasgow at the end of August 1820, afterwards giving him a pauper's burial 'as a last mean mark of contempt'. That night his daughter and niece disinterred his body and took him home to Strathaven. He had wanted to be buried 'in the dust of his fathers'.

John Baird and Andrew Hardie were hanged at Stirling just over a week later, on Friday, 8 September 1820. Eighteen other Radical leaders had been transported to Australia, but Prime Minister Viscount Castlereagh had called for a 'lesson on the scaffold'. Now in the National Library of Scotland, a contemporary broadside costing one penny gave a report of the execution:

> Yesterday, 8th September, 1820, the preparation for the execution of these unfortunate men having been completed the previous night, this morning the scaffold appeared to the view of the inhabitants. On each side the scaffold was placed a coffin, at the head of which was a tub, filled with saw-dust, destined to receive the head. To the side of the tub was affixed a block.

The prisoners, it was noted, were 'respectably dressed in black'. Decency at executions was much prized. This was not bloody murder. This was justice. Well guarded by soldiers, they were marched out of Stirling Castle and down to the prison. The authorities were nervous, fearing trouble from the crowd. Although they had ensured that was smaller than it might have been, people did have to be there to witness the proceedings. How else would the lesson be taught?

When they reached the scaffold, 'Hardie looked up and smiled – Baird surveyed the dreadful apparatus with earnestness, but composure. Both prisoners, but especially Hardie, looked eagerly and keenly at their veiled companion, but did not address him.'

Their veiled companion was the executioner.

Three ministers were also in attendance. Prayers were said and a few verses of the 51st psalm, from the 7th verse, were 'sung by the prisoners and others present, Hardie giving out two lines at a time, in a clear and distinct voice, and sung the same without any tremulency'.

> Purge me with hyssop, and I shall be clean;
> Wash me, and I shall be whiter than snow.
> Make me to hear joy and gladness;

> That the bones which thou hast broken may rejoice.
> Hide thy face from my sins,
> And blot out all mine iniquities.
> Create in me a clean heart, O God;
> And renew a right spirit within me.

This was the same psalm which James Wilson had asked the crowd who witnessed his execution to sing with him before he was hanged.

'Some refreshment being offered,' says the broadside of the Stirling executions, 'Hardie took a glass of sherry, and Baird a glass of port.' Both men then mounted the scaffold. It was now about half past two in the afternoon. John Baird addressed the crowd first, advising them to study their Bibles. Andrew Hardie told them, 'I die a martyr to the cause of truth and justice.' Instead of going to the pub to drink to him and Baird, people ought to go home and pray. At about ten to three, on a signal from Hardie, the men were hanged:

> After hanging half an hour, they were cut down and placed upon the coffins, with their heads upon a block; the headsman then came forward; he was a little man, apparently about 18 years of age; he wore a black crape over his face, a hairy cap, and a black gown. On his appearance there was a cry of murder. He struck the neck of Hardie thrice before it was severed; then held it up with both hands, saying: 'This is the head of a traitor.' He severed the head of Baird at two blows, and held it up in the same manner, and used the same words. The coffins were then removed, and the crowd peaceably dispersed.

In *The King's Jaunt*, John Prebble says that this young headsman was a medical student. It was a long time since anyone in Scotland had been hung, drawn and quartered. The last in Britain had been the Jacobites executed after the '45, and they were all put to death at Carlisle, York and London. Perhaps Tam Young, the hangman at Stirling, baulked at carrying out the butchery.

The two men were buried in a single grave outside Stirling Castle. Almost 30 years later a group of Glasgow Radicals exhumed them and took them back to Glasgow. They reburied them in Sighthill Cemetery and raised a monument there to the Radicals of 1820.

Only 12 years after Wilson, Baird and Hardie were so barbarically and publicly put to death came the Great Reform Act of 1832, the measure which led the way to parliamentary democracy in Britain. Andrew Hardie's mother put these lines up on a card in her window:

> Britons, rejoice, Reform is won!
> But 'twas the cause
> Lost me my son.

In the 1840s the Chartists took up the fight. Seventy years on from their struggles there remained plenty of work for the Red Clydesiders to do, still a muddy and rough road to be travelled until real democracy was achieved. Some might say we're still on it.

Scotland's Radicals continue to inspire. They always have. In 1938, the Camlachie branch of the ILP produced a huge banner in support of the people of Spain fighting a civil war against fascism. It can be seen today in Glasgow's People's Palace. In large red letters, the legend reads:

THOMAS MUIR
BAIRD AND HARDIE
DIED
THAT YOU SHOULD BE FREE
TO CHOOSE YOUR GOVERNMENT

WORKERS IN SPAIN
ARE DYING
BECAUSE THEY DARED TO
CHOOSE THEIR OWN
GOVERNMENT

UNITE FOR THE STRUGGLE!

9

Halloween at the High Court

*It was afterwards found that the hard missiles thrown at the
Judge were apples.*

In 1911 suffragettes' hopes were both raised and dashed. First came the
announcement that a parliamentary committee was to draft a bill to
give women the vote. Towards the end of the year, Prime Minister Asquith
announced the bill was to be shelved for the time being.

As the frustration of many suffragettes boiled over into anger, direct
action and much smashing of windows, one Glasgow glazier famously
found a silver lining. James Caldwell's advert in the *Forward* in 1912
advises potential customers that 'SUFFRAGETTES MAY BREAK
WINDOWS, BUT I AM THE WEE BOY [THAT] CAN PUT THEM IN.'

The destruction soon escalated way beyond the breaking of windows.
In Scotland, militant suffragettes burned down the railway station at
Leuchars in Fife and the mediaeval church of Whitekirk in East Lothian,
planted a bomb at Glasgow's Botanic Gardens and tried to blow up Burns
Cottage at Alloway. In June 1913 English suffragette Emily Davison
stepped out in front of the King's horse at the Derby and sacrificed her
life to the cause.

Many women were appalled by violent tactics and set their faces
completely against them. Others seem to have been ready to carry out
acts of terrorism without a qualm. Others again had to do some real soul-
searching before they could contemplate less violent but still destructive
acts. Helen Crawfurd of Glasgow was one of those. Militant suffragettes
were planning a window-smashing raid in London, to take place over
three days in March 1912. When Scottish suffragettes started talking
about heading south and joining in, she sought guidance in her husband's
church.

Alexander Crawfurd was a powerful preacher, with a sonorous voice and a dramatic delivery. That Sunday he chose to weave his sermon around the story of Christ throwing the moneylenders out of the temple. All unknowing, he led his wife to her decision. If Christ could be militant, then so could she. She went to London, smashed a few windows, was arrested and tried and sentenced to one month in Holloway. It was another eye-opening experience for her and often a distressing one, giving her an insight into the lives of the poor London women who were her fellow inmates.

While all this breaking of glass might sound pointlessly destructive, the suffragettes did have a point to make. The law dealt very severely with crimes against property. In contrast, crimes against people, especially young girls who were raped or sexually abused, were often dealt with very leniently. In their destruction of property, the suffragettes were making a lot of noise to draw attention to their cause but also protesting against this injustice.

Helen Crawfurd was in Holloway with other suffragette friends from Glasgow, including Janie Allan and Frances and Margaret McPhun. When Janie Allan went on hunger strike, she was force-fed for a week. Ten thousand people in Glasgow signed a petition protesting against her imprisonment and ill treatment.

The government which had not had time to discuss a bill bringing in female suffrage found time to pass a new law which became known as the Cat and Mouse Act. This allowed the authorities to release suffragettes on hunger strike on licence. Once they had spent time at home eating normally and regaining their health, they were re-arrested and the whole cycle began again.

Ethel Moorhead was one of those who did time in Holloway after the window-smashing raid. Born to Irish parents, she lived for many years in Scotland, working as an artist at her studio in Dundee. She earned a fearsome reputation as one of Scotland's most militant suffragettes, as her entry in *The Biographical Dictionary of Scottish Women* relates:

> When her father died in 1911, Ethel Moorhead joined the WSPU. Using a string of aliases she smashed windows in London and a showcase at the Wallace Monument in Stirling; threw an egg at Churchill and pepper at the police; attacked a teacher with a dog whip; wrecked police cells and was involved in several arson attempts.

It was attempted fire-raising which brought her to the dock at the High Court in Glasgow in October 1913, on trial with her co-accused, Dorothea Chalmers Smith. Helen Crawfurd was one of their many friends filling the public gallery.

Dorothea Chalmers Smith was a doctor, mother of six children and wife of the minister of Calton Parish Church, in Glasgow's East End. She and Ethel Moorhead stood accused of having attempted to burn down a large empty house in Glasgow's West End. As the indictment read:

> . . . the charge against you is that you did, on July 23, 1913, break into an unoccupied dwelling-house at No. 6 Park Gardens, Glasgow, and did convey or cause to be conveyed thereto, a quantity of firelighters, firewood, a number of pieces of candles, a quantity of paper, cotton wool, cloth, and a number of tins of paraffin oil and did place these, along with three venetian blinds, at or against a wooden door in a passage on the first floor of said house, and this you did with intent to set fire to said door and burn said house.

Dr Chalmers Smith and Ethel Moorhead refused to plead either guilty or not guilty. The judge told them he'd take that as a plea of not guilty and suggested they ought to have got themselves a legal adviser. Ethel Moorhead's sharp retort drew laughter from their friends in the public gallery: 'We generally find that they make a muddle of it. We prefer to defend ourselves.'

The trial proceeded. One witness testified that he had been taken to Duke Street Prison to see if he could identify the woman who had called at the solicitor's office where he worked asking to be shown around the big empty house in Park Gardens. He couldn't be sure; when he had visited the prison, both of the accused had been in bed and had refused to get up. Not to be outdone by the troublesome females in the dock, the judge tried for a laugh. Now he saw her fully dressed, could the witness identify the woman who had called at his place of employment? The witness could. The two would-be arsonists were found guilty and sentenced to eight months' imprisonment. It was at this point that pandemonium broke out in the court.

The suffragettes in the public gallery had risen to their feet as soon as the judge had pronounced the sentence. Now they began shouting, 'Pitt Street! Pitt Street!' They yelled the name over and over again. They hurled projectiles down into the court. The *Glasgow Herald* was horrified by what it called this 'scene of indescribable disorder and confusion . . . creating a disturbance probably without parallel in a Glasgow Court of Justice'.

Some two weeks earlier, a much more lenient sentence had been handed down in a Glasgow court. A brothel at Pitt Street near Charing Cross had been raided and the rumour going the rounds was that several of Glasgow's prominent citizens had been found there enjoying what the house of ill repute had to offer. Yet they had suffered no censure and the husband and wife who ran the brothel had been sentenced to only two weeks in prison.

The *Glasgow Herald's* sister paper, the *Evening Times*, gave a less formal account of the noisy protest at the court. 'Judge Pelted', read its headline. Under a subtitle of 'Pelting the Bench', it described the uproar which broke out as soon as the sentence was passed:

> A storm of protest from most of the women present was immediately raised. In chorus they shouted 'Shame, shame,' and, without further warning, a missile was hurled at the bench by someone near the front of the area. It struck the woodwork below the judge's seat with a resounding blow and fell to the floor.
>
> So sudden was the attack that Lord Salvesen involuntarily raised his arms as though to protect his face. The first missile was followed by a second which just missed the head of the clerk (Mr. Slight) and also struck the front woodwork of the bench.
>
> A scene of wild confusion followed.

Neither the *Glasgow Herald* nor the *Evening Times* reported that the women had shouted 'Pitt Street, Pitt Street!' as well as 'Shame, shame!' What the *Evening Times* did solemnly tell its readers was, 'It was afterwards found that the hard missiles thrown at the Judge were apples.'

So the suffragettes had gone prepared. Helen Crawfurd did note that the apples were small ones. Whether they chose these because the trial took place a fortnight before Halloween and there were plenty around or because small apples might hurt less – or perhaps more – she doesn't say. Glasgow, as it always does, saw the humour in the situation.

Like the other Glasgow newspapers, the *Glasgow News* carried a report on the trial the day after it took place and, the day after that, a cartoon depicting the scene in the courtroom. The story was obviously too good to let go. Whoever drew the cartoon must have witnessed the mayhem at first hand. The drawing perfectly depicts Mr Slight, the clerk of the court, ducking to avoid the flying apples. Some artistic licence allows both the wigged and gowned judge and prosecuting lawyer to get one in the eye while gripping a fork between their teeth as though they were dooking for them at a Halloween party.

What happened after that was not so comical. In February 1914 Ethel Moorhead, who had been released and re-arrested under the Cat and Mouse Act, became the first woman in Scotland to be force-fed. This happened at Perth Prison. Many had believed Scotland would never resort to such horrific treatment of prisoners, especially when those prisoners were women. When, in the summer of 1914, it emerged that two suffragette prisoners in Perth had been force-fed *per rectum*, the public recoiled in horror. A vigil was held outside the prison to protest, and Helen Crawfurd was one of those who took part.

Freed by her husband's death in May 1914 to become more active in her political endeavours, she was now living in the West End of Glasgow with her brothers William and John and her sister Jean. They had put their money together so as to be able to rent a flat in Hyndland and hire a housekeeper to look after them. She was in Perth in July 1914 when the King visited the fair city as part of a Scottish tour. One placard displayed at a window extended a mock invitation to the royal visitor: 'Visit Your Majesty's Torture Chamber in Perth Prison.' Then the news came through that two suffragettes had tried to blow up Robert Burns's cottage in Alloway.

Force-feeding of suffragettes had garnered much public sympathy. The assault on Burns' Cottage threatened to swing the pendulum as far back in the other direction as it could possibly go. The *Glasgow Herald* described the attack as a 'dastardly outrage':

Alloway Outrage
Attempt to Blow up Burns's Cottage
Suffragist in Custody

A dastardly attempt was made in the early hours of yesterday morning by suffragists to fire and blow up Burns's Cottage, Alloway, the birthplace of the national poet, which is annually visited by thousands of pilgrims from all parts of the world. The attempted outrage was fortunately frustrated by the timely appearance on the scene of the night watchman, but the fact that an attempt was made to destroy a shrine that Scotsmen in all parts of the world regard as sacred has roused in the locality the most intense indignation.

There was further outrage when one of the two suffragists responsible – 'suffragette' had still not entirely caught on – was found to be Frances Parker, niece of Lord Kitchener, the man whose eyes were to follow people from the First World War recruiting poster telling them that their country needed them. Fanny Parker's accomplice at Alloway escaped by bike, leaving behind two canisters containing 4 lb of gunpowder apiece.

Engaged to address the crowd at Perth that evening after the news had broken, fearing there might be people within the throng feeling hostile towards all suffragettes as a result, Helen Crawfurd summoned up her courage and the ghost of Robert Burns. She started by telling her listeners it was his words which had inspired her to be able to speak to them after the shock of the attempted destruction of his childhood home. In illustration, she quoted from 'Scots Wha Hae':

> Wha wad be a traitor knave,
> Wha wad fill a coward's grave
> Wha sae base as be a slave
> Let him turn and flee

She explained that the two suffragettes who had tried to destroy Burns Cottage were not Scottish and simply could not understand the high esteem in which all Scots, men and women, held him. She finished by quoting Burns on the subject of the emancipation of women:

> While Europe's eye is fix'd on mighty things,
> The fate of Empires and the fall of Kings;
> While quacks of State must each produce his plan,
> And even children lisp the Rights of Man;
> Amid this mighty fuss just let me mention,
> The Rights of Woman merit some attention.

Giving Scotland's suffragettes the stalwart support he always did, Tom Johnston quoted Helen Crawfurd's speech to the crowd at Perth in full in the *Forward* of 18 July 1914.

Tried at Ayr Sheriff Court, Fanny Parker also quoted Burns, as the

Glasgow Herald wearily put it, 'at some length'. She also declared, 'You Scotsmen used to be proud of Burns; now you have taken to torturing women.'

On 29 July 1914 Glasgow's *Daily Record* announced that the Austrians had declared war on Serbia. This dramatic news shared the front page with news much closer to home. The previous evening, Mrs Pankhurst had visited Glasgow, where she spoke to a large audience in St Andrew's Halls. The *Daily Record*'s headlines were dramatic:

WILD RIOT IN GLASGOW
MRS PANKHURST ARRESTED
REVOLVER SHOTS IN ST ANDREW'S HALLS
Amid a scene of wild riot in St Andrew's Halls, Glasgow, last night, Mrs. Pankhurst, the suffragette leader, was arrested. The meeting, which was held under the auspices of the W.S.P.U., had an audience of about 5,000, the vast majority of whom were ladies.

Mrs. Pankhurst, despite the vigilance of the police, entered the hall by one of the main entrances wearing a large picture hat with a yellow feather and trimmings, and a thick black veil.

You wonder how they could have missed her. Janie Allan was convinced the revolver shots were an indicator that a government conspiracy was afoot to assassinate Mrs Pankhurst. In the event, the war between the government and the suffragettes was resolved by the conflict which was about to engulf Europe.

On 4 August 1914 Britain declared war on Germany. The suffragettes immediately called a truce with the British government.

Red Clydeside, however, was just about to initiate hostilities.

10

Not in My Name

This murder business.

As Red Clydesider Willie Gallacher wrote in his vivid autobiography, *Revolt on the Clyde*:

> What terrible attraction a war can have! The wild excitement, the illusion of wonderful adventure and the actual break in the deadly monotony of working-class life! Thousands went flocking to the colours in the first days, not because of any 'love of country,' not because of any high feeling of 'patriotism,' but because of the new, strange and thrilling life that lay before them. Later the reality of the fearsome slaughterhouse, with all its long agony of filth and horror, turned them from buoyant youth to despair or madness.

Yet there were thousands who were passionately opposed to the war from the outset, many of them on Red Clydeside. On 15 August 1914, above another cartoon by Robins Millar depicting a ferocious and wild-eyed female warrior headed 'Europe Goes Stark Mad', *Forward* published a report on a peace demonstration held on Glasgow Green, estimating that 5,000 people were there. There's no way of corroborating those numbers, as only the socialist newspaper covered the story, subtitling their piece 'Boycotted by Press'.

The peace demonstration was organized by the ILP and the Glasgow branch of the Peace Society. *Forward* was at pains to assure its readers that the demonstrators had come from a broad social spectrum:

> The gathering was Cosmopolitan in character and included doctors and dock labourers and rebels of every possible brand from mild

peace advocates to the wildest of revolutionaries.

One thing was made obvious by the meeting: that the war is unpopular with people who think, while the rise in food prices is tempering the bellies of those who don't think.

One of the speakers was John Wheatley of the ILP, who had now been elected Councillor Wheatley. Another was his fellow ILP member Patrick Dollan. All the speakers condemned the war, telling the crowd that 'the working people [of Britain and Germany] had no quarrel with each other'. This was reiterated by the chairman of the Peace Society, a Miss Adams. After she and her fellow members of the society had spoken, resolutions were read out which had been agreed upon:

> . . . by huge gatherings of workers in Austria, Germany and France against war. These workers did not want war, and yet, in spite of their friendship for each other, the shadow of Death overcast Europe. Few homes in Europe would escape scathless from the passage of that shadow.

As we all now know, Miss Adams was proved horribly right in her prediction. At the time, many other people really did believe it would all be over by Christmas. Harry McShane was one of them. In his autobiography, *No Mean Fighter*, he wrote that, when the First World War broke out in 1914, 'everyone, including the socialists, thought it would be fought by professional armies and volunteers'.

Those volunteers continued to flock to the colours. Conscription had not yet been introduced, nor did there yet seem any need for it. McShane too described the overheated atmosphere at the start of the war:

> A terrible war fever developed. Men rushed to join the army hoping that the war wouldn't be all over by the time they got to the front; they had to march in civilian clothes because there weren't enough uniforms to go round. Many young people, particularly those who were unemployed, were caught up in the adventure of the thing. On every hoarding there was a picture of Kitchener, the Secretary for War, pointing his finger, and saying 'Your Country Needs You'. There he was, and then along came daft middle-class women with white feathers trying to drive young men into the army.

As the cenotaph in Glasgow's George Square tells us, 200,000 went from Glasgow alone. Standing guard over the names of thousands more are Clydebank's beautiful art deco war memorial and, around the country, all the other impassive stone angels and sad soldiers, heads bowed over their rifles. Those who refused to be caught up in the war fever were swimming against a rushing tide. As many of them were to find out, on a personal level they were also treading a dangerous path.

The ILP was split over the war, although Keir Hardie knew exactly where he stood: he had always been against it. By 1915 he was failing fast, his ill health exacerbated by his efforts to prevent the slaughter having been in vain. In his biography of James Maxton, Gordon Brown offers a poignant vignette of Keir Hardie: 'It is said that latterly, because of his staunch opposition to the war, many of his old friends would ignore him or refuse to shake his hand.'

Willie Gallacher was another of those who spoke out against the war from the start. So was John Maclean, who called the fighting 'this murder business'. In her biography of him, his daughter Nan Milton describes how he and other socialists and Marxists helped gather together those who were against the war.

From as early as the end of 1914, Maclean organized open-air Sunday-evening meetings on the corner of Renfield Street and Bath Street. His friend and fellow socialist John MacDougall left a description of these, referring to himself at the end of this quote in the third person:

> From the very first the meeting attracted large numbers of Socialists. Sunday by Sunday it grew, as the seriousness of the War situation became plain to even the meanest intelligence, and after a number of weeks it had grown so large that the casual passers-by in Renfield Street were attracted. It is a broad street. It was packed from side to side so that a child could have walked on the heads of the people, and that condition extended a long distance down the street. Week after week there was to be seen a vast body of men and women, standing in tense silence, their attention riveted on the speakers for two or three hours on end, while a succession of speakers kept the meeting going. Maclean's principal assistants were MacDougall, George Pettigrew, Mrs Helen Crawfurd of the ILP and a famous suffragette, and William Gallacher.

The suffragettes might have declared a truce with Lloyd George and the government over votes for women, but during the First World War Helen Crawfurd was one of many women who turned their energies to campaigning for peace. In June 1916 she, her friend Agnes Dollan and others established the Women's Peace Crusade, hanselling the new organization with another mass meeting on Glasgow Green.

James Maxton was another Red Clydesider who was always bitterly opposed to the war. In August 1914 he wrote to his girlfriend Sissie McCallum, saying, 'There's no chance of me volunteering. I'm working for peace for all I'm worth.' Sissie was also a teacher, she and Maxton having met while working as colleagues at a school in Glasgow.

Like Maxton, John Maclean brought all his skills as a speaker to the fight against the war. At the Bath Street meetings, standing on a table in the middle of the crowd, he repeated what he and many socialists believed. War was 'the continuation of the peace competition for trade and for markets already carried on between the powers before hostilities broke out'. He told his audiences that capitalists and employers were the real enemy and that they should not join up to fight in a capitalist war:

> The men they were asked to shoot were their brothers, with the same difficulty on Saturdays to find a rent for their miserable dwellings, who had to suffer the same insults and impertinence from their gaffers and foremen. What did it matter if they looked a little different? And spoke a different language? The Scottish miners when on strike had often received financial help from the German miners. The international solidarity of the working-class was not only the highest moral sentiment that existed in the world, it had already found expression in many ways.

None of them was ever going to get away with any of this. As John MacDougall put it when writing about John Maclean:

> His hearers knew that for these precious words of exhortation and of hope the man would have to pay, and pay dearly. Would he be shot? Would the traditions of British Liberalism stand the strain of this unprecedented test when the British Empire was standing with its back to the wall? Nobody knew. Would he be drafted into the army like Karl Liebknecht?

Liebknecht was a German Socialist, much admired by his British counterparts. James Maxton had a dog called Karl, named not after Marx but Liebknecht.

The Bath Street protests continued. Pushing it even further, John Maclean raged against the 'British Junkers' who had introduced DORA, the Defence of the Realm Act. This imposed all kinds of wartime restrictions on freedom of speech and action. A new Munitions Act also enforced draconian rules and regulations.

For the duration of the hostilities, strikes were made illegal. Ships and armaments manufactured on the Clyde being crucial to the war effort, nobody in what was now designated the Clyde Munitions Area was allowed to change their job without permission. This was enforced by having to secure a leaving certificate to show to a new employer. The Clyde's workers referred to this as a slave clause, depriving workers of their few hard-won liberties.

At the beginning of 1915 Willie Gallacher and fellow shop stewards, including Davie Kirkwood and Arthur McManus, formed themselves into the Clyde Workers' Committee (CWC). The CWC was soon to clash head-on with the minister for munitions, Mr David Lloyd George. For them, Maxton, Maclean and MacDougall, the fight against the war and for workers' rights was soon to become very personal indeed.

11

A Woman's Place

My good lady, go home and sit still.

Traditional ideas of what constituted women's work and acceptable female activities and behaviour took a hammering during the First World War. The men who marched off to war left huge gaps behind them. These were felt right across the social spectrum, the lack, of course, emotional as well as practical.

During the Glasgow Fair holidays of the summer of 1915, a poignant cartoon appeared in *The Bailie*, Glasgow's normally humorous weekly newspaper. Against the backdrop of a pier on the Firth of Clyde, a young woman sits on a bench under a tree, alone and thoughtful. The caption reads: 'THE "FAIR" WITHOUT THE BRAVE.' *The Bailie* also informed its readers that moonlit cruises doon the watter had been suspended for the duration.

The absence of men threw up some unexpected benefits. *The Bulletin* was a sister paper to the *Glasgow Herald* which specialized in bright and breezy articles accompanied by lots of photographs. Showing lots of smiling young Glasgow gels driving, cranking their open-topped cars into action and inflating their tyres, in August 1915 it reported on this new phenomenon:

> Since the chauffeur went away to the war the motoring girl has come by her own.
>
> Many ladies could drive cars in the old days, but the motoring girl may be truly said to be a product of the war. These types seem to enjoy all the little troubles that afflict the chauffeur, and only refrain from burrowing beneath the car because nowadays that is unnecessary.

This new ease of movement allowed middle-class women and girls a much greater social and personal freedom. Writing in the woman's page of *The Bailie* in July of that same year, the unnamed reviewer of a book called *The Street of the Seven Stars* recognized this new development. Undoubtedly a lady reporter, she was still rather uncomfortable that a couple in the book were depicted as spending lots of time together *'sans chaperone'*, which meant it 'wasn't quite the thing for a Sunday School prize book'. In the same column she made the interesting observation that the current shortage of men meant women were having more opportunity to socialize together and were finding that they enjoyed one another's company.

Language and the codes by which it indicated class was another preoccupation:

> Some years ago a London barrister referred for the first time to his charlady, and now the word he introduced in jest is allowed to describe a very useful section of the community. Within recent weeks we have seen 'lady' car-conductors, 'lady' lamplighters, and later, I suppose, 'lady' scavengers. Even the dignified newspaper just round the corner in Buchanan Street speaks of the 'ladies' appointed to such branches of public work. And why not?
>
> Meantime we have 'female' teachers and 'women' doctors and, instead of clerks 'clerkesses,' a word that offends me only a little less than 'chairman,' when it would not be in the least awkward to say 'chairwoman,' and would convey a sensible meaning without disturbing anybody's prejudices.

Some of us might agree with her on that last point, finding it risible that the political correctness of our own days reinforces gender inequality by choosing the masculine form of a noun as the superior version. When it isn't turning human beings into pieces of furniture.

The Bailie's writer didn't believe the use of the word 'lady' could 'make two classes into one'. It wasn't that she was a snob. She believed completely that 'one woman is as good as another but that doesn't alter the fact that there are differences'.

> As to the 'lady' conductors, I like them; and they haven't yet begun to bully women as some of the gentlemen conductors certainly did when the women were elderly and of good social position. The car ladies

are exceedingly pleasant, and now that they have left off wearing earrings and lace neckties they are good to look at too.

A week later *The Bailie* reported again on the lady tram conductors, who don't yet seem to have become 'conductresses', the name by which future generations knew this fearsome form of Glasgow womanhood. The First World War variety were to be dressed in long skirts of Black Watch tartan, allowing *The Bailie* to go off on a flight of fancy that maybe they should also wear sporrans and carry skean dhus. A month later *The Bulletin* took a more serious look at the women working on the trams.

Allegations had been made that the new lady conductors were being overworked. *The Bulletin*'s lady reporter, again, of course, unnamed, was following up on a story which had appeared in a London newspaper. According to this interloper from south of the border, women working on Glasgow's trams were being asked to put in the same number of hours as the men they had replaced.

'The natural result' of this on one lady conductor was that 'after a few weeks she had to rest, because the strain was too great'. Even worse than that, when she took the time off to have that rest, she'd been sacked. With the distinct feeling that national pride was at stake here, *The Bulletin*'s intrepid lady reporter picked up her sword of truth:

> Manifestly it was a matter to be investigated, and Mr James Dalrymple, manager of the Corporation Tramways, was the man to see. So I went up to the flag-bedecked building in Bath Street, and the recruiting sergeants standing at the door grinned as I passed in. I suppose they imagined I was one more applicant for the green and tartan uniform!

Mr Dalrymple laughed off the story. So did the lady conductors to whom he gave the lady reporter full access:

> 'Of course we are treated as men in the matter of working hours,' said one woman whose husband is in the trenches, 'but we took up the work on that understanding, and – what is more important – we are treated as men in the matter of wages, too.'

The lady conductors worked six days a week, eight hours a day. At a total of 48 hours, this was a lot less than the 74 hours and more which waitresses in Glasgow's tea rooms were putting in. After interviewing a few more lady conductors, the lady reporter declared herself satisfied they did not feel they were being exploited and seemed to enjoy their work. One woman who had been in domestic service said working on the trams was infinitely preferable to doing housework all day long.

More traditional skills were still being valued. On the same page on which they carried the story about the new lady conductors on the trams, *The Bulletin* reported on the knitting achievements of an Ayrshire woman. Anticipating the arrival of winter and the consequent need for comforts for the troops, a smiling older lady is offered as a shining example for other women to follow:

> Mrs Ross, who resides at Darvel, is one of those whose industrious fingers have gone constantly since the first demand went forth. To date she has knitted 60 pairs of heavy sox [*sic*] for the boys at the front, and declares her willingness to knit more if need be.

The Bulletin returned to the 'sox' and comforts issue three weeks later, making an appeal to patriotism with just a touch of advertorial in it and another poignant observation: that there were more soldiers on the front line now, so more women needed to start knitting for them. With winter again approaching, the women's page tells its readers:

> . . . we women must set to work again, and knit and sew as hard as we did last winter – and even harder still, because we have more men to knit and sew for than we had last year. It is obvious that a Tommy warmly clad and comfortable must be a more efficient fighting man than a Tommy who is cold and shivering and miserable. And that is just where we women come in. Nowadays, we never hear of the girl who used to announce boastfully that she 'couldn't knit a pair of socks to save her life.' The war has changed all that, and the girl who has reason to boast in these days of war is the one who can knit a 'record' number of socks or mittens or scarves for Tommy within a given time.

The Scotch Wool and Hosiery Stores were happy to give 'special discounts to work-parties buying large quantities of wool', and a free hundred-page booklet of knitting patterns could be had from any of their branches. They had 260 of those all over Scotland, 14 in Glasgow alone. Or you could get the booklet by writing to their head office at the simple address of The Worsted Mills, Greenock.

The First World War freed many working-class women and girls from the drudgery of domestic service. Faced with the unthinkable prospect of having to make their own tea and put a few lumps of coal on their own fires, the middle classes whinged about that for the next 20 years, firing off irate letters to newspapers about the 'servant problem'.

Without an army of housekeepers, cooks and maids, a side effect of just not being able to get the staff these days was the encouragement it gave the inventors and manufacturers of labour-saving devices. These did not come cheap. Adverts which appeared in Glasgow newspapers during the First World War offered electric vacuum cleaners for five guineas. One of those tea room waitresses working for Mr Kerr, the military caterer, would have had to hand over her entire pay for three months to be able to buy one.

Old attitudes continued to die hard, especially when women started working alongside men in industries which had previously been exclusively male preserves. Probably this is why Beardmore's provided a separate canteen for their 'girl munition workers'. They and their canteen gave *The Bulletin*'s lady reporter another subject to write up.

Beardmore's had converted a 'light, bright room' into a canteen for their 300 female workers. Since they worked in shifts around the clock, meals were served throughout the day and night. The food was substantial. On the day the lady reporter went, dinner at one o'clock consisted of lentil soup, meat and potatoes, with rice pudding for dessert.

Wearing 'neat holland overalls and frilled caps', the cooks and canteen staff were unpaid, doing their bit for the war effort. Glasgow College of Domestic Science, 'the Do School' for short, was one of the organizations which recruited and supplied the volunteers.

Given a glamorous makeover, the female munitions worker in her brown overall and unflattering matching hat became one of the war's poster girls throughout Britain, encouraging other women to do their bit. This archetypal figure is remembered in a beautiful stained-glass window at what was the headquarters of the North British Locomotive Company and then Springburn College. As Flemington House, it is now the Abbey Mill Business Centre.

Other women from Glasgow, Clydebank and elsewhere in Scotland went off to war themselves, working as nurses, nursing auxiliaries and orderlies. Some joined the Red Cross, whose ambulance train toured

Scotland before leaving for France. People queued for hours at Glasgow Central, Paisley Gilmour Street, Greenock, Stirling and elsewhere to view it and make a donation.

Voluntary Aid Detachment nurses served in both world wars. The VADs themselves liked to say that the letters stood for 'Virgins Almost Desperate'.

The Scottish Women's Hospitals grew out of the Scottish Federation of the NUWSS, the National Union of Women's Suffrage Societies. Their moving spirit was Elsie Inglis. She was an Edinburgh doctor and suffragette, one of those vehemently opposed to the use of violence to get the vote. When the war broke out she immediately offered her services to the War Office.

The reply she got is almost magnificent in its breathtakingly dismissive sexism: 'My good lady, go home and sit still.' Elsie Inglis did the exact opposite. The Scottish Women's Hospitals were soon well established at Royaumont, in France – treating casualties from the Western Front – in Serbia and in Russia. They appealed regularly for donations via adverts in the Scottish newspapers.

The Bulletin carried these frequently, as well as stories and pictures of the Scottish nurses and doctors, all women, in their field hospitals on the front line. They were looking for £100,000 to help them care for the wounded. By September 1915, one year into the war, they were able to tell the folks back home they had already cared for more than 1,250 injured soldiers, and they detailed what they needed so they could tend to more:

1. To MAINTAIN the HOSPITAL at ABBAYE DE ROYAUMONT, near Creil (200 beds), under the FRENCH RED CROSS SOCIETY.
2. To establish the new hospital at Troyes (200 beds) under the FRENCH MILITARY AUTHORITIES.
3. To SUPPORT TWO UNITS now at work in SERBIA under the SERBIAN RED CROSS AND MILITARY AUTHORITIES (600 beds).
4. To MAINTAIN an AMBULANCE FLOTTANTE AT WORK between the Firing Line and the Two Hospitals in France.
5. To PROVIDE MOTOR AMBULANCES for these hospitals. It is hoped that the motorists of Scotland will assist in this appeal.
6. To SUPPLY COMFORTS, MEDICAL NECESSARIES, Etc., to the

TROOPS in FRANCE AND SERBIA.
£50 WILL NAME A BED FOR A YEAR.
£350 WILL PROVIDE AND EQUIP A MOTOR AMBULANCE.

Donations could be sent to Mrs Laurie of Greenock or to Dr Elsie Inglis in Edinburgh. *The Bulletin* backed up the advert with photographs of a Dr Butler and her husband, 'two Glasgow lady doctors', a group of Scottish nurses attached to Royaumont, and an approving editorial from its 'Paris correspondent':

> The Scottish Branch of the National Union of Women's Suffrage Societies, the non-militant section of the movement, has done splendid work in various directions since the war began, but in none more than in the equipping and staffing of military hospitals in France.

Dr Butler had graduated with flying colours from Glasgow University in 1890 and had been working on a cancer research project in Austria when war broke out. Her husband worked as a chauffeur at Royaumont.

While the suffragettes were doing their bit for the war effort, the storm of war continued to rage and conflict began to brew on the Clyde. For a brief moment in 1915, however, the clocks stopped.

12

Death of a Hero: The Funeral of Keir Hardie

He got more Socialism from Burns than from Marx.

On 26 September 1915 the ailing Keir Hardie died. Many believed the outbreak of the European war he had worked so hard to prevent was what really killed him. Tom Johnston was sure of it. His tribute on the front page of the *Forward* on 2 October 1915 spelled it out. Headlined 'The Passing of Keir Hardie', the article's subheading was unequivocal:

> He Died of a Broken Heart
> By THE EDITOR
> A Stroke. A Seizure. Pneumonia! Call it what you will, James Keir Hardie died of a broken heart. I know.
>   He died of a heartbreak at seeing his cherished dreams, his fondest hopes, his firmest faith shattered in an hour. He had given his all to the building of a Labour Party and to the making of that Labour Party a national wing in the International Army of Labour: he spent his energies and his health rushing feverishly on trains to forge the worker's weapon that would cease, for evermore, international murder: he organised, instigated, encouraged, and toiled for 'the Day' – 'the Day' when the masses of Europe would no longer be pawns in the great crime of war.

It was a heartbreaking end to the life of a man who had known much sorrow but had risen above it to devote his life to the fight against poverty and the achievement of a lasting peace among the nations of the world.

James Keir Hardie, founder of the Labour Party, was born into poverty at Legbrannock near Motherwell in Lanarkshire in 1856, the illegitimate son of a farm servant called Mary Keir. Before he was three, his mother married David Hardie and the family moved up to Glasgow. David Hardie, a ship's carpenter to trade, found work in the Govan shipyards but was laid off five years later during a prolonged strike.

Young Keir, who had little formal schooling, had already started work. An accident in the shipyard had previously put his adoptive father out of commission. With no money coming in, his parents had no choice but to send their eldest child out to earn what little a boy could. He was only eight years old when he took on his first job as a message boy with the Anchor Line Shipping Company in central Glasgow. He moved on to heating rivets in the shipyard and there were hopes of his becoming an apprentice. However, his mother took fright when two other boys died in an accident in the yard and pulled him out of this workplace. His next job was less dangerous but no less arduous, working full-time as a delivery boy for a local baker, starting at seven o'clock in the morning and finishing when the shop closed in the late afternoon or early evening. He earned four shillings and sixpence per week, his family's only income while his stepfather was still out of work.

In later life Keir Hardie was to recall what happened when he was late for work one morning. He had the saddest of excuses. Another of the Hardie children, nearest in age to him, was dying of what is described only as a fever. An exhausted Mary Hardie was pregnant with another child. Keir sat up during the night with his dying brother, allowing his mother to get some rest. Hardie's friend and first biographer, William Stewart, allowed his subject to tell the story of what happened next:

> One winter morning I turned up late at the baker's shop where I was employed and was told I had to go upstairs to see the master. I was kept waiting outside the door of the dining-room while he said grace – he was noted for religious zeal – and, on being admitted, found the master and his family seated round a large table. He was serving out bacon and eggs while his wife was pouring coffee from a glass infuser which at once – shamefaced and terrified as I was – attracted my attention. I had never before seen such a beautiful room, nor such a table, loaded as it was with food and beautiful things. The master read me a lecture before the assembled family on the sin of slothfulness, and added that though he would forgive me for that once, if I sinned again by being late I should be instantly dismissed, and so sent me to begin work.

How awful it must have been for a ten-year-old boy who'd left the house with no breakfast that morning to be in the midst of all this plenty. He was filled with a burning sense of injustice at the baker's heartless treatment of him, made all the worse because there was no way he could express it. If you wanted to keep your job you didn't talk back to the master, especially not if you were a child.

Two days after this incident, young Keir was once more late for his work. Once again he'd been doing his best to help his mother and comfort his dying brother. Whether the baker had any knowledge of the tragedy which was being played out in the Hardie home is not clear but he had issued a threat and he carried it out. The boy was dismissed on the spot. Not only that, the baker told him he was fining him his last fortnight's wages as a punishment. This was a disaster for the whole Hardie family, whose ability to buy food and fuel and pay the rent rested solely on the small shoulders of one young boy.

Immediately aware of the crisis now facing his family, Keir Hardie began to cry, pleading with the woman who served in the shop to help change the baker's mind. Sympathetic to the child's plight, she spoke to the man from a speaking tube which linked the shop and the house:

> . . . presumably to the breakfast room I remembered so well, but he was obdurate, and finally she, out of the goodness of her heart, gave me a piece of bread and advised me to look for another place. For a time I wandered about the streets in the rain, ashamed to go home where there was neither food nor fire, and actually discussing whether the best thing was not to go and throw myself in the Clyde and be done with a life that had so little attractions.
>
> In the end I went to the shop and saw the master and explained why I had been late. But it was all in vain. The wages were never paid. But the master continued to be a pillar of the Church and a leading light in the religious life of the city!

How Mary Hardie reacted when Keir eventually went home is not recorded. Did she hug her tearful boy, tell him it wasn't his fault, that they would manage somehow, throw herself on the mercy of a kind neighbour?

The disaster of losing their sole source of income forced a prolonged separation on the family. Whether he had fully recovered from his accident or not, David Hardie went back to sea and Mary Hardie returned to stay near her mother in Lanarkshire. Keir, still only a boy of ten, went down the pit.

He did a boy's job below the ground, working as a trapper. They made sure the mine was well ventilated by opening and closing a trapdoor, sending air flowing along the passages where men were hewing and digging out the coal. The job was both lonely and cold, although on his first day a 'kindly old miner . . . wrapped his jacket round him to keep him warm'.

> It was an eerie job, all alone for ten long hours, with the underground silence only disturbed by the sighing and whistling of the air as it sought to escape through the joints of the door. A child's mind is full of vision under ordinary surroundings, but with the dancing flame of the lamps giving life to the shadows, only a vivid imagination can conceive what the vision must have been to this lad.

Thousands of working-class children in late-nineteenth- and early-twentieth-century Scotland had such heart-rending tales to tell. Thousands of us whose families lived through such hard times will have heard their stories and shed a tear for the sorrows and struggles of our forebears, been angry on their behalf over the injustices they endured. When Keir Hardie as a grown man spoke to and for those living lives blighted and narrowed by poverty, shared experience forged a powerful link. Education was the key. The belief that learning and self-improvement would open the door to a better life was an article of faith among working-class Scots, who stretched themselves to the limit to get the education poverty had denied them, for themselves and for their children.

Keir Hardie worked down the pit for ten hours a day but still managed to attend night school at Holytown near Motherwell, where the pupils had to bring their own candles so as to be able to see during winter evenings. Even while he was in the pit, he taught himself Pitman's Shorthand. Down in that Stygian gloom, he used the wick from a miner's lamp to see by.

At home his mother sang him the old Scottish ballads, told him traditional stories of days gone by and encouraged him to read widely. *The Pilgrim's Progress* by John Bunyan was a great favourite in the Hardie household, as were Tom Paine's *Age of Reason* and, of course, the poems of Robert Burns. As his biographer, William Stewart, put it, 'He got more Socialism from Burns than from Marx: "The Twa Dugs," and "A Man's

Man for a' that," were more prolific text books for his politics than "Das Kapital.'"

Although she retained the strong religious faith of her childhood, the experience with the baker changed Mary Hardie's outlook on organized religion forever. From then on she would tolerate no religious hypocrisy, priding herself and her family on being freethinkers. As William Stewart put it, 'All the members of the family grew up with the healthy habit of thinking for themselves and not along lines prescribed by custom.'

This was another characteristic of Red Clydeside at its best. Everything was open to question. Everyone had the right to ask why – and who and what and where and how. That society was arranged as it was, 'the rich man in his castle, the poor man at his gate', with the great mass of the population working long hours for little money and trudging wearily home to overcrowded houses and an inadequate diet, was not only manifestly unfair, it could no longer be tolerated. That it might have 'aye been' like this was no justification for not trying with all your might to change it.

James Keir Hardie did more than most. After some time working with the pit ponies – his pocket watch apparently bore the teeth marks of his favourite cuddy – he spent a dozen years underground, becoming a skilled miner, a hewer of coal. At the same time he continued to educate himself, became a lay preacher, a temperance campaigner and an active trade unionist. Around the time of his marriage to Lillias Balfour Wilson he came up from the pit for the last time. Ironically, Lillie was the landlord's daughter, her father the owner of a pub in Hamilton.

Hardie started a small shop, a not uncommon way of trying to make a living in mining communities, and began writing articles for the newspapers. His union activism had been too much for the local pit manager, who sacked him out of hand when he found out about it: 'We'll hae nae damned Hardies in this pit.'

Over the next ten years, he led the first strike of Lanarkshire miners, which saw bloody clashes with the police at Blantyre, founded a miners' newspaper and became ever more involved in wider politics. He had been a staunch Liberal, speaking from the platform at political meetings, but began to move farther to the left. He also began to travel, meeting people with radical views like R.B. Cunninghame Graham, the romantic and dashing 'Don Roberto'. Through him, while on a visit to London, he met Friedrich Engels. Although Keir Hardie never became a Marxist, he did become a socialist and, with Cunninghame Graham, father of the Labour Party.

It's a quirk of history – and snobbery – that this Scotsman steeped in the history of his native country never sat in the House of Commons for a Scottish seat. The Liberals of Mid Lanark rejected him as a parliamentary candidate in favour of a wealthy London barrister who'd been parachuted into the constituency.

Keir Hardie first entered Parliament in 1892 as MP for West Ham in London. He stood on an Independent Labour ticket, and the following year helped form the ILP. A few years later again, in 1899, he was one of those who helped found what grew into the modern Labour Party, of which he became the first leader.

After he lost the West Ham seat he stood in Merthyr Tydfil in Wales where in 1900 he was elected as one of only two Labour MPs in Parliament. By 1906 there were twenty-six and by 1910 forty. Still the sitting MP for Merthyr in 1915, he came back to Scotland and to his home at New Cumnock to die. His younger brother David Hardie described how the end came:

> That Keir was only 59 will come as a surprise to most people. He always looked more than his years, but the last 15 years of intense work and consequent strain gave him an aged appearance . . . The outbreak of war found him physically weak, and more rest was ordered. He made every effort to rest, but rest by effort is useless. The great crisis was ever present in his mind. It hung over him like a dark cloud . . . There is nothing more certain than that the great slaughter of his fellow-beings in the present European holocaust was the seat of his final trouble. The idea of a world-wide peace and good will was not to him a mere pious opinion, but a holy crusade, to which he had dedicated his life's work.

Keir Hardie died peacefully, his wife and daughter at his bedside. Thousands mourned his passing, although it rated the merest nod of acknowledgement in most of Glasgow's newspapers. *Forward* offered a lyrical description of his funeral and cremation at Maryhill in Glasgow. It's unsigned but the words sound as though they flowed out of Tom Johnston's typewriter:

> A fitful sunshine on a late September day. A hearse and carriages behind, filled with wreaths. Then comes a long seemingly endless trail of cabs. Crowds line the Maryhill tramway route. Thousands doff

their hats and caps as the black hearse passes: soldiers salute. The cortege turns off to the Western Necropolis, and behind the cabs fall in a long procession of Labour and Socialist representatives, four deep. It is the funeral of Keir Hardie.

Cunninghame Graham was one of the mourners. The service was led by Reverend Forson, a friend of Hardie. Once it was over, another friend stepped forward. He was Bruce Glasier, who had succeeded Hardie as chairman of the ILP. Tom Johnston noted how ill Glasier looked. He was himself suffering from the cancer which would kill him five years later.

Glasier put his hand on his friend's coffin and made an emotional appeal to the mourners to dedicate themselves afresh to the cause to which Keir Hardie had devoted his life. 'But he was pulled up suddenly as with a shock when the coffin began to be automatically lowered.' Fighting his grief, Hardie's brother George thanked everyone for coming. Outside, on the steps of the chapel of the Western Necropolis, a few more words were said to men and women reluctant to leave. 'And then the cabs refilled, and the crowd trekked home, and the tramway cars clanged again. Hardie had gone.'

On Sunday, 3 October 1915, a memorial service was held at St Andrew's Halls. Thousands gathered to listen to the three speakers. One was Mary Macarthur, trade unionist and dedicated member of the ILP. She'd married and become Mrs Anderson four years before but seems to have continued to use her maiden name in her political life. She told funny little stories about Keir Hardie, remembering that, when he found that a 'capitalist newspaper' had said something complimentary about him, he would go very quiet before asking what he had done wrong to be praised by the likes of them.

Another of the speakers was Bob Smillie, the leader of Scotland's miners who later became MP for Morpeth in Northumberland. Smillie spoke with great passion, 'in ringing tones'. He was scathing about the official 'we're all in this together' line currently being peddled about the war. *Forward* reported both Smillie's speech and the audience's reaction to it:

> They tell you, he cried, that you and they are one, that after the war
> the Sutherlands, the Breadalbanes and the Durhams will be one with
> the wounded and torn working class, back from the trenches. O, do
> not believe them. Do not believe them. When the war is over our real

fight with our real enemies will begin. And every time he raised the slogan of Socialism and Peace the cheering, round after round of it, became more vociferous and more compelling.

Ramsay MacDonald also spoke. The audience in the packed hall gave him a standing ovation before he had even said a word. MacDonald threw away his notes and spoke from the heart:

> Here lies one, he said, quoting Morton or John Knox, who never feared the face of man. And MacDonald went on to describe the boy Hardie running errands in the rain, wandering about in sorrow because he had no wages for his mother; as a youth scraping shorthand characters on the smoke of a pit wall . . .
>
> In him the spirit of the Covenanter lived again – Airds Moss tempered with the lyrics of Burns. From Hardie's mysticism: from the great invisible creative power in him came his persistency and his perseverance, his power of seeing above and beyond.

In his written tribute too, MacDonald said that, if Keir Hardie had ever written the story of the long struggle of the Labour movement, he would have begun with the Covenanters. He might have had their faults of obstinacy and dourness but he had also had 'the simple mind of a child' and an other-worldly mysticism.

With Hardie, wrote Ramsay MacDonald, you always got the feeling that he saw the world as ephemeral and 'that at any moment the vain show would melt into mist, and the spiritual substance of being resolve itself'. He went on:

> Such a man will offer his hand to every struggling and unpopular cause. But the personalities and powers cannot prevail against him. He will start great movements, he will reveal to men their own best qualities, he will be despised and rejected, but he will make more changes in the world than generations of others. Such a man was Keir Hardie.

13

Mrs Barbour's Army:
The Rent Strike of 1915

We are not removing.

As the war progressed, British industry found itself working at full-tilt to produce the ships, other hardware and munitions required to fight it. Many factories were turned over for the duration to the making of munitions, the Singer plant at Clydebank just one of them.

With the economy roaring up onto a war footing when so many men on Clydeside had already marched off to the trenches, an influx of labour was required to man – and woman – the munitions factories, shipyards and workshops. Concentration on the war effort had put an abrupt stop to the building of new houses. Accommodation in Glasgow was soon at a premium.

Realizing demand now outstripped supply, many of Glasgow's private landlords saw an opportunity to increase their profits by raising rents. If the sitting tenant couldn't pay the increase, there were plenty of people queuing up to take over the tenancy. What the landlords hadn't reckoned with was the fighting spirit of Glasgow's housewives.

In 1914 they had already formed themselves into the Glasgow Women's Housing Association, whose aim was to improve the tenement homes in which they all lived. Their opposition to the rent rises the landlords tried to impose in 1915 was both practical and a matter of principle. So many fathers and sons were away at the war and food prices had risen sharply. Household budgets were under strain and the improvements needed still hadn't been carried out.

Although the rhetoric of the time was that everyone had to pull together for the sake of the war effort, landlords and the factors who acted for them were ruthless about evicting tenants unable to come up with the extra rent. In March 1915 one case hit the headlines. Mrs McHugh of William Street in Shettleston had fallen into arrears. She owed less than one pound. She also had a husband wounded in the war, two sons serving in France and five children at home.

When the factor arrived with the eviction order, he found himself dealing with not only one woman but also several hundred of her neighbours. Local councillor John Wheatley stood at the head of the crowd. The factor retreated, and Wheatley addressed the angry people gathered in William Street.

Fired up, they headed off in pursuit of the would-be persecutor of defenceless women and children. By the time they caught up with him, they had acquired an effigy which they burned in front of the windows of his office. Later, they pursued him to his house and smashed some of its windows. As the *Forward* reported, John Wheatley gave them a gentle telling-off for that, pointing out:

> ... that they were not there to organise the wrecking of homes, but to prevent homes from being wrecked, and while they had been marching away to the Factor's residence, the Bailiffs might have ejected Mrs. McHugh. (Cries of 'We had enough left here to prevent that!') Anyway, he said, the burning of effigy business was wasted time and so were the demonstrations at the Factor's house. He knew, for if they remembered they had done it once to him. (Laughter, and cries of: 'Never mind! You're aye here yet!')

On the advice of the police, the eviction order on Mrs McHugh was not served. Her case became a cause célèbre. As the *Forward* told its readers, it even reached the 'English Sunday Press'. Other Glasgow newspapers picked up on it too. Landlords and factors scored a spectacular own goal every time they tried to turn a soldier's wife and children out into the street. Many of those threatened with eviction were also munitions workers, people whose labour was crucial to the war effort.

The ILP quickly offered support but it was the tenants themselves who led the fight. Willie Gallacher described the strategy adopted by women like Mary Barbour of Govan and Mrs Ferguson of Partick:

> In Govan, Mrs. Barbour, a typical working-class housewife, became the leader of a movement such as had never been seen before, or since for that matter. Street meetings, back-court meetings, drums,

bells, trumpets – every method was used to bring the women out and organize them for the struggle. Notices were printed by the thousand and put up in the windows: wherever you went you would see them. In street after street, scarcely a window without one: 'WE ARE NOT PAYING INCREASED RENT.'

Actually, what the notices read was 'WE ARE NOT REMOVING'. They cost one penny each and had a polite request printed on them: 'Please tack this to top of lower sash of window.' Thousands of people did. The rent strike was on.

People made up their own placards too. One was held aloft at a rent strike demonstration in Partick:

> Partick Tenants' Strike
> Our Husbands, Sons and
> Brothers are fighting the
> Prussians of Germany.
> We are fighting the Prussians of Partick.
> Only alternative
> MUNICIPAL HOUSING

Helen Crawfurd also wrote in some detail of the strategy women deployed in rent strike skirmishes to stop their neighbours from being evicted:

> One woman with a bell would sit in the close, or passage, watching while the other women living in the tenement went on with their household duties. Whenever the Bailiff's Officer appeared on the scene to evict a tenant, the woman in the passage immediately rang the bell, and the women came from all parts of the building. Some with flour, if baking, wet clothes, if washing, and other missiles. Usually the Bailiff made off for his life, chased by a mob of angry women.

The factors tried some strategies of their own. A favourite ploy was to convince individual housewives everyone else in the close had paid the increased rent until they had all been fooled into doing so. On one occasion when this was tried, Mary Barbour drafted in the men from Govan's shipyards. She led them to the factor's office and demanded the amount of the increase be returned.

'On the factor being shown the thousands of black-faced workers crowding the street,' wrote Helen Crawfurd, 'he handed it over.' Now a committed socialist, she addressed many meetings during the rent strike. She used her time on the platform to speak out against the war too, and argue the case for socialism.

It was by no means only socialists who supported the rent strikers. In September 1915 *The Bulletin*, sister paper to the *Glasgow Herald*, published an article very sympathetic in tone:

> The revolt against the increase of house rents in Glasgow threatens to become a very big problem. In three different districts strikes have been resorted to by tenants – first in Shettleston, then in Govan, and now in Partick. These movements have widespread sympathy and, given the slightest provocation, will assuredly spread.

The Bulletin made a suggestion that sounds very like a recommendation: since so many of the families involved were munitions workers, maybe the government would intervene. It wrote approvingly of the tenants in Partick who were involved in the rent strike. There were around 100 of them and they lived in different closes in Hurlet Street, Thornwood Avenue, Clyde Street, Rosevale Street and Exeter Drive:

> The large majority of the tenants are of the respectable artisan type – steady workers employed in the local shipyards and engineering shops. In one of the closes, in which there are 13 tenants, no fewer than nine of them are engaged in war munition work.

No long-haired and wild-eyed revolutionaries here then. The women who ran the rent strike were well aware of the value of presenting a respectable face to the world. Look at the photos of the protests and demonstrations and you'll see neatly dressed women, men and children, all in their Sunday best. Big hats at dawn.

On 16 October 1915, the rent-striking tenants living in Thornwood Avenue and Clyde Street were due to be evicted. The 'WE ARE NOT REMOVING' placards were up in the windows, the tenants came out onto the street and 'the ranks of the demonstrators were swelled by a contingent of women from Govan'. Mrs Barbour and her army were on manoeuvres. Probably they crossed the river on the Govan ferry, the wee boat which used to come right up the steps of the landing stage.

Mary Barbour's counterpart on the north bank of the Clyde was Mrs Ferguson, secretary of the Partick Rent Strike Committee. She seems to be the same Mrs Ferguson involved with Helen Crawfurd and Agnes Dollan in the Women's Peace Crusade. She had gone right to the top, contacting Lloyd George. As minister for munitions, what was he going to do about these evictions of soldiers' wives and munitions workers? She really thought he should send a message about this to the tenants of Partick. Lloyd George's telegram in reply to Mrs Ferguson was read out to the assembled company. As *The Bulletin* informed its readers, it did not go down well. The Minister for Munitions advised that the Secretary of State for Scotland was setting up a committee to look into the matter.

Supporting the striking tenants, local councillor Mr Izett said angrily that he 'wished the soldiers could see and know that while they were defending the trenches abroad, the women folk were defending the trenches at home'.

Patrick Dollan declared that 'the law of humanity was higher than the law of the property owners' and that there was no way they were going to allow the threatened evictions to take place.

Mrs Ferguson got the best response when she told everyone that 'the men in the shipyards had asked that immediately there was any attempt to put the ejections into force word should be sent to the men, and they could come out on strike in a body'.

It was also decided that patrols be set up to guard the houses where the evictions had been threatened and that these should go on until confirmation was received that the eviction orders had been withdrawn.

What the landlords did then was go to law. They would circumvent people power by not confronting it. Once again, they had reckoned without the determination of Mrs Barbour, Mrs Ferguson and the Glasgow Women's Housing Association. The men in the shipyards made good on their promise too, swelling the ranks of Mrs Barbour's army. It was Willie Gallacher who gave that name to the people who marched on Glasgow Sheriff Court on 17 November 1915 in support of the Partick rent strikers:

> From early morning the women were marching to the centre of the city where the sheriff's court is situated. Mrs. Barbour's army was on the march. But even as they marched, mighty reinforcements were coming from the workshops and the yards. From far away Dalmuir in the West, from Parkhead in the East, from Cathcart in the South and

Hydepark in the North, the dungareed army of the proletariat invaded the centre of the city.

Like a latter-day Pied Piper, Mary Barbour led her troops up and across the Clyde and into the centre of Glasgow, calling first at Lorne Street School in Govan to pick up John Maclean. He had just been sacked by Govan School Board for his antiwar activities. The army was a noisy one, adding to the pounding of its feet with tin whistles, hooters and a dilapidated old drum. Following on behind, Willie Gallacher describes how, as they marched along Argyle Street near to Central Station they passed a group of soldiers heading for France:

> Some of the young chaps gave us a cheer as we passed, but many others looked pathetically towards us as our fellows shouted 'Down tools, boys,' and gave the impression that very little persuasion would have brought them over into our ranks.

But the young soldiers kept on going, filing into the station to board the trains which would carry them to the mud and blood of Flanders.

When they reached the city centre, the marchers assembled in front of the City Chambers in George Square before going the short distance along Ingram Street to the Sheriff Court. It was then in its old home at the City and County Buildings. Impressive even when its stone was still covered in a layer of dense black soot caused by industrial pollution, the large neoclassical building occupied a whole block bounded by Ingram Street, Hutcheson Street, Wilson Street and Brunswick Street. It still does.

Their approach not having been exactly stealthy, and not meant to be, the police were waiting for the marchers and would not let them into the court. Mrs Barbour's army marched round the building before stopping in Hutcheson Street. According to *The Bulletin*, they were noisy but good-humoured. There were speeches from John Maclean, Willie Gallacher and Helen Crawfurd. Makeshift platforms were raised so they could be seen and heard above the heads of the crowd.

Reporting the next day on the 'Glasgow Rent Agitation', *The Scotsman* allowed that 'though the crowd was large there was nothing in the nature of disorder calling for the drastic interference of the police, who allowed the impromptu meetings to proceed for a time'. This and other contemporary newspaper reports back up Willie Gallacher's description of the scene. His account might contain a whiff of exaggeration and a little too much socialist bombast, but it's still vivid and convincing:

> Into the streets around the Sheriff's Court the workers marched from all sides. All the streets were packed. Traffic was completely stopped. Right in front of the court, John Maclean was on a platform addressing the crowd as far as his voice could reach. In other streets near the court others of us were at it. Our platforms were unique. Long poster-boards had been picked from the front of newspaper shops. These were placed on the shoulders of half-a-dozen husky, well-matched workers and the speaker was lifted on to them. It was a great experience, speaking from a yielding platform and keeping a measure of balance while flaying the factors and the war-makers.

Dressed in that Sunday best, the tenants had posed for photographs outside the court. Their children held up placards. Smart in his Norfolk jacket and well-starched white shirt collar, a young boy carried one which read, 'My father is fighting in France. We are fighting the Huns at home.'

Inside the court, 18 tenants were about to begin the legal battle with their factor Mr Nicholson. All parties had agreed there would be one test case and that the Sheriff's decision on it would apply to all eighteen.

The Bulletin reported the next day on what it headlined as:

> THE RENT STRIKE
> EXTRAORDINARY SCENES
> MINISTERIAL INTERVENTION
> A PACIFIC SHERIFF
> Considerable excitement prevailed in Glasgow Small Debt Court yesterday when additional petitions for the ejectment of householders who refused to pay increases of rent were down for hearing. The court was crowded to overflowing by those chiefly interested and their sympathisers, and a number of policemen were called in to preserve order. The proceedings took an unusual course.

That unusual course began with Sheriff Lee trying to persuade Mr Nicholson, the factor, and his lawyer, Mr Gardner, to drop the legal action on 'patriotic grounds'. There was a war on, after all, and munitions workers were pivotal to winning it.

The packed court started sitting at ten o'clock. By noon, with the Sheriff still in his chambers trying to knock heads together, people were becoming restive. *The Bulletin* noted that those in the gallery 'evinced considerable impatience at the delay'. To loud cheers, Councillor Izett walked forward to the bar of the court and asked who was in charge. In the name of the workers present, he protested about the delay:

> The protest evoked a loud outburst of cheering, which brought the Sheriff from his chambers into court. He sternly rebuked the demonstrators, and threatened to have the court cleared if there was a renewal of the disturbance.

One of the tenants came forward and asked His Lordship if he would receive a deputation which might help resolve the situation. Sheriff Lee was clearly a pragmatic man. Although he pointed out that 'his position was purely a legal one, and he had no authority to mix himself up with any political questions', these were exceptional times. He spoke privately with four of the tenants, after which the test case was heard. Mr Reid, whose first name was not given by *The Bulletin*, was secretary of the Tenants' Defence Committee.

Mr Reid stated that before the war had started his rent had been £1.18s per month. It had subsequently risen to £1.19s.2d. On 10 September, he had been given notice that it would rise still further to £2 per month, making a total increase since the outbreak of hostilities of two shillings per month.

On 14 September a number of tenants including Mr Reid had stated they would not pay the increase. They were then given two weeks' notice to quit, required to leave their houses by 28 September. It was now more than three weeks later and Mr Reid and the other tenants were still in their houses and refusing to budge. The Commission of Inquiry was due to offer its opinion in another two weeks again, issuing its findings at the end of November.

Mr Gardner the solicitor chose that moment to inform the court that his client had received a direct request the day before from Mr Lloyd George asking him to either drop the legal action or at least suspend it till everyone heard what the Commission of Inquiry had to say. Sheriff Lee grew a little tetchy, understandably so if the solicitor had not told him during all that time in his chambers of this request from the Minister for Munitions. Besides which, the law was the law. Once set in motion, it could not be started and stopped on a whim.

Seizing his opportunity, Mr Reid told the Sheriff he and his co-defendants had decided they needed a decision today, whatever that decision was going to be. He weighed in with a pointed and patriotic observation:

> Munition workers were involved in 15 of the cases, and they did not wish to stay off work to come there and discuss the question of rent. They had a bigger battle to fight in the workshops, and they wanted to fight loyally there.

Those few words seem to have swung it as far as Sheriff Lee was concerned. He knew very well that munitions workers who stayed away from their work could be fined or even put in prison. The national interest surely required that the other side should drop the legal action. As this challenge hung in the charged air, it's easy to imagine every pair of eyes in the court swivelling round to Mr Gardner the solicitor.

He agreed to drop the action, on one condition: the defendants had to agree to accept whatever the Commission of Inquiry said about rents. The Sheriff, who by this stage in the proceedings sounds as though he was completely on the side of the rent strikers, said that of course they would:

> The people affected by this rent dispute knew what was going on. They had observed that in many directions since the war began there was special legislation to meet particular cases of hardship or of difficulty due to the war, and they thought, rightly or wrongly, that the case of rent was one of those difficulties, and that there ought to be special legislation to deal with it.
>
> They [the rent strikers] thought their case called for special legislation, but he did not understand for a moment that if special legislation was passed they would dream of opposing it. They had appealed to the justice of their country, and when the country declared through Parliament their decision they would abide by it at once.

Mr Gardner and Mr Nicholson confirmed their agreement to drop the cases. As *The Bulletin* reported, 'The intimation was received with loud cheering.' The Sheriff told Mr Reid he hoped he would use his influence to see there would be no 'denunciations antagonistic to the petitioner'. Presumably he meant no triumphalist taunting, variations on 'Yah boo, sucks to you, we just won and you just lost.'

The rent strikers were too dignified for that. Mr Reid assured the Sheriff there would be no such trouble, 'and the proceedings ended by those in court giving a hearty cheer for the Sheriff'.

Final victory went to the tenants. The Commission of Inquiry recommended that rents be restricted for the duration of the war. Although there were rent strikes in other parts of Britain, it was the Glasgow rent strike which brought about this decision which made a difference to the lives of ordinary people throughout the country. Even the *Glasgow Herald* was impressed by the action taken by Mary Barbour, Mrs Ferguson and their supporters:

> Thanks to the fine stand made by the Glasgow women and the determined attitude of the Clyde munition workers, the Government has introduced a Bill to legalize pre-war rent during the war and for six months thereafter.

Mary Barbour continued to make a difference, becoming a town councillor and Glasgow's first female bailie and helping to establish Glasgow's first family planning clinic. In 1921 she stood for election in Govan's Fairfield Ward as a member of the ILP. Her fellow candidates were Manny Shinwell and Thomas Kerr and they issued a joint manifesto which stated their policies on housing, local rates, the cost of living and unemployment:

> As a Socialist, and the nominee of the Independent Labour Party, I have been selected to contest the Fairfield Ward as one of the Candidates of the Local Labour Party. I have been resident in Govan for over 20 years and during that time I have taken a keen interest in the public business of the town. My time and energies have all been spent in the working-class movements for the Social betterment of the whole community.
>
> I do not wish to draw any distinction between men and women's questions, because essentially they are the same, but I am convinced and have always advocated that women should take their full share of public work.
>
> Mrs. M. Barbour.

Above the names of all three candidates, the manifesto ends with these words: 'We have the honour to be your fellow citizens.'

14

Christmas Day Uproar: Red Clydeside Takes on the Government

*Mr Lloyd George came to the Clyde last weekend
in search of adventure. He got it.*

The First World War was a voracious consumer of men and munitions alike. This led naturally to a shortage of skilled labour just when it was most needed and the introduction of unskilled labour to compensate. The process was known as dilution, short for dilution of skilled labour, and it gave rise to roars of protest on Clydeside. It was the engineers still working in the yards and workshops who were most vociferous in their opposition to dilution, loathing the very idea of unskilled workers coming in to do skilled jobs.

One of their biggest fears was that many of these unskilled workers, known by the unattractive name of 'dilutees', would be women and that this would inevitably drive wages down across the board. They were right, of course. A woman might be doing exactly the same job as a man, but everyone knew you didn't have to pay her the same wages. Margaret Irwin had pointed that out back in the 1890s.

It's a chilling statistic that twice as many British soldiers died in the First World War as in the Second. The demand for munitions so British troops could inflict the same slaughter on the Germans climbed with the terrible toll of death and horrendous wounds. For some reason, this obscene idiocy made sense to the people in charge at the time.

David Lloyd George had been chancellor of the exchequer for seven years by 1915, serving first in the Liberal administration of Prime Minister Herbert Asquith and then in the wartime coalition government. In May 1915 he became Minister for Munitions, giving him a newly created portfolio and the task of persuading the skilled workers of Britain to accept dilution of labour. The wartime economy was going to grind to a halt without it.

Lloyd George was a wily operator but he came seriously unstuck in Glasgow, outwitted by the Clyde Workers' Committee. Arthur McManus, he of the millions of sewing machine needles, was one of the members of the CWC, as were Willie Gallacher and Davie Kirkwood. The shop stewards of the CWC were elected by their workmates at regular factory floor meetings. People had grown impatient with long-serving union officials. They were too cautious, unwilling to fight the workers' corner against the government.

For the duration of the war it was now illegal to strike, to try to persuade anyone else to strike or to change jobs without the permission of your existing employer. Any workers who did any of these things had not only broken civil law but had also placed themselves under the jurisdiction of the military. They could therefore be tried by court martial, which had the power to sentence any man, soldier or civilian, to be shot by firing squad.

None of this was ever going to sit well with the men of the Clyde. They were mentally and physically tough, intelligent, eloquent, full of cynical humour, angry and raring to go, so it's not surprising Lloyd George wasn't keen on having to confront too many of them in one room. This may be why he and his staff arranged the Local Trade Union Officials Munitions Conference at which he would speak at St Andrew's Halls in Glasgow for the morning of Christmas Day. In 1915 that fell on a Saturday.

The Minister for Munitions and his officials may or may not have known that Christmas Day was not much celebrated in Scotland at the time. After the Reformation, the Kirk had done its best to stamp out what had once been enthusiastic revelry at both Christmas and New Year, the time traditionally known as the Daft Days. Although some Scots in the early 1900s were beginning to reclaim the old traditions, other than children hanging up their stockings in the hope of some sweets or an orange, most people considered 25 December to be a normal working day like any other. Lloyd George and his staff would certainly have known that Saturday mornings were part of the working week and that taking one off meant forfeiting half a day's pay.

Lloyd George's team had another trick up their sleeves which might stop the Minister from having to confront too many angry men. They would control the issue of tickets for delegates to the conference. Referring to the Byzantine manoeuvring which ensued, the *Forward* wrote, 'Not even Mr. Sexton Blake, the eminent detective, could unravel *that!*'

In *Revolt on the Clyde*, Willie Gallacher recounts the tale of how the CWC outfoxed Lloyd George. He tells the story of the run-up to the Christmas Day conference with a mixture of anger, humour and unholy glee. Two days before, on Thursday, 23 December 1915, the CWC called a meeting in Glasgow. An executive member of his union, which was also meeting that evening, Gallacher got there late. He found three of his fellow CWC members handing out tickets for the Christmas Day conference at St Andrew's Halls.

They explained to him how the tickets were to work: 'The Minister had agreed to pay each shop steward 7s 6d for expenses, so that they would have to be careful in distributing tickets, as each one represented that amount.' Hang on a wee minute, said Willie Gallacher, seeing at once that the business with the expenses and the careful handing out of the tickets was a way of reducing how many people would be at the conference. Besides which, the CWC hadn't decided yet whether it was even going to attend.

Harry Hill – no, not that one – came angrily back at him. 'By Christ, I never met your equal for making trouble!' A furious Hill, shop steward in the shipwrights' union, then threw the tickets down on the table and stomped off. His method of departure was so outrageously dramatic everybody laughed at it. Gallacher spoke up again:

Have we no sense of responsibility to the organizations we represent? Are we to be at the beck and call of this avowed enemy of the trade union movement? To what are we being reduced when this man can send along tickets and instruct us to organize a meeting for him?

He managed to convince them the Christmas Day meeting should be boycotted but as soon as it was clear the vote was likely to go that way, one of the other CWC members ran out into the corridor and phoned the Central Station Hotel, where, as Willie Gallacher put it, 'Lloyd George, with his tame trade union and Labour Party officials, had his headquarters.'

On the other end of the phone, Arthur Henderson was asking them to stay where they were. He wanted to come over and speak to them. Henderson was a member of the wartime coalition government, the first Labour MP to hold cabinet office. Nicknamed 'Uncle Arthur', he had previously been a union leader. As far as Willie Gallacher was concerned, in both capacities Uncle Arthur definitely fell within the definition of a tame official.

Nevertheless, he jokingly suggested they should agree to wait if they could all get taxis home paid for after the meeting was over. The message relayed over the phone from Henderson was, 'He thanks you very much, and he has instructed his secretary to order a fleet of taxis.'

'Yes, sir,' wrote Willie Gallacher – whose vigorous turn of phrase often shows the evidence of the year he spent in the United States as a young man, visiting two of his sisters, who had settled in Chicago, and learning how revolutionary syndicalist trade unions worked with the Wobblies – 'they had money to burn.'

Arthur Henderson arrived a few moments later and made 'a pathetic appeal to us to assist Lloyd George in the great fight he was making to win the war'. Willie Gallacher wiped the floor with him:

> Isn't it clear that Henderson isn't here as a free agent? He is permitted to come and speak to us as the servant of one of our worst enemies. How is it possible that a man can fall so low? Fellow members, let us send him back with a message to his master that the Clyde trade unionists are not the lackeys of the workers' enemies!

The decision to boycott the Christmas Day meeting stood. Gallacher and the others rode home through the December night in the fleet of taxis which was waiting for them, laughing all the way back to Paisley.

The late night was followed by an early morning. On Christmas Eve Willie Gallacher rose at his usual time of half past four, the early start he needed to cross the Clyde to start work at six. When he arrived at the Albion Motor Works in Scotstoun where he worked as a fitter, he found the place buzzing with anticipation. Everyone was wondering if Lloyd George might come to the factory to plead the case for dilution directly to the workers and their increasingly influential leader. Willie Gallacher was beginning to get himself noticed. He rather liked that.

Sadly for the other employees, that excitement was not to be. Instead, the Albion's manager took a phone call which asked if Gallacher would go up to the Central Hotel to meet Lloyd George. He took the tram for this trip. When he arrived at the luxurious station hotel, he found some fellow members of the CWC but as yet no sign of the Minister for Munitions. Tables had been arranged in a square and everyone sat down.

It was Lord Murray of Elibank who took the lead. A Liberal politician and a tactful man, he appealed to the CWC to support the national interest at this time of international crisis. Davie Kirkwood described him as having a face that would thaw an iceberg, one of those 'imperturbable gentlemen whom nothing can harass'.

Britain needed men to serve at the front and Britain needed munitions. Dilution was necessary. Lloyd George sympathized with the workers – of course he did – but there was a war on. Surely the members of the CWC wanted to help their country win it? Once Lord Murray had finished speaking, all eyes turned to Willie Gallacher. As usual, he called it as he saw it:

> None of us here is prepared to accept the statement that Lloyd George is, or ever was, a friend of the workers. If he's so keen on winning the war, let him tackle the employers, stop their profits. They're piling up profits at our expense. However, that's *our* war, the war against the employers. We don't mind him being with them. It's what we expect, but when he asks us to assist him in carrying through their plans, that's treating us cheap, to say the least of it. We stand for the workers we represent, and while there are employers reaping profits we'll carry on the war against them.

A Glasgow bailie leapt to his feet and declared that Gallacher was 'out for bloody revolution' and didn't care whether the war was won or lost. After some shouting, Lord Murray managed to call the meeting to order. It then emerged that Gallacher's own union had collected tickets for the Christmas Day conference and was ready to hand them out, which is when Lloyd George himself slid out of the woodwork. Dismissing everyone else, he asked Willie Gallacher to wait behind.

Lloyd George proceeded to treat the bloody revolutionary as though he were his new best friend. Could Mr Gallacher possibly arrange for him to meet representative members of the CWC that evening? No problem, said the wee man who lived in a tenement flat in Paisley to the mighty Minister for Munitions as they stood in one of Glasgow's most exclusive hotels, we'll see you here at seven o'clock tonight.

Lloyd George started the Christmas Eve meeting with the smaller CWC group by exercising his well-known charm, circulating a box of cigars. His own staff all took one. The workers of the CWC brought out their proletarian pipes. 'That's right, boys,' Lloyd George said, digging his own pipe out of his jacket pocket. 'Why should we be formal? If we are going to talk, let us be comfortable; and what's more comforting than a good pipe?' As Willie Gallacher observed, the Minister for Munitions was never one to miss a trick. Wreaths of cigar smoke and clouds of pipe tobacco: the air in that room must have been quite delightful. The two women who were present probably didn't smoke. Even if more ladylike cigarettes had been on offer, only fast women smoked in public.

Willie Gallacher tells us that the two women spoke but not what they said, a bit remiss for a man with such apparently accurate recall for dialogue. Socialists could be sexists too, and frequently were. It's an intriguing thought that one of those women might have been Jane Rae of the Singer's Strike. She certainly attended the Christmas Day conference, keeping her ticket as a souvenir.

Through the tobacco smoke, Lloyd George launched into what Gallacher called a 'typical propaganda speech', explaining that:

> . . . munitions were the key to victory. We were short of men to man the factories at present operating; new factories had to be built. Therefore thousands of workers were needed, and we had to find them. He looked to us for support. As he looked at us he could see that strong spirit of independence that would never tolerate the military domination of Germany. Yes, he knew that we were the very men to rely upon in a crisis.

Lloyd George had told the newspapers a few days before that he would have absolutely no truck with the CWC. Now he was trying to schmooze them. They took their revenge via the eloquent words of one of their number, another shop steward from the Albion Motor Works called Johnny Muir. Willie Gallacher fair cries him up:

> Johnny was masterly in the handling of the subject. He dealt very briefly with the development of capitalism and with the fact that the one and only concern of the employers was profit; that in pursuit of profit every change in the method of production was used to cheapen the cost, and that this took the form of continually introducing new types of semi-skilled or unskilled labour at the lowest possible rate of wages. Thus he showed that dilution had always been a feature of capitalist development.

However, Muir continued, since it was obvious to everyone there was currently a shortage of labour, the CWC was prepared to accept dilution for the time being. On one condition: the government had to take the factories out of the hands of the employers and allow the workers to run them through factory committees.

It was an astonishing suggestion, yet this revolutionary idea did not immediately provoke a spluttering response from Lloyd George. Willie Gallacher described 'the pompous little peacock at the top of the room' as appearing not even to be listening to Johnny Muir. Instead, he was stroking his moustache and luxuriant hair, whispering to Arthur Henderson.

Gallacher exploded, demanding they should have the courtesy to listen to Muir. Lloyd George insisted that he was listening. After Johnny Muir had said his piece, Davie Kirkwood, Arthur McManus and the two female shop stewards spoke, all of them supporting Muir. As far as they were concerned, this was 'a war for trade and territory, a war carried on for the purposes of imperialism', and they were completely opposed to it. The only question they were prepared to address was who was going to administer dilution of labour and who was going to run the factories while the war continued to rage and cause the labour shortage.

Again according to Gallacher, Lloyd George praised Johnny Muir for his eloquence but told the CWC he could not agree to the demands that the workers should control dilution. That would be a revolution and they couldn't have a revolution in the middle of a war. As Willie Gallacher drily put it in *Revolt on the Clyde*, 'It was only a couple of years later, however, that Lenin and the Bolsheviks showed him just how that very thing could be done.'

Although many of the details in this story sound authentic, the tone of the interchange doesn't quite ring true. It seems unlikely that Lloyd George would sit for so long to be lectured on the iniquities of capitalism. Perhaps it wasn't quite so clear-cut as Willie Gallacher describes it. Be that as it may, the CWC did agree to attend the Munitions Conference at St Andrew's Halls the following day.

So, on the morning of Christmas Day 1915, shop stewards gathered where, as Gallacher put it, 'the modern St. George was going to slay the dragon of unrest and conquer the unruly Clyde'. David Lloyd George was famously and proudly Welsh, speaking that language before he ever learned English, the son of a race which cherishes the dragon as one of its most revered symbols. Presumably Willie Gallacher was thinking of the government the Welshman represented, seeing that as English rather than British.

Although he does not mention the personal detail in his memoirs, Gallacher turned 34 on Christmas Day 1915. His birthday treat was coming right up. As *Forward* put it:

> The best paid munitions worker in Britain, Mr. Lloyd George (almost £100 per week), visited the Clyde last weekend in search of adventure.
>
> He got it.

Trouble clearly being expected, rows of policemen and barricades were lined up in front of the platform at St Andrew's Halls. The delegates filing into the hall reacted by breaking into song, a rousing rendition of 'The Red Flag', keeping this up as the platform party arrived. According to Davie Kirkwood, this started up in response to a choir singing 'See the Conquering Hero Comes' as the Prime Minister entered the hall. 'As Mr Lloyd George sat down, a lock of hair strayed over his brow. Shouts of "Get your hair cut!" came from all quarters.'

As soon as the singing finished, Arthur Henderson, on the platform with Lloyd George, rose to his feet. The crowd roared its disapproval at him, drowning out whatever he was trying to say. Henderson gave it up as a bad job and Lloyd George stood up. Willie Gallacher, a hostile witness to be sure, described the Minister's attempts to get the audience to quieten down: 'He pranced up and down the platform; he waved his arms; he stretched them out in mute appeal.'

It was all to no purpose. The crowd continued to yell out its protest. Lloyd George tried to quell the tumult, shouting out, 'I appeal to you in the name of my old friend, the late Keir Hardie!' That he dared to take that sacred name in vain only made the audience angrier. They started singing 'The Red Flag' again, refusing to allow Lloyd George to speak. Accounts of what happened after that vary.

There's the official report of Lloyd George's speech to the conference. Issued to the Press Association the day before, it says nothing about any trouble. It was published in most newspapers exactly as they received it, as they had been asked to do: 'Mr Lloyd George will address meetings at Glasgow, and it is particularly requested that no report other than the official version of his speech should be published.'

In this official version, the one which appeared in the newspapers on the Monday after Christmas, Lloyd George puts his arguments to the delegates. They all listen attentively, clap politely and then everyone goes home. *The Scotsman* did report that there were interruptions and 'some singing of the "Red Flag". The interrupters, however, were in a distinct minority, and the meeting was, on the whole, good-humoured.' As we might by now expect, that's not the way Willie Gallacher tells it.

He has Johnny Muir jumping up onto a chair and the whole hall immediately falling silent to listen as this supremely eloquent speaker begins to discuss the issues around dilution. In this version Lloyd George, Arthur Henderson and the rest of the official party walk off the platform and the meeting continues without them.

Remarking that the audience was pitiless, Davie Kirkwood says that he called out from the body of the hall for Lloyd George to be given a hearing. *Forward* confirms this, telling the story in some detail. They had a reporter there; Tom Hutchison took everything down, word for word, what the platform party said and what the audience hurled back at him in response.

Hutchison reported that Arthur Henderson did manage to make himself heard, although he was heckled throughout. His appeal to patriotism and how Britain had gone to war to save gallant little Belgium was given short shrift, with cries of 'That's enough! We don't want to hear that! Get to the Munitions Act! Come awa' wi' Davy!' That last comment might imply some respect and even affection in the hall for David Lloyd George. Indeed, as Henderson told the audience the Minister for Munitions would shortly address them on the subject of dilution of labour, there was hissing and booing but also some cheering.

Arthur Henderson struggled manfully on with his introduction: 'The scheme of dilution that Mr Lloyd George will recommend to you did not come from any employer. It came from a Committee upon which there were seven Trade Unionists.'

Henderson's no doubt well-meaning but misguided assurance brought forth cries of 'Traitors!' and a demand that those trade unionists be named. He gave them the names, including that of Miss Macarthur, who 'certainly knows how to deal with the women workers'. Cue a cry of 'Miss Macarthur's the best man o' the lot!' This was the same Miss Macarthur who had spoken at Keir Hardie's memorial service some two months before. Same venue, very different kind of gathering. There was laughter, but there was immense frustration too. Delegates felt they were being talked at, not allowed to express their own opinions on dilution. It didn't help when they were told any questions they had for the Minister would have to be written ones, passed up to the platform.

When Lloyd George began to speak, the anger in the hall was too hot to allow him to do so unchallenged. In line with his approach to the CWC the night before, he appealed to patriotism and national unity at this time of crisis: 'Let me put this to you, friends: while we are comfortable at home on a Christmas Day . . .' he began, and was immediately interrupted by shouts of 'No sentiment! We're here for business!'

Lloyd George kept doggedly to his prepared speech, '. . . while we are comfortable at home on a Christmas Day there are hundreds and thousands of our fellow-countrymen, some of them our sons, some of them our brothers, in the trenches facing death'.

'You're here to talk about dilution of labour!' came another exasperated shout.

The Welshman tried to pacify his listeners by dropping another famous Scottish socialist name, that of Ramsay MacDonald, 'one of my greatest friends'. That got some cheers but not much else. This is when Davie Kirkwood intervened, asking the delegates to give Lloyd George a fair hearing, but the heckling and heated interruptions continued.

'The responsibility of a Minister of Munitions in a great war is not an enviable one,' Lloyd George told the hall. 'The money's good,' came the cynical response. Becoming ever more exasperated, the Minister responded to the derisive laughter which greeted that sally with an eloquent few words about the war, telling the delegates what he thought it would mean for everyone:

> There will be unheard of changes in every country in Europe; changes that go to the root of our social system. You Socialists watch them. It is a convulsion of Nature; not merely a cyclone that sweeps away the ornamental plants of modern society and wrecks the flimsy trestle-bridges of modern civilization. It is more. It is an earthquake that upheaves the very rocks of European life.

In no mood to listen to this purple prose, the delegates continued to hiss and boo. Lloyd George announced that he would now begin answering the written questions. He might not get through them all, though, because he had an engagement at twelve o'clock. It was an astonishingly crass thing to say and may indicate just how badly this smooth operator had been rattled by the noisy and hostile reception he got at St Andrew's Halls.

Room de Luxe, the Willow Tea Rooms, Glasgow. (The Willow Tea Rooms)

Mother and Child in Glasgow, 1912. (Glasgow City Archives)

'A Cottage for £8 a Year.' J. Robins Millar, *Forward*, 1913. (By courtesy of the Mitchell Library, Glasgow City Council)

A Cottage for £8 a Year.

Here is a picture of the city dwellings the Glasgow Labour Party wishes to build for the workers. Isn't this something better than a room and kitchen up a dingy close? This means health for your children, happiness for your wife, and comfort for yourself. Do you want it? *Vote Labour!*

'Left out! The Tragedy of the Worker's Child." J. Robins Millar, *Forward*, 1913. (By courtesy of the Mitchell Library, Glasgow City Council)

Left Out! The Tragedy of the Worker's Child

Remember that, so long as you remain a slave, surrendering to the masters the wealth you yourself create, your children are every day being robbed of the natural joys of childhood. Dare to be a Socialist! Dare to demand for your own child the little happinesses you provide for the children of the shareholders who control your foreman.

Singer Sewing Machine Factory, Clydebank, c. 1908.
(Courtesy of Clydebank Library)

Thomas Muir of Huntershill. (By
courtesy of East Dunbartonshire
Leisure & Culture Trust)

Tom Johnston.
(Herald and Evening Times)

Auld Scotch Street, Scottish
Exhibition, 1911. (Author's collection)

Glasgow First World War Female
Munitions Worker. (Glasgow
Digital Library, based at the
University of Strathclyde)

'Hallowe'en at the High
Court.' *Glasgow News*,
1913. (By courtesy of the
Mitchell Library, Glasgow
City Council)

Glasgow Rent Strike, 1915. (Herald and Evening Times)

Willie Gallacher. (Courtesy of
Gallacher Memorial Library,
Glasgow Caledonian University)

John and Agnes Maclean
and one of their daughters.
(Herald and Evening Times)

Tanks in the Trongate after Bloody Friday, 1919. (Herald and Evening Times)

Helen Crawfurd with Children in Berlin, 1922. (Courtesy of Gallacher Memorial Library, Glasgow Caledonian University)

Mary Barbour in her Bailie's robes.
(Courtesy of Gallacher Memorial
Library, Glasgow Caledonian
University)

Davie Kirkwood.
(Author's collection)

The *Queen Mary* Leaving the Clyde, 1936. (From the collection of the
Scottish Screen Archive at National Library of Scotland © NLS)

VOTE FOR MAXTON
AND SAVE THE CHILDREN.

Published by John Taylor, Election Agent, 88 Canning St., Bridgeton.
Printed by James Hamilton, Ltd., 213 Buchanan Street, Glasgow.

James Maxton Election Postcard. (University of Glasgow Library, Department of Special Collections)

Leaving Radnor Street, March 1941. (Courtesy of Clydebank Library)

According to Tom Hutchison of the *Forward,* this was when Johnny Muir jumped onto the chair and demanded to put forward the facts of dilution of labour as the CWC saw them. However, in this account an instantaneous and respectful silence does not fall: 'As it was impossible to hear either the Minister or Mr. Muir, the Chairman closed the proceedings, and the meeting broke up in disorder.'

Lots of sound and fury but nothing achieved for either side: and the mailed fist was just about to appear from beneath the velvet glove.

15

Dawn Raids, Midnight Arrests & a Zeppelin over Edinburgh: The Deportation of the Clyde Shop Stewards

Banished to Edinburgh!

Tom Johnston's newspaper was first in the firing line. Years later, long after the heat of battle had cooled, he took the same mischievous delight in telling the story as he did when he originally reported it. Make that as soon as he was *allowed* to report it.

In his *Memories*, he recalled one of the many interchanges of that faraway but well-remembered Christmas morning when Lloyd George had dolefully declared his burden as a minister of the Crown in wartime was a heavy one and had the reply thrown at him that the money was good.

'All this,' wrote Johnston, now himself a highly respected elder statesman, 'was too much for Mr. Lloyd George, who completely lost all sense of proportion and ordered a complete raid of all copies of the *Forward* in every newsagent's shop in Scotland; he even had the police search the homes of known purchasers.'

In the first few days of 1916 the military as well as the police were deployed to censor the upstart newspaper, raiding its offices in Howard Street, off St Enoch Square. This was carried out by 'high ranking police and military officers smelling through wastepaper baskets and old correspondence files in an endeavour somehow or other to find evidence *post facto* for an amazing and petulant and wholly illegal act of suppression'. The newspaper was banned from publishing until further notice.

Questions were asked in the House of Commons about this suppression of free speech. Tom Johnston was quite sanguine about the whole affair, having just been handed some brilliant free advertising. He played the game all the same, making as much noise as he could and demanding compensation. Eventually, 'after five or six weeks of this hullabaloo Mr. Lloyd George bowed before the storm of ridicule'.

The young editor was invited to London to meet the Minister for Munitions. He took his solicitor with him. He was Rosslyn Mitchell, a dapper, charming and radical Glasgow lawyer who later became Labour MP for Paisley.

Just as with Willie Gallacher, Lloyd George greeted Tom Johnston effusively, 'as if I were a long lost brother, and shaking my hand like a pump handle'.

> 'My dear Johnston, you mustn't get me wrong. You really mustn't. I am the last man on God's earth to suppress a Socialist newspaper.'
>
> I laughed.
>
> 'My dear young man' (he was so ostensibly pained and distressed at my unseemly mirth). 'My dear young man, don't you believe my word? Why do you laugh?'
>
> 'Well, Mr. Minister, you say you are the last man on God's earth to suppress a Socialist newspaper. You are. You did it six weeks ago, and no one has done it since!'

They sat down to discuss the situation and at the end of their chat Johnston 'walked out free to start again, and "it had all been a mistake, and these happen in the best regulated families, Ha! Ha! And we must see more of each other and be better friends in future."'

This avuncular approach did not extend to the other Clydeside socialists who had declared war on the Munitions Act. Perhaps some class distinction was operating. Or perhaps Lloyd George did not think Tom Johnston and the *Forward* were nearly so dangerous as the CWC.

Believing Tom Johnston disapproved of the CWC and wasn't giving them enough support in his newspaper, Willie Gallacher and Johnny Muir had started up their own. The first edition of *The Worker* appeared in the middle of January 1916, while the *Forward* was still officially forbidden to publish.

In a story he could only have got from Tom Johnston, Willie Gallacher maintained Lloyd George had shown the former a copy of the new paper during that visit to London. According to Gallacher, Lloyd George told Johnston he had thought *Forward* was bad until he saw *The Worker*.

'Should the Workers Arm?' That was the article that did it. The piece actually said that the workers shouldn't but Gallacher and Muir were arrested anyway. John Wheatley and Davie Kirkwood visited them in prison, the latter telling them not to worry. He'd engaged a good lawyer to fight their case. Step forward once again Mr Rosslyn Mitchell. Willie Gallacher gives us one of his word pictures on him:

> He was a dapper little gentleman with a beaming, cultivated smile. Someone had told him that he resembled Lord Rosebery, and he tried to live up to the part, with winged collar, spats and all.

Gallacher and Muir appeared in court the following morning to hear the charge against them:

> Having on or about January 29th at 50 Renfrew Street or elsewhere in Glasgow attempted to cause mutiny, sedition or disaffection among the civilian population, and to impede, delay and restrict the production of war material by producing, printing, publishing and circulating among workers in and around Glasgow engaged on war materials, a newspaper entitled *The Worker*.

Rosslyn Mitchell got them released on bail but it was only a temporary reprieve. When their case came to trial, Muir got a year, Gallacher six months and the printer three. According to Davie Kirkwood, at least one innocent man was locked up. He told the story in *My Life of Revolt*, claiming that Johnny Muir was not the author of 'Should the Workers Arm?':

> John Muir was charged with having written the article. He did not write it nor did either of the other two arrested men. The man who wrote the article was married and had a family of five children. John Muir was unmarried. He accepted the responsibility. There were only three persons who knew the author – John Wheatley, Rosslyn Mitchell, and myself. It was suggested that Muir should reveal the secret. He refused, saying: 'Some one [*sic*] is going to jail for this because the Military has read it the wrong way. If . . . . . goes, there will be seven sufferers. If I go, there is only one so I am going.'
>
> Many years later, John Muir was elected to Parliament and became

Under-Secretary to the Ministry of Pensions. To the day of his death he never by word or suggestion went back on his word, nor did the others who knew his secret.

The government's Dilution Commission had visited Glasgow at the beginning of 1916. They held meetings with employers and the Amalgamated Society of Engineers (ASE), the engineers' union, to hammer out the details of how dilution was to work but refused to meet with the CWC or allow shop stewards to approve new dilutees. Workers at Beardmore's, where Davie Kirkwood was a shop steward, promptly went on strike in protest.

Three other Glasgow munitions factories came out in sympathy, including Weir's of Cathcart, where Arthur McManus was one of the shop stewards. Presumably Lord Weir was unaware that he was nursing such a socialist viper in his bosom. The government took swift and decisive action. On Friday, 24 March 1916, the shop stewards regarded as the main ringleaders were arrested and deported to Edinburgh.

Despite observing that the 'Minister for ad-Munitions' had given them the new motto of 'gang *Forward* warily', there was no sign of caution in the howl of outrage Tom Johnston splashed all over his front page on Saturday, 1 April 1916:

BANISHED!
Kirkwood and other Clyde Shop Stewards
Expelled from West of Scotland
Taken from their Beds

It was a dawn raid. Or, as Davie Kirkwood put it in *My Life of Revolt*, 'During the night Lloyd George struck.'

On March 25, 1916, at three o'clock in the morning, I was sleeping the sleep of the just. I was awakened by a violent rat-tat-tat at the door.

My wife said: 'That's them for ye noo.'

The same thought flashed through my mind. I went to the door and asked who was there. A voice answered: 'The police. Open the door.'

'I will do nothing of the kind,' I answered.

'You'd be better to open it. We have a warrant under the Defence of the Realm Act to take you to the Central Police Office. If you do not open the door, we shall batter it in.'

I opened the door. There were four detectives with revolvers at their sides. I gave them the dressing-down of their lives.

None of the policemen involved having written their memoirs, we'll have to take Davie's word for it that he told them in no uncertain terms they had no right to arrest a man who had done nothing wrong. He was, he declared, neither a savage nor an anarchist. He'd read about these sort of things happening in Russia (where the Tsar still had a year left to rule) but never in his wildest dreams had he thought they could happen in Scotland. How could Scotsmen stoop so low as to 'arrest another Scotsman who had done nothing, but simply was standing up for his rights and the rights of his fellows'?

Friendly but firm, the police told him to get dressed and come with them. They reiterated that they were acting under the authority of DORA, the Defence of the Realm Act, and on the instructions of the competent military authorities.

After a cold night sleeping on the floor of a prison cell without even a blanket, Kirkwood discovered he had been court-martialled the day before in Edinburgh and sentenced to be deported. Understandably furious, he demanded to know how he could have been court-martialled without even having been there or knowing anything about it. He had never in his life been in trouble with the police. Where on earth was he supposed to go, anyway?

A Colonel Levita told him he could 'go to San Francisco or anywhere you like, so long as it is outside of the Clyde Munitions area'. Plucking his destination out of the air, Kirkwood said he would go to Edinburgh. After another night on his own in the cells, he was collected by two detectives who took him home to Parkhead to collect some clothes.

Sparing no expense, they took him by tram. By the time they had walked from the stop to his home, a crowd of people were following him and the policemen. Perhaps fearing trouble on the streets, that evening the police used cabs to transfer the court-martialled shop stewards between the Central Police Station and Queen Street Railway Station. Police officers rode shotgun above and below the cabs.

'In Queen Street Station,' wrote Kirkwood, 'I was handed a single ticket for Edinburgh and a ten-shilling note, and put inside the barrier. We were cast adrift.'

Bemused, their only instruction being to report to Edinburgh's Chief Constable immediately upon arrival in the capital, the six men on the train were stunned by the speed with which they had been wrenched away from their homes and families. One of those men was Arthur McManus.

Worried about how his wife and six children were going to manage without him, Kirkwood was worried for himself too. On the journey through to Edinburgh, he wondered if he might be destined to face a firing squad. Dublin's Easter Rising had happened only two weeks before, and his friend James Connolly had been shot for his part in it. Meeting the same fate must have seemed a real possibility.

They came up out of Waverley into a blizzard. It had stopped the trams, and the deportees stood for a while in the swirling snow, watching some men trying to reconnect one tramcar to the overhead electric cable. Kirkwood thought they could be in Russia: '. . . an antiquated method of engineering and transport, a blinding snowstorm, and my emotions outraged at being lifted in the middle of the night without any charge preferred against me'.

Things began to look up when they reached police headquarters. Captain Ross, the chief constable, was polite and kind, asking them where they were going to stay. They were permitted to live anywhere within a five-mile radius of the city centre.

None of them had much money. They did have friends in Edinburgh though, and eventually they settled on John S. Clarke, later to become a Labour MP and subsequently a Glasgow town councillor. So it was that four of the dangerous revolutionaries of Red Clydeside deported under the draconian terms of the Defence of the Realm Act walked out through the snow to douce Morningside.

Known to his friends as 'John S.', Clarke was living in Edinburgh with his wife, son and mother. He came originally from Northumberland and was a member of a circus family. To describe him as a colourful character would be something of an understatement, as the title chosen by his biographer, Raymond Challinor, shows: *John S. Clarke: Parliamentarian, Poet, Lion-tamer*. Davie Kirkwood thought Clarke's house was more like a museum than a home, full as it was of stuffed birds and animals.

John S. was not at home but his womenfolk were very hospitable, taking the refugees from Glasgow in until they could find work and seek out alternative lodgings. Finding work proving not so easy, the exiles had lots of time on their hands.

One day they walked out to take a look at Roslin (usually now spelled Rosslyn) Chapel and Castle. Reverend Morrison, the minister there, hated their politics but he and his wife gave afternoon tea to 'the wild men from the Clyde'. Davie Kirkwood said that as they all sat round the table in the manse they were 'as meek and gentle as schoolchildren at a Sunday School party'.

Banned from any political activity or attendance at public meetings though he was, one evening he just happened to be passing the Mound while Helen Crawfurd, 'well known as a militant suffragist, pacifist, and Communist', was addressing a meeting urging a negotiated peace to end the war. When a couple of Australian soldiers threatened to get violent with the speaker who followed her, Kirkwood intervened, defusing a potential riot.

Barely two weeks after he and his fellow shop stewards arrived in Edinburgh, the horror of war came to the Scottish capital. Once again ignoring the ban on political activity, they were in the ILP hall in Edinburgh 'when the lights were gradually lowered'. This happened three times, and on the third occasion the lights stayed out. 'The Edinburgh people knew what it meant,' wrote Kirkwood. 'They whispered: "Zeppelins!"'

There had been Zeppelin raids on London which had caused fatalities and injured hundreds and there was a great fear the Germans might attempt a raid on Scotland. The warning drill had been well rehearsed:

> Very silently we stole out into the pitch-dark streets. We walked to Morningside, a mile and a half, speaking in whispers, careful not to let our heels click too hard on the pavement. At last we reached the house where we were staying. Six of us entered. The only occupants were Mr Clarke's mother and her little grandson.

Midnight came and went. Clarke's mother-in-law took herself and her grandson off to bed. And then it happened: 'Suddenly a terrifying explosion occurred. Windows rattled, the ground quivered, pictures swung. We all gasped. I ran to the window and saw Vesuvius in eruption.'

Everyone but Kirkwood ran out of the house to see what had happened, not even stopping to put their boots back on. Mrs Clarke reappeared in her dressing gown, concerned the noise of the explosion might waken the wee boy. Kirkwood smiled at her and told her that was probably it, and she went back to bed, but the Zeppelin raid was by no means over:

I opened the window. A great flash greeted me from the Castle and then, above the roaring, I heard the most dreadful screeching and shouting. The inmates in the Morningside Asylum had started pandemonium. Another bomb exploded, but nearer Leith, then another, followed by a fire.

When I was a young man I had read Dante's Inferno, which came out in parts at 4 ½d. each. Here it was in reality.

And the old lady in bed and the little boy slept peacefully through it all!

The men who had rushed in their stocking soles out into the night gradually came back to the house, the last of them not until three o'clock in the morning. Kirkwood didn't like this man, describing him as a braggart who was now gabbling away, the shock of the raid making him talk nineteen to the dozen.

He told the other men he had not only seen the Zeppelin, he had heard the gunners being ordered to shoot him. Davie Kirkwood remarked drily that he must have learned German gey quick to be able to understand what was being said. He doesn't name this man but takes two more sideswipes at him:

> That fellow turned up at the forty hours' strike. While some of us were being batoned, he cleared away, and, like Johnnie Cope, didn't stop running till he reached England.
>
> A few years later he put all Britain into a panic.

Could Kirkwood be referring here to Arthur McManus and the notorious Zinoviev Letter? Published by the *Daily Mail* in 1924, this purported to be orders from Soviet Russia to Britain's communists and socialists, urging them to work towards revolution. It was signed by the Russian Zinoviev and Arthur McManus, by then British representative on the Communist International. The resulting reds-under-the-bed panic helped bring about the defeat of the first Labour government in 1924.

The Zeppelin which bombed Edinburgh on Sunday, 2 April 1916 killed 11 people and injured many more. The bomb dropped at Leith hit a whisky bond, setting fire to the spirit and lighting up the night sky. Bombs were dropped on Marchmont and Causewayside, where a five-storey building was completely destroyed, although with no loss of life. In the Grassmarket a bomb hit the pavement outside the White Hart Inn, killing one person and injuring three more. An engraving on the paving stones now marks the spot.

The raid was a shocking event, both physically and psychologically. It wasn't only that Scots had thought themselves too far away to be bombed. It was the reality of the Germans bringing death and destruction to Scottish soil. Anti-German sentiment intensified after the Zeppelin raid, feeding the flames of jingoism. This was bound to have an effect on how people regarded those, like Helen Crawfurd, John Maclean and James Maxton, who were speaking out against the war.

The deportation of the shop stewards had provoked an angry demonstration on Glasgow Green on Sunday, 26 March, two days after they had been dispatched to Edinburgh. It was here that James Maxton, who was in enough trouble already, blithely got himself into some more.

It was midnight when they arrested him.

16

Prison Cells & Luxury Hotels

*This is the vagabond, though he's mair like
a scarecrow nor a Russian revolutionary.*

In December 1915 permission was refused for St Andrew's Halls as a venue for a demonstration 'in support of free speech and against conscription'. The meeting was switched to George Square. When they were told they couldn't hold it there, the speakers went up into North Hanover Street and addressed a crowd of around 2,000 people from the traditional platform of the back of a lorry.

Those speakers were Manny Shinwell, John Maclean, Willie Gallacher and James Maxton. They were arrested for causing an obstruction, fined 20 shillings each and released. The incident did not help Maxton's increasingly strained relationship with the Glasgow School Board, which took a dim view of his antiwar activities and the amount of time he was spending outside the classroom in order to pursue them.

When he wanted even more time off to attend the Labour Party Conference in Newcastle in April 1916, he offered John Maclean as a substitute for himself. Since Maclean had already been dismissed by the Glasgow School Board for his own involvement in antiwar activity, it's hard not to see Maxton's suggestion as deliberate provocation. The School Board reacted by transferring him from his school at Dennistoun to one in Finnieston and putting him on a final warning. Any more trouble and he would be sacked.

When conscription came into force at the beginning of March 1916, Maxton was called up. He applied for exemption as a conscientious objector and appeared before a tribunal in Barrhead to state his case, launching into an eloquent argument as to why he should be allowed to claim this status. After he had finished speaking, he was asked why his employers had not put in a good word on his behalf, as they had done for other teachers.

The answer was simple. The Glasgow School Board had made good on their threat. The troublesome Mr Maxton had received his letter of dismissal. The tribunal asked if he would consider joining the army as a medic. His retort was immediate and unequivocal. No, he would not consider that: 'It's all part of the game, and you know it.'

The tribunal said they would give their decision in a fortnight. By that time Maxton had got himself arrested over the deportation of the shop stewards to Edinburgh. At the angry demonstration on Glasgow Green on Sunday, 26 March 1916, he was one of those who addressed the crowd:

> It is now for the workers to take action and that action is to strike and down tools at once. Not a rivet should be struck on the Clyde until the deported engineers are restored to their families. In case there are any plainclothes detectives in the audience I shall repeat that statement for their benefit. The men should strike and down tools.

Typical James Maxton. Passionate. Defiant. Challenging. Reckless.

Plain-clothes policemen were indeed present, taking down every word. They waited a few days before they came for him, until midnight on the following Thursday. Maxton had just got home after visiting his friend John Maclean, who himself was out on bail after having been arrested for the speeches he had been making against conscription.

James Maxton's dog Karl was ready to go for the policemen but his master restrained him and went quietly. Well, probably not at all quietly, but peacefully at least. After Maxton's arrest, Karl the dog was stoned to death by thugs claiming to be patriots objecting to his master's antiwar stance.

James MacDougall, with whom Maxton had shared a platform at Glasgow Green, was also arrested. Both men spent the next four weeks in Glasgow's grim Duke Street Prison, charged with 'attempting to cause mutiny, sedition and disaffection and with impeding, delaying and restricting the war effort'.

Maxton was desperately worried about his girlfriend Sissie and his mother Melvina, who now had two sons in prison. John Maxton had also claimed exemption from military service as a conscientious objector but was refused. After a court martial, he had been sentenced to imprisonment in Wormwood Scrubs.

Outwardly, James Maxton put on a brave face. Unable after all to attend the ILP conference in Newcastle in April 1916, he sent his apologies. In the letter read out to the delegates he explained he was unable to attend owing to the unfortunate circumstance of currently being confined to his room:

> People in the movement here have done everything they could to make me as comfortable as possible. The prison officials have been very decent and have shown every respect and consideration. It is a valuable and instructive experience and everyone should have at least ten days in prison annually for the good both of their health and their immortal souls.

While he was confined to his lonely cell, he was thinking deeply about life, his and Sissie McCallum's in particular. She was allowed to visit him in Duke Street and it was in prison that he proposed to her and was accepted. She must have really loved him, for he certainly wasn't much of a catch: out of work, in prison, facing a trial for sedition and an even lengthier prison sentence. Understandably, Sissie's parents were not exactly over the moon about their daughter's choice.

She had to buy her own ring, although her new fiancé did arrange to get the money to her for that. He wrote movingly to her on 4 May 1916:

> My own dearest lass,
> We've got our marching orders quicker than I expected so yesterday was our goodbye, I fancy for some time now. Whatever the time may be it will soon pass and then see how glad we'll be when we meet. Always look forward til then and things won't seem so bad. I'll make up to you for every sorrow you've suffered and every tear you've shed in every way I can.
>
> I've only realised in the last four weeks what a woman's love means, and I'm sure that's one good thing prison has done. I never believed it possible in any other circumstances that any woman would do what you've done for me, or stick so loyally through thick and thin. I shall never forget it, and every power, every ability I have, and I'm afraid they're not many, will be used henceforward for your sake.
>
> I haven't so much time as usual for this note so I'll cut off here. Keep cheery, enjoy yourself as much as possible, have as many

friends as possible, and I'll be with you again soon.

Yours ever,

Jim

They were both thirty at the time of their engagement and it was another three years before they could be married. A major reason for the delay was that it was only Sissie who now had a regular income. The bar on female teachers being married meant she would be obliged to give up work as soon as they wed.

Maxton and MacDougall were tried at the High Court in Edinburgh, sitting in Parliament House, off the Royal Mile. Their legal team on Thursday, 11 May 1916 included the indispensable Mr Rosslyn Mitchell and both defendants took the advice to plead guilty. The core of their defence was the strength of their feelings over the deportation of the shop stewards of the CWC. They had felt this was a grave injustice and that was why they had spoken out so passionately against it. They realized now they should not have said what they had done.

The Lord Advocate, prosecuting, was having none of it. Maxton and MacDougall had incited the workers to strike while 'the flower of our British manhood' was fighting a war to save Britain from the Germans. Given the strong anti-German sentiment in Edinburgh after the death and destruction caused by the Zeppelin raid, the sentence imposed was considered lenient: one year's imprisonment.

The two men served their time in Calton Jail. Perched on the cliff which rises above the main railway line to London at Waverley Station, this occupied the site of today's St Andrew's House. There's not much left of the prison now apart from one of its fanciful Victorian towers, complete with battlements. Maxton joked about it being his ancestral home.

Conditions were pretty grim, with a monotonous diet of porridge and buttermilk, little comfort in terms of bedding and nothing to read except the Bible and a hymn book. The prisoners were isolated too, despite now having other friends occupying cells in the same building. Willie Gallacher and Johnny Muir were also in Calton Jail. So, briefly, was John Maclean.

Maclean too had been tried and found guilty of sedition, sentenced to a harsh three years' penal servitude. He was soon transferred from Edinburgh to Peterhead, on the windswept Buchan Coast north of Aberdeen. If the authorities hoped thus to put him out of sight and out of mind, they had badly misjudged the esteem in which thousands of people held him.

The prisoners in Edinburgh had friends outside the jail. Davie Kirkwood and the CWC shop stewards were still in Edinburgh:

> Another of our interests was to go to Calton Hill, overlooking the Jail, and wave to James Maxton, William Gallacher, John W. Muir, Walter Bell, and James McDougall [*sic*] when they came into the yard for exercise.
>
> Let it be said in honour of the good-nature of their jailers that, when it was discovered that we were sending greetings, the officers found something to attract their attention elsewhere for that one precious minute a day. It was an open secret that every one in Calton Jail learned to love James Maxton.

The warders certainly warmed to him. As Gordon Brown put it, he 'persuaded some of them to form a branch of the Police and Prison Warders' Trade Union and even inveigled a few into the ILP'.

Outside the prison walls but their internal exile enforced by having to report to the Edinburgh police three times a day, the CWC deportees spent varying amounts of time in the capital. The ASE, of which they were members, refused to give them any help, although some came from other quarters.

When rank-and-file members of the union elected a member to attend the Labour Party Conference in Manchester in January 1917, Davie Kirkwood won by a mile. After various shenanigans and the intervention of Colonel Levita, he was allowed to go. He told the Colonel that when he was finished at Manchester he was going home to Glasgow. The Colonel dared him to do it. Kirkwood did.

The Glasgow police called on him as soon as he got there, asking him to sign a document promising that in future he would interfere in no way with the production of munitions. He indignantly refused, on the grounds that he never had done. On the contrary, he had helped keep production going. Not quite sure what to do with him, the police asked him to give his word of honour that he would not leave home for the next 24 hours.

When they hadn't returned four days later, a bemused Kirkwood consulted with John Wheatley and Tom Johnston. Seeing that he was under the weather physically, they advised a short rest, and 'it finished up with me being packed off in my best clothes with bag and umbrella to Crieff Hydropathic'.

It was a new experience for me. I had never before been in a hydropathic or any similar resort of the well-to-do. I was astonished to find that, as the old woman said, 'the place was fair polluted wi' meenisters.' It was like a ministers' guest-house. I was still more surprised in the evening to see the ministers and their lady friends dancing or sitting at a dozen tables, playing cards! So innocent was I of the fashionable world that I thought ministers looked upon card-playing as a sin and a folly. I could not play cards. I thought it strange to have dancing and card-playing during the War.

The police caught up with him the morning after his arrival. He had eaten a hearty breakfast, sung hymns at a morning service and was thinking good thoughts about everyone around him when the Chief Constable of Perthshire turned up and arrested him. The platoon of soldiers the Chief Constable had brought with him to the Hydro were to escort Kirkwood to Edinburgh Castle.

'All right,' said the dangerous revolutionary, 'but I'll need to go upstairs for my bag and my umbrella.' Although outwardly he remained calm, seeing the soldiers had shaken him badly. 'They had come for me at last,' he wrote. Not only was this mere months after the Easter Rising, they were also in the middle of a war where terrified young men suffering from shell shock were shot at dawn. Facing that firing squad must once again have seemed a real possibility.

His senses clearly heightened, Kirkwood looked out of the window of his fifth-floor room in Crieff Hydro and observed how beautiful the surrounding countryside was:

The Chief Constable looked, and said he had no idea that Crieff was such a beautiful place and that he had never seen it from such a height.

Then he turned to me and said:

'Kirkwood, you're a queer fish. I can't make you out at all. If I were you, I should have something more on my mind than looking at the ordinary things of Nature.'

They took me from the Hydro by a back door, lest I should give the place a bad name or disturb the peace of the ministers.

He had nothing but praise for the 'utmost kindness and good will' with which the Perthshire police treated him before he was sent off to Edinburgh: 'One of Britain's greatest achievements is the creation of a police force which performs its duty with efficiency and retains an attitude of detachment.'

When they offered him bread, butter and tea he told them he was a lot hungrier than that. What he wanted was 'steak, potatoes and a vegetable, and then a pudding'. The police burst out laughing, and obliged:

> These things were sent for, and a fine Scots lassie brought them in. I enjoyed my dinner.
>
> The train arrived. The Chief Constable shook hands and wished me good luck, and my soldier escort and I boarded the train.
>
> In little more than an hour I was in a dungeon in Edinburgh Castle, sitting on my bag, with my umbrella propped up in a corner!

The two weeks he spent there were dark in more ways than one:

> The Castle of Edinburgh is of great age. It was built at a time when oppression drove the people in rebellion and then cruelly crushed the rebellious.
>
> My new habitation was a vault far below the ground, into which the only light entered from a small grated window high up near the roof. Above my vault were the guards' quarters, occupied by German and Austrian officer-prisoners. They were a noisy crew, singing, shouting, and scrapping day and night. They seemed to want for nothing.
>
> I thought it strange that I, who was innocent of any offence, should be in a dungeon while the captured enemy should be so cheerfully housed up above.
>
> I was a done man. My mind refused to think. My body seemed incapable of exertion. I wondered what was to happen next.
>
> Hours passed in utter loneliness.

On his third day, a soldier flung open the cell door, slapped the revolver at his belt and threatened to dispatch him: '. . . I'd raither use it to shoot you nor a German. You're David Kirkwood o' the Clyde.' Kirkwood drew his own weapon in defence: words and reasoned argument. They soon got onto the Bible:

I was grateful to Joseph – he occupied fully twenty minutes! Then we passed to Pharaoh and Moses, and the very pleasant story of the mother who made Pharaoh's daughter pay her for being a nursemaid to her own child. After that it was easy to tramp through the desert, though it took the Israelites forty days and forty nights. By the time we had reached the Land of Promise, in which I was more fortunate than Moses, I was becoming exhausted, but I was grateful to the minister whose Bible class I had attended in my youth!

The soldier had long since stopped menacingly patting his revolver. Davie Kirkwood spent two hours talking to the man about the Bible and made a shrewd observation:

He was more interested in the Bible than in shooting me, although he had come for that purpose. I have often noticed that people who are attracted by the blood stories of the Old Testament are inclined to look upon weapons of destruction as instruments confided to their care for carrying out what they believe to be the purposes of the Almighty. It is a kind of brain affection that has put a blight on religion through the ages.

When the guard changed, Kirkwood told the soldier going off duty that maybe one day he would see the light, that 'this was a capitalist war' and after it he might very probably find himself out of a job. Years later, Kirkwood met that soldier again. He came up to him at an open-air meeting, shook his hand and told him that he had indeed now seen the light. Kirkwood had converted him that day in Edinburgh Castle.

Unable to coerce him into signing any undertakings that he would cause no trouble in the future, an exasperated Colonel Levita released the stubborn Mr Kirkwood but reminded him that he was still under sentence of deportation and could not therefore return home to Glasgow. Kirkwood walked out of Edinburgh Castle into the fresh air of the outside world. He remembered to take his umbrella.

Once again he sought refuge with John S. Clarke. He told Kirkwood he should head south to Moffat Hydro. The CWC had already sent James Maxton, Willie Gallacher and James MacDougall there to get their strength back after their months in prison. The group stayed at Moffat for two weeks, the cost funded by a collection of the faithful taken up by John Wheatley, doing what he so often did and quietly making the necessary arrangements. Kirkwood's train was met by another chief constable:

> How had he known I was coming? He saluted and said: 'Good afternoon, Mr Kirkwood.' It was a most generous greeting. I raised my hat and said: 'Good afternoon, Chief.' It was like Stanley's meeting with Livingstone in Africa. The Chief Constable ought to have said: 'Mr Kirkwood, I presume?' He turned away and I went on to the Hydropathic – the second time I had been in such a place.

Davie Kirkwood once observed that James Maxton always looked so ill nobody noticed when he really was unwell. That Maxton kept body and soul together on a diet which consisted mainly of cigarettes and tea probably didn't help. At Moffat, worried by his friend's persistent cough, Kirkwood insisted on taking him to see a local doctor. Dr Park was reassuring about Maxton's health but damning of the wild men of the Clyde everyone was talking about:

> 'Traitor of the deepest dye,' he called Kirkwood, and said Maxton was a vagabond. It was a good thing they were both safe within the walls of Edinburgh Castle. We kept back our laughter with difficulty.
> As we were saying our good-byes, Jimmie said, pointing to me:
> 'This is the traitor of the deepest dye.'
> 'And this,' I said, 'is the vagabond, though he's mair like a scarecrow nor a Russian revolutionary.'

Dr Park's mouth fell open. Then he began to laugh, the traitor of the deepest dye and the vagabond joined in and they all parted the best of friends. Davie Kirkwood made another astute observation: 'Like so many people who thought they hated us, he did not hate us. What he hated was his own idea of us.'

Relations with the many wounded officers staying at Moffat Hydro were not so cordial:

> It was tragic to see them, splendid men, hobbling about. Of course they knew who we were, but they paid no attention to us. They gave a good example of self-control, for I am sure that in their distress they must have hated us.
> In all the fortnight only two of them spoke to us.

One of those who did was a Cameron Highlander who swayed up to their table one night when he was drunk and 'full of insulting remarks'. When the Red Clydesiders refused to rise to the bait, the soldier tried harder:

> Then he ruffled Maxton's hair, saying: 'Look at his hair. He's more of a Frenchman than a Scot.' That was too much for me. I rose up and said: 'Look here, Captain, if you don't go over to your own table, I'll smash your jaw for you, and the whole British Army won't protect ye.' He gave a silly wave of the hand and went away like a child. The other officers looked, but said nothing.

Still a deportee, Kirkwood had to go back to Edinburgh when he left Moffat Hydro. Desperately worried about his wife, who was expecting a baby, he had a crisis of conscience as to whether to sign the documents which would allow him to go home. When his son sent a telegram to say his mother had given birth to a baby girl, Kirkwood 'ran to the Scottish Command'.

Although Kirkwood continued to refuse to sign the documents, Colonel Guest, the new commander, told him he was a married man himself and would do his best to get him home. Kirkwood went to Waverley, bought a single ticket to Glasgow and packed his bag. Once again, he did not forget his umbrella.

Despite all sorts of complications, Colonel Guest was as good as his word, accompanying his prisoner through to Glasgow on a special late-night train. Kirkwood was horribly afraid the Colonel's kindness meant his wife had died and that the military man was only waiting for the opportunity to break it to him gently:

> At Queen Street, Glasgow, the station seemed to be full of soldiers, all drawn up in parade order. It was now one o'clock in the morning. Glasgow was silent and dark.
>
> I was led to a motor-car in front of which were two soldiers. Colonel Guest sat beside me. We drove to my home. At the close-mouth he stopped and, in the gentlest way, said:
>
> 'I think you had better go upstairs by yourself. If I appear in these regimentals, it might give Mrs Kirkwood a shock. Go up and see how things are, and then come down and let me know.'
>
> I ran up three steps at a time and chapped on the door in the way

we both knew so well. Then I pushed open the letter-box and heard
my wife say:

'There's Davie at the door.'

I think in all my life I have never heard anything so wonderful as
that phrase.

When Kirkwood returned to the close-mouth where Colonel Guest was
standing in the gloom of the night and told him mother and baby were
both doing well, the soldier threw his arms about his prisoner and hugged
him: 'I was speechless. We looked at each other. We clasped hands. He
saluted, and moved away to his car in the darkness. I waved to him as he
went.'

Impressed that Kirkwood had not exaggerated how ill his wife was in
the hope of gaining his own freedom, Guest gave it to him anyway,
confirming that by letter at the end of May 1917.

All but one of the Red Clydesiders who had challenged the government
were now free. A welcome-home social was held for them at St Mungo's
Hall in June 1917. Everyone was still tremendously excited by the news
of Russia's February Revolution and the overthrow of the Tsar.

Everyone also agreed that the priority now was to get John Maclean
out of prison.

17

John Maclean

*I am not here, then, as the accused: I am here
as the accuser of capitalism, dripping with
blood from head to foot.*

John Maclean dedicated his life to teaching people about Marxist economics, the history of the working classes and the class struggle. For him, revolution was the only way to end poverty and injustice. The working classes must rise up and seize the power which, as the producers of society's wealth, was rightfully theirs.

Passionately opposed to the First World War, he spoke out against it at meeting after meeting and was arrested under the Defence of the Realm Act. His first prison sentence lasted less than a week but resulted in instant dismissal from his teaching post. This happened at the end of 1915. Mrs Barbour and her army collected him from the last school he taught in on their way to the Sheriff Court to protest during the rent strike.

Losing his job was a financial disaster for him and his family but freed him to carry on urging revolution, teaching outside the formal school system and protesting against the war and conscription. This got him arrested again in February 1916 under DORA, when he was imprisoned briefly in Calton Jail with James Maxton, James MacDougall, Johnny Muir and Willie Gallacher, and then by himself in Peterhead.

When his wife was allowed to visit him there in the summer of 1916, they discussed the petition which was being mooted to try to secure his release. Maclean was adamant that he would not beg for leniency. Any petition should focus on securing rights for him as a political prisoner. If countries like Germany, Russia and England recognized this category, why was Scotland insisting on treating him like a common criminal?

It wasn't much of a visit. Husband and wife were permitted to spend only twenty minutes together, had to talk under the supervision of two guards and were not even allowed to clasp each other's hands through the bars which separated them. Another visit would not be permitted until Maclean had served a year of his sentence.

Letters were also strictly limited. Agnes Maclean visited in July. She and her husband were not allowed to write to one another until the following November. He was allowed one book a week but no newspapers. Sentenced as he was to three years' penal servitude, he had to work out of doors in all weathers. The often harsh climate of the Buchan Coast was to take its toll on his health.

A campaign was mounted on his behalf: a demonstration on Glasgow Green, questions asked in Parliament, letters to the Home Secretary. Socialists in other countries asked their ambassadors in Britain to enquire into the case of John Maclean. Why had this man been dealt with more severely than others?

Sales of work were held and donations made to a fund to give financial support to Mrs Maclean and the couple's two daughters. Agnes Maclean wrote to her husband in November 1916: 'It would take pages to tell you of the people who are always asking about you and thinking of you.'

His continuing imprisonment had become a cause, one which fired up thousands. The burning sense of injustice found a focus at the end of June 1917, when Lloyd George, now prime minister, returned to Glasgow to be given the freedom of the city. That such an honour should be conferred on him was not a universally popular move on Red Clydeside.

Willie Gallacher remembered how Lloyd George was driven through Glasgow in an open carriage, surrounded by soldiers and policemen on foot and horseback, to St Andrew's Halls where the ceremony was to take place. Was the venue coincidental or was the Prime Minister hoping to lay the embarrassing ghost of the Christmas Day Munitions Conference? The Welsh Wizard was on top form, at his charming best:

> At the top window of a block of flats overlooking the west entrance to the hall used on this occasion, an old stalwart of the movement, Mrs. Reid, her white hair crowning a face alight with the flame of revolt against the mad slaughter of the war, was waving a great red flag.
>
> From the distant place to which we had been forced back Kirkwood was shouting encouragement to her at the top of his stentorian voice, while the crowd gave her cheer after cheer. Before entering the hall,

> Mr. Lloyd George, always acutely conscious of the mood of the crowd,
> stood up in the carriage which had drawn to a stop, looked up at our
> comrade bravely waving the scarlet banner, raised his hat and gave
> her one of his most gracious bows. Then he looked over the heads of
> the military and police, towards the mass of workers, nodding his
> head as though to say, 'You see, I'm a bit of a Red Flagger myself.'

Whether by chance or design, John Maclean was released from custody
the morning after Lloyd George was given the freedom of Glasgow.
Returned to the city the day before, he was freed from Duke Street Prison.
He got his own welcome-home reception, chaired by Tom Johnston.
When a telegram of congratulations was read out from the Petrograd
Soviet, the cheering raised the roof.

It wasn't long before Maclean was back at the barricades. In October
1917, like so many on Red Clydeside, he drew strength and inspiration
from the second Russian Revolution. This saw the triumph of the
Bolsheviks under Lenin and the establishment of a Communist state.
Men like Maclean and Willie Gallacher and Arthur McManus longed to
achieve the same in Scotland, with society run by workers' and soldiers'
committees.

At the beginning of 1918 Lenin appointed John Maclean soviet consul
for Scotland. It was a dubious honour. No country was as yet prepared to
give official diplomatic recognition to the new Soviet workers' republic.
Nothing daunted, Maclean opened a Russian consulate at Portland Street
in Glasgow.

In April 1918 the police raided the premises and once again arrested
him under DORA, charging him with sedition and attempting to spread
disaffection among the civilian population. He was tried in Edinburgh on
9 May 1918 and the speech he gave from the dock that day has acquired
legendary status. This ringing denunciation of capitalism took him more
than an hour to deliver:

> It has been said that they cannot fathom my motive. For the full period
> of my active life I have been a teacher of economics to the working
> classes, and my contention has always been that capitalism is rotten
> to its foundation, and must give place to a new society. I had a lecture,
> the principal heading of which was 'Thou shalt not steal; thou shalt
> not kill', and I pointed out that as a consequence of the robbery that
> goes on in all civilised countries today, our respective countries have

had to keep armies, and that inevitably our armies must clash together. I consider capitalism the most infamous, bloody and evil system that mankind has ever witnessed. My language is regarded as extravagant language, but the events of the past four years have proved my contention.

Looking at the carnage which had engulfed Europe in those past four years, you didn't necessarily have to be a revolutionary socialist to agree with him:

I wish no harm to any human being, but I, as one man, am going to exercise my freedom of speech. No human being on the face of the earth, no government is going to take from me my right to speak, my right to protest against wrong, my right to do everything that is for the benefit of mankind. I am not here, then, as the accused: I am here as the accuser of capitalism, dripping with blood from head to foot.

The jury did not retire but gave their verdict through their foreman: guilty on all charges. The Lord Justice General turned to Maclean and asked him if he had anything to say. 'No,' he said, 'I think I have said enough for one day.'

The judge told him he was not going to dwell on the gravity of his having been found guilty again of an offence under the Defence of the Realm Act, '... because you are obviously a highly educated and intelligent man, and realise the thorough seriousness of the offence you have committed'.

The Lord Justice General sentenced Maclean to five years' penal servitude, an even tougher sentence than the last time. In her biography of him, his daughter Nan Milton described what happened next. Maclean turned to friends in the court and told them to 'Keep it going, boys, keep it going'. As he was being led out of the court, he turned and waved his hat to his wife and friends, who shouted back to him, 'Ta, ta, Johnnie! Good old Johnnie!' before standing up and belting out 'The Red Flag'.

Once again a campaign swung into action to demand his release. It gathered huge momentum, especially after the armistice which ended the First World War was signed on 11 November 1918. Lloyd George called an immediate election. The release of John Maclean was on the agenda at every political meeting in Glasgow and beyond.

Freed on 3 December, he had served only seven months of his five-year sentence but was not a well man, weakened by going on hunger strike while in Peterhead and being force-fed. Bruised and exhausted, he wrote to Agnes Maclean saying she was the only person he wanted to meet him at Buchanan Street Railway Station, but word got out. Thousands were there to greet him when his train pulled in.

The welcoming party had hired a horse-drawn carriage so as many people as possible could see him. Someone handed him a red flag. The horse and the carriage driver picked a careful path through the sea of supporters thronging the city streets. Worn out though he was, a defiant Maclean stood up and waved the red flag above his head. Now, there was a moment. 'Never in the history of Glasgow,' wrote Willie Gallacher, 'was there such a reception as John Maclean got that night.'

The joy so many people felt at John Maclean's triumphant return to the Clyde and the legendary position he continues to occupy in the history of Red Clydeside are reflected in two exuberant anthems written long after that December night in 1918, Hamish Henderson's 'John Maclean March' and Matt McGinn's 'The Ballad of John Maclean (The Fighting Dominie)'.

When the Communist Party of Great Britain was founded in April 1920, Scotland's most famous Marxist did not join it. He wanted a Scottish communist party, not a British one, so he founded the Scottish Workers' Republican Party. One newspaper advert for it was cheerfully combative: 'Roll-up, Glasgow Reds, and join the new Revolutionary Party for a Scottish Workers' Parliament, allied to Russia, one big industrial union, Marxian education under the Scottish Labour College.'

Maclean served two more prison sentences, in 1921 and 1922. In both cases he was again charged with sedition, firstly for advocating that the miners of Airdrie should lead a workers' revolution and secondly for saying the post-war unemployed should steal food rather than starve. The first sentence lasted three months, the second a year.

When he was released from prison in 1922 he had little more than a year to live. Once a robust and healthy man, his prison terms, endless teaching and public speaking had seriously damaged his health. He spent the last months of his life working to build up his Scottish Workers' Republican Party.

He fought every local by-election he could, convinced as always that patching up capitalism was never going to be the answer. Only revolutionary socialism could sweep away poverty, injustice and war:

I come before you at this election at the request of many members of your ward as a COMMUNIST or RED LABOUR candidate. Pink Labourism is of no use to the workers, never will be. Your poverty and misery are more intense today than ever before. Thirteen out of every hundred in Glasgow are getting Parish Council Relief, and the number is growing. World developments are bound to make things still worse, even if Britain is lucky enough to avoid another world war.

Maclean's manifesto goes on to damn unemployment as 'a weapon to cow the workers into accepting lower wages and a longer week'. His solution to the lack of jobs was a scheme to 'reclaim all the moorland lying round Glasgow, and establish a system of co-operative or collective farming on scientific lines'.

He called for a Scottish Parliament, one completely divorced from Westminster. Only a Scotland independent from England had any hope of becoming a country where the workers were in charge. England, he feared, would not be ready for communism before the war Maclean believed was coming:

I therefore consider that Scotland's wisest policy is to declare for a republic in Scotland, so that the youth of Scotland will not be forced out to die for England's markets.

The Social Revolution is possible sooner in Scotland than in England . . . Scottish separation is part of the process of England's imperial disintegration and is a help towards the ultimate triumph of the workers of the world.

The young members of the Scottish Workers' Republican Party loved John Maclean. In an age much more formal than our own, he insisted they call him by his first name. He encouraged them at every turn, building up their confidence so they could stand up and address a public meeting. 'In the winter all felt it their cardinal duty to attend the economics and industrial history classes,' wrote Nan Milton, adding that his students acquired the nickname of 'John Maclean's bright young things'.

Maclean remained a teacher to the end, giving his classes on economics and taking a close interest in the education of his elder daughter Jean. At the beginning of 1922 she was coming up to her 12th birthday. Her father's advice was that she should start reading the papers and finding out what was going on in the world:

> A good geography book and an atlas should always be at your side to enable you to know as much about the earth as possible. A general history of the world in all times should prove useful. Perhaps your aunt may be able to tell you about the great civilization of ancient Egypt, the mummies, and the tombs of the Pharoahs [*sic*] or emperors, and of the recent discoveries at Luxor on the Nile where the tomb of King Tutankhamen has just been found and is causing excitement all over the world.

He did not scruple to tell young Jean that people were already saying there could be another European war but he told her there was a way to stop war:

> The only way to end war and prevent all wars is for the wage workers of the whole world to unite and tell the wealthy that the workers themselves will rule the world. For advocating that, your father was sent to gaol and may be sent again. But sooner or later the workers will do as your father wishes them to do.

Sylvia Pankhurst was a friend and supporter of Maclean. On a visit to Glasgow she went to his home in Pollokshaws, where he was living by himself and eating little more than porridge and dates. He had given what money he had to pay for food and a doctor for a sick child.

Some regard John Maclean as a secular saint, the tragic martyr of Scottish socialism. Heart, head and soul, he was devoted to his cause. He viewed those troubled years immediately following the national trauma of the First World War as opening a door to the revolution he so believed in. Convinced that door would not stay open for long, he could not allow himself to rest until he had done everything in his power to make the revolution happen.

For that goal he sacrificed everything, including his own health and family life. Seeing how he was driving himself into the ground, Agnes Maclean had taken their two daughters and left him, telling him she would come back only if he stopped his political activities.

Maclean wrote to tell her that although he was on a shortlist for the paid post of tutor at the Scottish Labour College, he couldn't pursue it, as the college was insisting the tutor should not be actively involved in politics. That restriction was something he simply could not contemplate. Agnes should also know his enemies were using her living apart from him as a stick to beat him with. She had to come home and be seen out and about with him:

> If you cannot come I'll be blackened worse than ever, and will be economically damned. If that is so, I have made up my mind for the worst – that we'll never come together again.
>
> If I go down, I must go down with my flag at the mast-top. Nothing on earth will shift me from that. Now, there's the tragedy for you, as clearly and bluntly as I can put it.
>
> If it's your duty to be here, as I maintain it now is, I contend it is your duty to stand shoulder to shoulder with me in the hardest and dirtiest battle of my life. If we have to go under we had better go under fighting together than fighting one another.
>
> Realizing that this is the greatest crisis in our lives I cannot find words to say more.
>
> If you come I'd prefer you to come at once and walk right in.
>
> Whatever course we follow, remember that you are the only woman I love and can now love.

In June 1922 Maclean won a seat in the local elections for Glasgow's Kingston Ward. His printed election address warns of the rise of the 'Fascisti' in Germany and Britain. He also warned voters off reforms which might seem to be to their benefit but in reality were only applying those patches to capitalism. Once again it all comes down to economics: 'The worker who votes for the upholders of the system of society that allows him to be robbed of the larger part of the wealth produced by him and his fellows, is clearly a simpleton.'

Right to the end, he kept faith with Marxism, as his final election address shows:

> For the wage-earning class there is but one alternative to a capitalist war for markets. The root of all the trouble in society at present is the inevitable robbery of the workers by the propertied class, simply because it is the propertied class. To end that robbery would be to end the social troubles of modern society.

Elated by his success in the municipal election, he decided to contest the Gorbals as a Labour candidate at the upcoming general election. His decision plunged Agnes Maclean into despair: 'It is just throwing yourself away, and money that is needed to keep your family.'

Her own health was not too good at the time but she had decided she would 'go in for nursing or something that will give me some independence and that will be a bit cheerier. We will need to arrange about the children in some way.' Angry and upset, she told him it was his duty to stand by her and leave politics alone for the moment. Perhaps hoping to persuade him, she agreed to go back to him.

She found him at a low ebb physically. It was November, month of freezing fogs, but he was still addressing meetings, many out of doors. He had loaned his only coat to a black friend from Barbados who was shivering in the cold of a Scottish winter.

Determined to work until his last breath to get his message across, John Maclean was on a platform at an open-air meeting when he collapsed and had to be carried home. He was found to be suffering from double pneumonia. He died on St Andrew's Day, 30 November 1923, at the age of 44.

Tens of thousands of people turned out to see him make his final journey, his friend James Maxton one of the pallbearers who carried the coffin out of the house to the horse-drawn hearse. Afterwards money was collected which gave Agnes Maclean and her daughters a reasonable weekly income for quite a number of years. She died in 1953, 30 years after her husband.

The Soviet Union remembered John Maclean on the centenary of his birth. In 1979 they produced a postage stamp in his honour. In 1973 a cairn in Pollokshaws was erected to commemorate the 50th anniversary of his death. The inscription reads, 'Famous pioneer of working-class education, he forged the Scottish link in the golden chain of world socialism.'

The revolution he called for never came. Yet there are still those today who continue to make the pilgrimage to that cairn and to his grave in Eastwood Cemetery, paying their respects and taking inspiration from John Maclean, the man whose dedication to his cause was absolute.

18

Bloody Friday 1919: The Battle of George Square

Military Ready to Deal with Clyde Rioters.
We didn't regard the Forty Hours Strike as a revolution.

The year started with a tragedy. On Hogmanay 1918, HMS *Iolaire* put out from Kyle of Lochalsh, heading for Stornoway on the Isle of Lewis. On board were almost 300 soldiers coming home from the war. In the early hours of New Year's Day 1919 the *Iolaire* struck notorious rocks a mile outside Stornoway Harbour. Valiant efforts saved many of the men on board but more than 200 drowned as the ship went down. It was a heartbreaking blow after four long years of war.

People were exhausted in 1919. The war was over but the peace had yet to be won. Promises had been made of a land fit for heroes but there were few signs this was about to arrive any time soon. After the strain and losses of the war, another blow was dealt when the influenza pandemic swept round the world.

Between May 1918 and the spring of 1919, Glasgow experienced three outbreaks which caused four thousand deaths. Many of those were of children under five, who were particularly susceptible. Around the world, millions died of the Spanish Flu. Yet it is almost a forgotten tragedy. After so many deaths during the previous four years, perhaps people simply could not absorb any more grief.

In politics, the Representation of the People Act of 1918 had given the vote to men over 21 and women over 30. Despite this hard-won and so long awaited extension to the franchise, the post-war election disappointed many. There was a widespread view that the poll had been rushed and nothing much had changed.

As Davie Kirkwood put it, 'In that election the Socialists went down like ninepins. The country had only one hero, Lloyd George, and only one object: "Make the Germans pay."' The Welsh Wizard had now become the Man Who Won the War.

A new coalition government was formed. Although the Conservatives under Andrew Bonar Law had more seats, Lloyd George's popularity with so many voters meant that he remained prime minister. The Labour Party had returned 57 MPs to Westminster, the greatest number yet, but they had little power in this new Parliament.

Frustration mounted as the wartime economy slammed on the brakes. There was no longer the need to go hell for leather on munitions and the Clyde's order books were beginning to look sparse. Thousands of demobbed servicemen were flooding into a labour market where there soon wasn't enough work to go round.

The STUC, Glasgow Trades and Labour Council and other trade unionists came up with an idea. Reducing industry's working week from 54 to 40 hours would allow what work there was to be shared out more fairly. Resistance to this idea from employers, the government and some unions led to calls for industrial action. The dispute became known as the 40 Hours Strike.

On Sunday, 26 January 1919, 10,000 people, some waving red flags, marched from St Andrew's Halls to the City Chambers. In their report the next day in which they gave their readers that information, the *Evening Times* quoted one of the speakers who addressed the marchers in George Square. Mr Cameron of the Discharged Soldiers' Federation said his organization was 'backing the workers this time and looked for the workers to back them. They had fought for their country and they now wanted to own it.' The next day St Andrew's Halls was again the focus. Three thousand people attended the meeting where the strike was officially called. Over the next few days the protest gathered momentum.

Workers at the Port Dundas and Pinkston power stations were among those who came out, cutting electricity supplies throughout Glasgow. They agreed to keep the lights on in the city's hospitals and streets and to keep Glasgow and their fellow strikers moving by keeping the trams running. By Friday, 31 January, 60,000 people had downed tools.

Putting the numbers of strikers at 40,000, the *Glasgow Herald* referred to them and their techniques as 'the methods of terrorism'. *The Scotsman* too referred to 'Terrorism on the Clyde'. *The Times* had sympathy for the exhaustion of working people after the strain of the war but no sympathy with the 'gangs of revolutionaries' it believed were exploiting them: 'The three firebrands named by the Lord Provost are notorious rebels against all social order.'

The three firebrands in question were Manny Shinwell, Davie Kirkwood and Neil MacLean. *The Times* noted that Manny Shinwell 'is described as a Polish Jew'. In fact, he was born to Jewish parents in the East End of London, moved to Glasgow with them and became an adopted Glaswegian. Formerly of Singer's, Neil MacLean was one of the 26 Scottish Labour MPs elected to Parliament in the previous month's poll. 'These are the men who have challenged the Government,' wrote *The Times* disapprovingly.

On Wednesday, 29 January a committee of strikers asked Glasgow's Lord Provost to intervene on their behalf with the government. James Stewart said he would do what he could and asked the committee to come back to see him on the Friday. They brought a few friends with them. Davie Kirkwood described George Square as 'black with men'.

Notices requesting their presence had been placed in *The Strike Bulletin, Organ of the 40 Hours Movement.* The news-sheet was published daily over the course of the dispute and cost one penny, 'although admirers say it is worth Threepence'. On Thursday, 30 January, their notice 'TO ALL STRIKERS' told everyone to come to George Square the following day at half past twelve: 'BE IN TIME AND BE THERE.'

Some say 60,000 people gathered in the centre of Glasgow that Friday. Other estimates put the number as high as 100,000. The famous photograph of the event which gives this book its cover is the classic image of Red Clydeside. The unknown press photographer who shot it certainly framed a surging mass of humanity, all crammed in together, all eyes on the City Chambers. If Scotland ever really did come close to revolution, this is the favoured moment.

Some men have shinned up the ornate lamp posts outside the City Chambers, Glasgow's seat of municipal power. Red flags have been unfurled. Manny Shinwell, Willie Gallacher and Davie Kirkwood were to the fore. John Maclean was not in Glasgow, fulfilling speaking engagements and attending political meetings in Cumberland, Manchester and London. James Maxton was in Glasgow but did not come to the square. For once in his life he chose to avoid trouble.

Winston Churchill was now secretary of state for war. The day before Bloody Friday, the *Evening Times* reported what he had to say about the 40 Hours Strike:

The present situation in Glasgow had been brewing for a long time. The disaffected were in a minority, and, in his opinion, there would have to be a conflict to clear the air. We should be careful to have plenty of provocation before taking strong measures. By going gently at first we should get the support we wanted from the nation, and then troops could be used more effectively. The moment for their use had not yet arrived. In the meantime the Defence of the Realm Act was still in force, and some of the leaders of the revolt should be seized.

At the same meeting of what was still called the War Cabinet, the Secretary of State for Scotland said it was clearer than ever that it was a misnomer to call the situation in Glasgow a strike. This was a Bolshevist rising. Raising the hare and the panic, perhaps seeking to justify those strong measures, he stated there were no more than 10,000 malcontents and he knew public opinion would 'support the Government in quelling any disorder'.

The Deputy Chief of the Imperial General Staff advised that six tanks and a hundred motor lorries with drivers were going north by rail that night. The War Cabinet discussed prosecuting the strike leaders under DORA but decided that 'for the moment no further action was necessary by the Government'.

It's no wonder the government was nervous of Glasgow's strikers. Not only had Red Clydeside earned a powerful reputation for its readiness to confront authority, what was going on in Europe must have sent a shiver down the spine. The shock waves pulsing out from Russia's October Revolution of not much more than a year before were still being felt. Even socialists and communists who had welcomed that with such jubilation had been astonished by how quickly and completely the Tsar and the apparatus and institutions of Imperial Russia had been swept away.

The German Kaiser had abdicated at the end of the war and Germany had just experienced its short-lived revolution. That ended in spectacular failure and death for its leaders, who included Karl Liebknecht and Rosa Luxemburg. On 15 January 1919, two weeks before the Battle of George Square, they were taken from the Adlon Hotel in Berlin and executed without trial. That the next European revolution might erupt on Red Clydeside could not be ruled out.

Yet few of the strikers seemed to have thought that. Harry McShane said, 'We didn't regard the Forty Hours Strike as a revolution. We saw it more as the beginning of things.'

Neil MacLean, Shinwell, Kirkwood and Harry Hopkins of the ASE went into the City Chambers to meet the Lord Provost and hear from him what the government had said. While they were in there, around noon, the men and women who'd made sure they arrived early in George Square began to get restive.

Nobody can quite agree on what happened next. What is undisputed is that, as Glasgow's *Evening News* put it, 'The police found it necessary to make a baton charge, and strikers and civilians – men, women and children – were felled in the melée that followed.'

The demonstrators responded with stones and bottles, taking those from a lorry which had got stuck in North Frederick Street. Sheriff Mackenzie came out of the City Chambers, saw what was going on and decided to read the Riot Act, a copy of which he had conveniently brought with him, ordering the crowd to disperse. It was the first time in 50 years it had been read and the last time it ever was read:

> Our Sovereign Lord the King chargeth and commandeth all persons, being assembled, immediately to disperse themselves, and peaceably depart to their habitations, or to their lawful business, upon the pains contained in the Act made in the first year of King George the First, for preventing tumults and riotous assemblies. God save the King.

Sheriff Mackenzie wasn't very far into it before his copy of the act was plucked from his hand by one of the strikers but he managed to complete the words from memory.

Tramcars had become marooned in the ocean of people. One female driver was stopped by men jumping up onto her platform and making off with the reversing handle. Afraid because of all the bottles that were flying about and because the windows of her car had been smashed, Mary Beattie left the tram.

She told her story at the trial of the strike leaders which took place at the High Court in Edinburgh in April 1919. One policeman giving evidence told the court, 'There was a dense crowd, and young men mounted the cars and were hanging on all over them like a Christmas tree.' This same policeman claimed to have heard Davie Kirkwood shout from a window in the City Chambers overlooking Cochrane Street, urging the crowd to rush the police: 'Never mind their batons.

Get into them.' Glasgow's Town Clerk told a different story, saying Kirkwood was doing his best to calm the crowd and had actually said, 'This is not the opportune time for us; our time will come.'

There's plenty of eyewitness evidence that Davie Kirkwood rushed out of the City Chambers and into George Square when he heard the noise of the disturbance and was almost immediately knocked unconscious by a police baton. Willie Gallacher was also injured and he, Kirkwood and Shinwell were arrested.

The fighting continued, spreading up into North Frederick Street and Cathedral Street and later developing into running battles down to the river at Clyde Street and along as far as Glasgow Green. Nobody died but both demonstrators and policemen were injured. Official figures put the wounded at 34 strikers and 19 policemen. Given the numbers in the square, this would seem to indicate most people in the huge crowd were not involved in the fighting. *The Scotsman* reported on some police officers who were:

> WORSE THAN FRANCE
>
> Sergeant John Caskie described how an inspector and himself were pinned up against the wall while the crowd threw missiles at them. Witness had his helmet bashed and received a severe blow with half a brick on the shoulder. The inspector was hit by a number of stones. They dodged the heavy ones and submitted to the lighter ones. (Laughter.) The attack on the inspector and himself would last about five or ten minutes.
>
> Constable Campbell Smart, who stated that he was hit on the head, hands, and feet, declared that while he had had some unpleasant experiences in France, where he had served in the Army up to the point of the Armistice, there was nothing worse than they had had in Cathedral Street.

Harry McShane agreed with that judgement of the situation up in Cathedral Street:

> Finally the police ran for it and the strikers went after them. There were a lot of closes in Cathedral Street and they rushed up these closes to try and get over the back wall. But there were men catching them by the legs and pulling them down. Some of them got a terrible hiding. I think the best fight was up in Cathedral Street.

Glasgow's *Evening News* was first with the report on the day, carrying it that night:

STRIKE BATTLE
RIOT ACT READ
Police Charge the Mob
WILD GLASGOW SCENES
About 30 Persons Injured
LEADERS ARRESTED

In the tense hours and days which followed, those army tanks which had been dispatched north rolled through the streets of Glasgow in a show of strength designed to impress and subdue the troublesome natives. It's part of the romance of the story that the troops who marched in with them were young English conscripts, it being thought too risky to deploy the Scottish troops in Maryhill Barracks. The chance of their changing sides was too high.

This may well be true, although Harry McShane recalled going 'to explain things' to some soldiers arriving at Buchanan Street, 'the main station for trains from the north'. That doesn't necessarily mean they were Scottish, of course, and McShane doesn't specify, more interested in them not knowing very much about the labour movement:

> They were quite prepared to use their weapons, about that there is no doubt. I'll always remember one of them pointing at his rifle and saying, 'This is better than bottles.' I tried to talk to them on the road down to George Square, but the officers were getting between us and the men. But those young soldiers were aggressive too.

The *Daily Record* did its best to diminish the demonstrators, presenting them as rowdy youths, mindless neds and thugs. Its report of the events of Bloody Friday refers to 'disgraceful scenes' and 'little groups of malcontents' who started assembling in George Square from early morning onwards:

> Singing snatches of their favourite 'Red Flag' as they swung along, the demonstration presented a menacing and truculent appearance. For the most part the ranks were composed of the prentice class, hefty young fellows upon whom a sense of civic responsibility has not yet dawned.

The *Glasgow Herald* was at least more honest about the fear the Battle of George Square struck into the hearts of the city's Establishment. John Wheatley might have stated quite clearly in 1918 that the ILP rejected revolution: 'The people of this country may have socialism when they consider it worth their vote.' Not convinced, the *Glasgow Herald* declared that the people who had caused the trouble in the square were Bolsheviks.

Bolsheviks, sometimes Bolshev*ists*, were entering popular culture as the villains of the piece. *Glasgow 1919: The Story of the 40 Hours Strike* includes among its press cuttings and Harry McShane's account of Bloody Friday and what led up to it an episode of a serial which appeared in the *Glasgow Herald* on 8 February 1919, one week later.

'Banished from the World' features 'Derek Clyde, the famous detective', a man who 'sauntered into the room in the cool, listless way that was habitual to him'. Naturally, the languid air is all a front. Our hero has already dealt with one of those cunning Russian revolutionaries:

> . . . when Vladimir Tolstoi, one of the six Russian Bolshevists who had been sent to England and Scotland to spread their pernicious doctrine, had met with a tragic death. He had been blown to fragments at his lodgings in the Gorbals by the explosion of an infernal machine with which he had meant to destroy a vessel that was lying off the Broomielaw.

The dramatic drawing which accompanies the serial shows an 'infuriated Bolshevist' pointing a gun at Derek Clyde, the famous detective: 'I mean to kill you! I shrink from nothing that is my duty. It will be no crime to destroy one who is the tool of tyrants and oppressors.' Adding to the mix that dash of casual anti-Semitism so common at the time, the story also includes 'a Jew named Finkelstein'.

By Sunday, 2 February *The Times*'s special correspondent was reporting that the troops on guard in Glasgow seemed to be teaching the strikers a lesson, as there were 'signs of returning reason. The futility of violence in the face of machine guns and rifles has been realized.' Those machine guns were mounted on top of the buildings around George Square, with a howitzer in the City Chambers. Would Lord Provost James Stewart really have been prepared to sanction the mowing-down of thousands of Glaswegians, his fellow citizens?

The Bulletin showed two soldiers in tin helmets and with fixed bayonets at the power stations, describing them as 'this formidable guard – equal in strength to the guard at a bridge-end on the Rhine', although it has to be said that they and many of the soldiers in the photographs of the aftermath of Bloody Friday do look very young.

Despite the soldiers, the tanks in the Trongate, the machine guns in George Square and the *Daily Record*'s headline of 'Military Ready to Deal with Clyde Rioters', Harry McShane said, 'There was no open threat and we learned to live with them.'

On Monday, 10 February the 40 Hours Strike was called off, with a recommendation that everyone should go back to work on Wednesday, 12 February. The *Glasgow Herald* was unable to resist a *de haut en bas* wagging finger, printing a 'WARNING TO REVOLUTIONARIES':

> The strike can hardly be said to have reached an official termination; it died a natural death because it had no moral or financial support, because so very few people wished it to live any longer, and because its continued existence was an obvious anachronism in a community which never took it seriously as a Labour movement, but which objected to it emphatically as a symptom of incipient revolutionary tendencies wholly foreign to the good sense and the political and social beliefs of the people.

Although James Maxton had not been in George Square on Bloody Friday, he rallied to the support of those who had. A touching little vignette from Davie Kirkwood illustrates the characters of both men:

> When I was arrested after the Riot of the Forty Hours' Strike, I was taken from the Central Police Station to Duke Street Jail in a Black Maria. Maxton was waiting outside the Central. As I passed he put something in my hand. It was a clean white handkerchief.
> He had remembered my great weakness for a clean hankey.

The 12 men tried in Edinburgh in April 1919 were charged with 'forming part of a riotous mob to hold up the traffic in the Square and adjoining streets, to overawe and intimidate the police force on duty there, to forcibly take possession of the Municipal Buildings and the North British Station Hotel'. Five of the defendants, including Kirkwood, Gallacher, Shinwell and Harry Hopkins of the ASE, faced additional charges of inciting a mob 'of 20,000 or thereby riotous and evilly disposed persons'.

One of the witnesses for the defence was Rosslyn Mitchell. As a town councillor, he had been on a balcony in the City Chambers watching the crowd, giving him an excellent view of what was going on. He thought the police had initially drawn their batons to push the crowd back to clear the way for a tramcar to pass and it had escalated from there. According to Mitchell's testimony as reported in *The Scotsman*:

> . . . some of the police poked the crowd. If the crowd had been determined to move forward with a vicious intent, the cars would have toppled over, and there would have been massacre. To his astonishment, the police charged the crowd at the double. In his view, there was no reason for that charge. After the charge the crowd took turf and daffodil bulbs from the plots in the square, and stones, and threw them. There was another baton charge, in which men were struck down indiscriminately, and a great many people were injured. It was some time after the second baton charge that the bottle-throwing began. After the first baton charge the attitude of the crowd was pretty ugly. There was no evidence of the crowd to do mischief that day.

King's Counsel Mr Constable also argued there had been no 'preconcerted design to do mischief on the part of the mob assembled in George Square' and that the trouble had largely been concentrated around the trams in one corner of it. Every time the police advanced, 'the people ran before them like sheep. The conclusion was irresistible, that some at any rate of the baton charges were made without any excuse or provocation'. Another of the advocates concurred: 'The real cause of the trouble on 31st January was the hasty action of the police.'

Conducting his own defence, Willie Gallacher was dismissive of the idea that what is now the Millennium Hotel, on the north side of George Square, was ever in any danger of being stormed by the crowd:

> . . . for good or ill he had referred to the North British Station Hotel, but no one paid any attention to it, and the authorities never thought there was going to be any interference with that hotel. There had

never been such a ridiculous case put up against a body of men, and whichever way the jury decided his conscience was easy, and he would sleep as well in a prison cell as at home.

In his final summing-up, the Lord Justice Clerk told the jury he was 'sure they were tired of the case, but he thought it right to say that in his judgment the case had not occupied any more time than it ought to have occupied'. Nor did His Lordship see much significance in the red flag having been carried by the strikers on the Monday before Bloody Friday:

> . . . he was not sure he knew what the red flag meant. But whatever it meant, it had the capacity, apparently, of exciting paroxysms of indignation and derision in some quarters, and exciting enthusiasm beyond bounds in others.

The crowd which had gathered in George Square had done so perfectly legitimately in order to hear from the Lord Provost what the Prime Minister had said. Be that as it may, rioting or inciting other people to riot was against the law.

Eight of the defendants were acquitted, including Davie Kirkwood. That he had been struck by a police baton and there was a photograph of him lying concussed on the pavement had earned him a lot of sympathy. James Murray and William McCartney were sentenced to three months in prison, as was Willie Gallacher. This was despite the jury recommending leniency in his case, as he had tried to get people to disperse peacefully. Manny Shinwell was given a sentence of five months.

The 40-hour week didn't come until the Second World War, although after the strike hours were reduced from 54 to 47. The biggest difference that made was to start times, meaning men and women no longer had to be at the yard or factory gates for six o'clock. That had always been a killer.

On 1 February, *The Strike Bulletin* gave what happened in George Square the name it's been known by ever since:

> Henceforth January 31, 1919, will be known to Glasgow as Bloody Friday, and, for the crime of attacking defenceless workers, the citizens will hold the authorities responsible. The police have once

more been used as hirelings to bludgeon the workers.

The workers will not forget.

The news-sheet also urged strikers to 'keep cheery'. It was a very Scottish affair, this revolution that never was.

19

The Red Clydesiders Sweep into Westminster

We were the stuff of which reform is made.

Another square in the centre of Glasgow, another massive crowd. As at George Square on Bloody Friday, estimates vary. Some say well over 100,000 men and women filled St Enoch Square and spilled over into Argyle Street and the other streets around it.

Those who'd got there first stood in front of the two sweeping carriageways which curved up into the grand Victorian railway station. Extra lamps had been brought to light up the gloom of the November night and two large red flags fluttered over the entranceway.

There was music, of course, as there always was. The William Morris Choir led the singing: 'The Red Flag', 'The Internationale', 'Jerusalem', Psalm 124. The Covenanters knew this as 'Scotland's Hymn of Deliverance':

If it had not been the LORD who was on our side, now may Israel say;
If it had not been the LORD who was on our side, when men rose up
    against us:
Then they had swallowed us up quick, when their wrath was kindled
    against us:
Then the waters had overwhelmed us, the stream had gone over our
    soul:
Then the proud waters had gone over our soul.
Blessed be the LORD, who hath not given us as a prey to their teeth.
Our soul is escaped as a bird out of the snare of the fowlers: the snare
    is broken, and we are escaped.
Our help is in the name of the LORD, who made heaven and earth.

The men going off to London had been given a sacred trust, one they acknowledged in a printed declaration distributed to their supporters at services of dedication held earlier in the day:

> The Labour Members of Parliament for the City of Glasgow and the West of Scotland, inspired by zeal for the welfare of humanity and the prosperity of all peoples and strengthened by the trust reposed in them by their fellow-citizens, have resolved to dedicate themselves to the reconciliation and unity of the nations of the world and the development and happiness of the people of these islands.

The election of 1922 might have returned a Conservative government to power but it also produced an earthquake which rocked the political landscape of Britain. For the first time ever, the Liberal Party was no longer the opposition: the Labour Party was. Its candidates and supporters had strained every sinew to win electoral success. This was an election fought with real passion. Tom Johnston wrote in the *Forward* of the many female volunteers who helped him win his seat in West Stirlingshire:

> They hustled the indifferent to the booths; they lent shawls and held babies: they carried the sick and dying to the polls on mattresses – and they won. May black shame fall upon the individual or the party, who, having the trust of these women, ever betrays it.

There were no Red revolutionaries or dangerous Bolsheviks here. This was all about using democracy and the parliamentary process to get into Westminster and start reforming the system from within.

James Maxton stood for Bridgeton in 1922, the constituency he was to represent at Westminster until his death in 1946. His election manifesto gives full details of where to vote and how to establish which ward you're in, providing the names of the relevant streets so you can work this out. Like other candidates, he spoke at numerous public meetings before the election to put his case. That was how elections were fought in those days.

Since he held two public meetings a night at different schools in the neighbourhood, all at eight o'clock in the evening, presumably he had a warm-up man or two, or quite possibly a warm-up woman. Under the details of the meetings is a polite encouragement to come along: 'All Electors cordially invited to attend. Ladies specially invited.'

Unemployment, housing and education were at the top of Maxton's list of issues. His experience as a teacher allowed him to strengthen the message:

> The welfare of children is of first importance to me. I have had experience of the children of Bridgeton, both as a teacher in the district and as a member of the Education Authority. I know that every year many clever and capable boys and girls lose the opportunity of developing their talents to the fullest through the poverty of their parents. It is the duty of the nation to see that opportunities of education are open to the children of the worker as to the children of the rich.

This was the first election to the Westminster government after the establishment of what was then known as the Irish Free State. Maxton's position on the Irish Question, of profound interest to all those Glaswegians of Irish extraction, was typically idealistic. He believed Britain should continue to give support to 'the Irish nation, both North and South. I look to the developing Irish Labour Party to put an end to the feuds that have rent Ireland asunder.' His manifesto finishes with his stance on Scotland: 'Scotland's commercial and social progress would be considerably quickened by the establishment of a Scottish Parliament.' Crystal clear there too.

His deep appreciation of the women of West Stirlingshire notwithstanding, Tom Johnston later claimed he never actually wanted to be an MP, offering a tongue-in-cheek defence for having done so which basically amounted to 'Jimmy Maxton made me do it':

> . . . it was not until James Maxton sent me a rather indignant letter saying he thought it most unfair that he should be landed for a contest in Bridgeton, while I should sit high and dry; in fact if fellows like myself were going to escape, he would jolly well get out too – not until then did I fall for the apparently 'hopeless' seat of West Stirlingshire. But I lived on the borders of the constituency: a hired car could bring me home every night: the constituency covered the field of Bannockburn, the Wallace Monument on the Abbey Craig, and parts of the bonny banks of Loch Lomond, and touched Loch Katrine; and above all there was not the remotest chance of winning.

They were in buoyant mood as they set off. One story attributed to Manny Shinwell has him telling the crowd the first thing they were going to do when they got to London was 'find the Prince of Wales and hang the bugger from the nearest lamp-post'. The Playboy Prince, briefly to become Edward VIII, did not lead the sort of life calculated to endear him to the working people of Red Clydeside.

The 1922 election returned 142 Labour MPs from constituencies throughout the United Kingdom, the highest number yet to sit in the Westminster parliament. The change in the political landscape of Glasgow and the west of Scotland, where ILP candidates had won 18 seats, was especially dramatic. In Glasgow alone, ten out of the city's fifteen constituencies returned ILP candidates.

Above a cartoon of a bemused St Mungo wondering why a respectable person like himself was now casting a queer kind of a shadow, that of the sinister Russian Bolshevik who had so seized the popular imagination, *The Bailie* informed its readers that 'Glasgow is now two-thirds red. Politically and geologically Glasgow stands on shaky ground. It is said that there is a serious "fault" under our feet. Earthquakes are predicted.'

Like a victorious rebel army, blue bonnets crossing the border, ten of the new MPs were to travel down to London together on the night mail from St Enoch. In *My Life of Revolt* Davie Kirkwood offered a summing-up of his comrades of 1922:

> What a troop we were! John Wheatley, cool and calculating and fearless; James Maxton, whose wooing speaking and utter selflessness made people regard him as a saint and martyr; wee Jimmie Stewart, so small, so sober, and yet so determined; Neil MacLean, full of fire without fury; Thomas Johnston, with a head as full of facts as an egg's full o' meat; George Hardie, engineer and chemist and brother of Keir Hardie; James Welsh, miner and poet from Coatbridge; John W. Muir, an heroic and gallant gentleman; and old Bob Smillie, returned for an English constituency though he was born in Ireland and reared in Scotland.

The Conservative prime minister, Sir Andrew Bonar Law, sat for a Glasgow constituency. It's probably a fair bet that the Right Honourable member for Glasgow Central chose to return to Westminster and Downing Street by a different train.

The Bailie was generous enough to observe that the 'ten wise men' deserved their electoral success:

A new spirit is abroad in politics. In one respect we give credit to the Labour Party. They take their politics seriously. Look at the send-off those Labour M.P.'s received on Sunday. Had the old parties shown the same enthusiasm the political complexion of Glasgow would have been very different to-day.

Putting the number of people in St Enoch Square at 50,000, *The Bulletin* too gave remarkably generous coverage to the send-off of the 'elated labourists'. Perhaps the newspaper realized many of its readers had to be among the vast crowd:

SEND-OFF SCENES
Enthusiastic Crowds at the Station
At both the Metropole Theatre, where an I.L.P. rally was held to celebrate the Labour victory, and at St Enoch Station later in the evening when the new M.P.'s were leaving the city for the opening of parliament today there were scenes of remarkable enthusiasm, the crowds of well-wishers attending the departure being of such dimensions that they choked up all approaches to the railway station.

At the Metropole Theatre meeting the auditorium was packed in all parts. As the names of the victors were mentioned as speakers by the chairman, Bailie Dollan, there were outbursts of tremendous cheering, though, one of the most cordial receptions was given to Mr. E. Rosslyn Mitchell and others of the unsuccessful candidates.

The Bulletin reported Tom Johnston's mischievous observation which 'raised a howl of laughter' that he was now the Duke of Montrose's representative in Parliament. He'd given the gentleman a fairly comprehensive doing in *Our Noble Families*. There were more speeches and more laughter at St Enoch Square, where James Maxton, Patrick Dollan and Neil MacLean, re-elected as Labour MP for Govan, addressed the crowd.

They did so from the parapet of St Enoch's sweeping carriageway, up above the metal advert which for years extolled to travelling Glaswegians the benefits of the pens produced by an Edinburgh firm: 'They came as a boon and a blessing to men, the Pickwick, the Owl and the Waverley Pen.'

For James Maxton, the euphoria of that send-off must have been bittersweet indeed. He and Sissie McCallum had married in the summer of 1919 and had a son two years later. Seriously ill through the first year of his life, the baby was nursed devotedly by his mother. The strain did not help her own health, which had never been robust. As young Jim returned to full health and strength, his mother weakened. Sinking fast, she died at the end of August 1922, leaving a distraught husband behind her.

Maxton's mother stepped into the breach, taking over the care of her baby grandson. His brothers, sisters and friends rallied round, whisking Jimmy off to the continent on a journey which was half a holiday and half a research trip into how conditions for working people were in France, Germany, Austria and Czechoslovakia. Ramsay MacDonald, who had also been widowed young and left with a young family, advised Maxton that the only way to cope with his grief was to throw himself into his work.

Doing just that, he made the crowd in St Enoch Square laugh by poking fun at Bonar Law, promising the Prime Minister wasn't going to know what hit him when the Scottish MPs arrived at Westminster:

> Bonar, seek not yet repose
> Cast that dream of ease away,
> Thou art in the midst of foes,
> Watch and pray.

After the parody of the hymn came the warning – and the battle cry:

> When they went to the House of Commons, he said, they would make some of the genial old Tories from the backwoods earn their £400 by the sweat of their brows. They could not work miracles, but they promised courage, hard work, genuine and strenuous service. They wanted to pass from the era of government by delusion to government by understanding.

Davie Kirkwood remembered that when he and John Wheatley reached Westminster and walked together from the House of Commons to the House of Lords, he saw the physical manifestation of the world of privilege they all so hated: 'Turning to John Wheatley, I said aloud: "John, we'll soon change all this."' Looking back on it all, Kirkwood summed up the enthusiasm and the optimism:

We were going to do big things. The people believed that. We believed that. At our onslaught, the grinding poverty which existed in the midst of plenty was to be wiped out. We were going to scare away the grim spectre of unemployment which stands grinning behind the chair of every artisan. We believed it could be done. We believed that this people, this British folk, could and were willing to make friends with all other peoples . . . We were the stuff of which reform is made.

20

The Zinoviev Letter

Another Guy Fawkes – a new gunpowder plot.

The new Scottish Labour MPs were sometimes lonely in London at the weekends. It was too far to go home, and too expensive. In those days MPs had to pay their own expenses, including railway fares between their constituencies and the House of Commons, out of their annual salary of £400.

They kept one another company, sometimes having a wander through the street market at Petticoat Lane. Speaking broad Scots, Davie Kirkwood was not always understood by the Londoners. He kept a guid Scots tongue in his heid in the House of Commons. Famously, in a debate on poverty in Clydebank, he was reprimanded by the Speaker for mentioning the King, reminded that the monarch must not be referred to by name in the House. Kirkwood thought for a moment and substituted 'the Prince o' Wales's faither'. The chamber erupted into laughter.

Sometimes on a Sunday a group of them went together to St Columba's, the Scots Kirk, and sometimes to an Anglican church in the East End where the parson 'always put up a fervent word for strength and courage to the men from Scotland who had come down to Westminster to fight against needless poverty'. The opportunity to do so came sooner than they had expected.

Prime Minister Andrew Bonar Law resigned due to ill health only a year after that triumphant send-off in St Enoch Square. Stanley Baldwin called another election, hoping to cement his new leadership of the Tory Party, but his confidence was misplaced. His party lost almost 90 seats, while Labour's share of the vote shot up to almost 200. Not considering his majority strong enough, Baldwin declined to become prime minister. King George V therefore asked Ramsay MacDonald to form a government.

Britain's first Labour government took office in early 1924. Its supporters had high hopes but these were swiftly to be dashed. MacDonald and other moderates within the Labour Party were anxious not to alarm middle-class voters by pursuing policies they might view as too radical. 'Alas,' Davie Kirkwood later wrote, 'that we were able to do so little!' One significant piece of legislation did come out of the first Labour government. John Wheatley's Housing Act started the building throughout the United Kingdom of half a million local-authority houses to be rented out to poorer families.

Manny Shinwell said hindsight showed that the Labour Party in 1924 was not ready to govern. Being in a position to change things had been a dream for so long but the reality brought with it some unpleasant truths. He thought one of those was that the Conservatives had lost public confidence rather than the Labour Party winning it. Their coats were on a shoogly peg.

Ramsay MacDonald gave Shinwell responsibility for mines, which were administered by the Board of Trade. It was a poisoned chalice. Miners and coal owners loathed each other so much they could hardly bear to be in the same room with each other, let alone sit down around a table and hold rational talks about wages and hours. In his memoirs, Manny Shinwell described how fierce the mutual hostility was:

> The miners were spoiling for a showdown with the owners. Both sides were frankly stubborn and suspicious, each regarding the other as enemies. For more than two years, the miners had worked under a sense of grievance since being forced to take a wage cut after the cessation of work, as much a lockout as a strike, in March 1921.

The miners were now threatening to strike. Shinwell coerced the mine owners into agreeing a wage increase of 13 per cent and the strike was averted. For now.

Despite his desire to avoid controversy and be seen as a safe pair of hands, Ramsay MacDonald was convinced Britain needed to officially recognize Soviet Russia. This was simply facing up to reality. Unhappy that he might have to receive people who had shot and killed his cousin the Tsar and his family and thrown them down that mineshaft in Ekaterinburg, King George V was reassured by Ramsay MacDonald this would never happen.

There was an economic argument for recognizing the Soviet Union. If diplomatic relations between the two countries were resumed, Britain might be able to collect on the debts Russia had owed Britain since before the Revolution. The Russians said yes, fine, but we'd like a new loan to help get our industry and our agriculture moving. Britain's bankers and financiers were not the only people in whom this provoked a very sharp intake of breath. Although the King had been brought round to recognizing the Russians, many in Britain were outraged by the very idea of it. The Soviet Union remained a bandit state, a lawless country brimming with brigands and Bolsheviks.

Led by press baron Lord Rothermere, a campaign was mounted against Ramsay MacDonald and the Labour government. In other words, the *Daily Mail* struck again. They soon found two great big sticks with which to beat Ramsay MacDonald.

John Ross Campbell was a socialist from Paisley, a member of the CWC during the First World War and in 1920 yet another Scottish founder member of the Communist Party of Great Britain. By 1924 Campbell was in London, editing the party's *Workers' Weekly*. In July of that year he published an open letter to British servicemen, urging them to 'let it be known that, neither in the class war nor in a military war, will you turn your guns on your fellow workers'.

The Attorney General advised Ramsay MacDonald to prosecute Campbell under the Incitement to Mutiny Act of 1797. The senior law officer changed his advice when it emerged that John Ross Campbell had served with distinction during the First World War and been awarded the Military Medal. It wouldn't look good to prosecute a war hero. That argument didn't wash with Lord Rothermere and those so fundamentally and viscerally opposed to the Labour government.

In September of 1924 MI5 intercepted the infamous Zinoviev Letter. This was apparently signed by both Grigory Zinoviev, chairman of Russia's Comintern, and Arthur McManus, formerly of Singer's and now the first chairman of the British Communist Party. The letter urged British communists and socialists to work towards revolution in Britain. At the same time, Ramsay MacDonald was dealing with a motion of no confidence in the House of Commons because he had declined to bring a prosecution against John Ross Campbell.

The Conservatives and the Liberals alleged he was under the influence of the Communist Party of Great Britain, even that of Soviet Russia. MacDonald lost the motion of no confidence and resigned, precipitating yet another general election.

Someone then leaked the Zinoviev Letter to *The Times* and the *Daily Mail*. Both newspapers published it four days before the election. The somewhat lengthy epistle was nicely summed up in the accompanying written protest from the British Foreign Office to the Soviet Chargé d'Affaires in London:

> The letter contains instructions to British subjects to work for the violent overthrow of existing institutions in this country, and for the subversion of His Majesty's armed forces as a means to an end.
>
> It is my duty to inform you that His Majesty's Government cannot allow this propaganda, and must regard it as a direct interference from outside in British domestic affairs.

It was incendiary stuff. Ramsay MacDonald described it as 'Another Guy Fawkes – a new gunpowder plot.' The resulting panic among voters sealed the downfall of the first Labour government. After the election, MacDonald returned to Parliament with 50 fewer seats, only 151 MPs as compared with the 412 now sitting on the Conservative benches.

Although Grigory Zinoviev always denied he had ever seen the letter which bears his name and claimed he had nothing whatsoever to do with it, the document remained controversial. When the late Robin Cook was foreign secretary in 1998, he ordered an investigation into it. While this stated it definitely was a forgery, the Zinoviev Letter continues to exert a fascination over conspiracy theorists.

In August 1925, 12 members of the Communist Party of Great Britain were arrested under the Incitement to Mutiny Act on the basis of the allegedly seditious articles they had written and the communist literature they had circulated. Willie Gallacher and Arthur McManus were among the defendants, sentenced to one year's and six months' imprisonment respectively. Arthur McManus died of a heart attack a year after he was released from prison. He was 38.

There's a conspiracy theory about these arrests too. Some believed they were a pre-emptive strike, an attempt to weaken the warriors of the Left. Another battle was brewing.

21

Nine Days' Wonder:
The General Strike of 1926

*Law abiding citizens should refrain
from congregating in the streets.*

E verything stopped at midnight. Even the cross-border trains between
Scotland and London ground to a halt, stranding their passengers
wherever that happened to be. Maybe those passengers should have had
a little more foresight. The General Strike of May 1926 had been well
advertised.

It was called by the TUC, asking workers throughout Britain to support
Britain's miners. Mine owners wanted them to take a cut in their wages
and an increase in their hours. The miners refused, going on strike on 30
April. Next day, at the annual May Day celebrations, thousands marched
through Glasgow and on to Glasgow Green, where a rally was held in
support of the miners. Their leader, Arthur Cook, had come up with a
catchy slogan: 'Not a penny off the pay, not a minute on the day.'

Workers in other industries – railwaymen, printers, engineers – saw
the miners' struggle as their struggle too. If the miners' pay was cut
today, their pay would be cut tomorrow. Britain's economy was in trouble,
and this was one solution to fixing it. It was not the strategy favoured by
the Left. John Wheatley summed up what was wrong with it:

> In 1920, the millions of ex-Service men who had returned to industry
> gave us, with the aid of the improved methods of production introduced
> during the war, an enormous output. The standard of wages did not
> enable the workers to buy up the goods as rapidly as they were
> produced. The inevitable consequence was a glatted [*sic*] market, a
> collapse in selling prices, industrial stagnation and growing

unemployment. Competitive Capitalism's only remedy for this was the paradoxical one of a reduction in wages when the obvious need was more purchasing power.

The coal owners were, however, adamant. The miners of the north of England, Wales and Scotland had to increase their working hours and take a cut in pay. There was a feeling that the men who worked below the ground had been singled out to take the punishment first. Many working-class people throughout Britain were already struggling to survive.

By the early 1920s, 5,000 people in Clydebank were unemployed. Others were on short time. When McAlpine's, the factors of the Holy City tenements, decided to raise the rents, a prolonged rent strike ensued. It was fought on the tenants' side by the Clydebank Housing Association. Among others, they were led by Andrew Leiper and David Cormack. Support came also from the ILP, the Communist Party and the National Unemployed Workers' Movement.

Women were once again to the fore, including Mrs Hyslop and Mrs Pickles, other female members of the ILP and the Co-operative Women's Guild. Manny Shinwell and Patrick Dollan were also involved, as was Davie Kirkwood, now Labour MP for Clydebank. Telling the tenants to put the rent money aside each week so that they could pay when the dispute was settled was not one of his smarter moves. None of them could afford to put any money aside.

Quoted in Seán Damer's *Rent Strike! The Clydebank Rent Struggles of the 1920s*, Mr Lambie of the Clydebank Housing Association, whose first name is not given, recalled that there were people on the verge of suicide because they'd lost their jobs at Singer's. Those still employed in the sewing machine factory were having their wages arrested by the company to pay the arrears of rent to McAlpine's, the factors.

The Clydebank Rent Strike did not win the victory Mrs Barbour's army had. The dispute dragged on and ended in defeat for the tenants. Many were evicted, six of them on Hogmanay 1925, the timing seen as deliberately vindictive. This renewed sense of class conflict was the atmosphere in which the General Strike took place.

The TUC first asked specific groups of workers to come out: transport workers and printers. On Clydeside as elsewhere the disruption to transport led to violent clashes on the roads and tramways and angry confrontations between strikers, non-strikers and the volunteers manning the trams and driving lorries and buses.

Those volunteers are often remembered as well-heeled university students having a bit of a lark. Glasgow Caledonian University's Red Clydeside website points out that the Students' Representative Council of Glasgow University declared itself neutral during the strike and that fewer students were involved in strike-breaking in Glasgow than at Edinburgh or St Andrew's.

That some Glasgow students were involved is recalled on the same website by an oral testimony given in 1970 by Bill Cowe of Rutherglen. A member of the National Union of Railwaymen, Cowe was one of those who went on strike in 1926:

> In Glasgow the Glasgow University students were arraigned by the working class as being the defenders of property and Toryism because the Glasgow students tried to break the General Strike.
>
> The young students, they drove tramcars in Glasgow that led to battles in the Glasgow streets where these trams were wrecked and students were manhandled because every action was a mass action and immediately a tramcar was surrounded by a mass of strikers the police could do nothing. The students foolish enough to do this job really let themselves in for a lot of trouble.
>
> To this day you'll get among good trade unionists an aversion to university students. Women in the street were encouraging their menfolk to really injure the students.

Class warfare was being waged here, and from both sides. Newspaper reports after the strike ended in failure exhibit an unmistakeable sense of crowing that the middle classes had turned out and managed to do jobs the workers normally did, as a report in *The Scotsman* of 1926 illustrates:

> So far as the Clyde Trust was concerned, they got on with their work at Princes Dock, which they had selected as it was easily protected, central, and with many advantages. Their operations went on extremely well, and he asked the Trustees to concur with him in expressing their gratitude to Col. Wingate and the men of his organisation who came and did that work for them. (Applause.)
>
> It demonstrated that men who had never been accustomed to manual labour, but had their hearts in their work, and wanted to get it through, in the course of a very short apprenticeship, did about just

as good work as the men who were employed from day to day. If that was not an object lesson in Trade Unionism he did not know what would be.

In Glasgow at least it feels like revenge was being taken for how scared the middle classes had been back on Bloody Friday in 1919. *Forward* apart, the city's newspapers were either part of that middle-class Establishment or highly deferential towards it. Three months after the end of the General Strike, in August 1926, the Institute of Journalists met in Glasgow. Its chairman was Sir Robert Bruce, editor of the *Glasgow Herald*.

He won applause from the floor when he stated that his institute did not want to 'be dominated at a moment of crisis by a cabal of militant Trade Union leaders'. The Institute of Journalists also sent a loyal message to the King, by telegram to Balmoral Castle.

The printers who produced the newspapers were a horse of an entirely different colour, a group of men with a long tradition of political Radicalism. One of the incidents which precipitated the General Strike was the refusal of those working on the *Daily Mail* to print an article calling the miners, and those who proposed to strike in sympathy with them, subversive revolutionaries.

With printers solid for the strike, Sir Robert Bruce and other newspaper owners and editors in Glasgow took a leaf out of Red Clydeside's book and got organized, producing the *Emergency Press*, which came out every day over the nine days of the strike. The papers which cooperated to get their side of the story out were the *Glasgow Herald*, the *Daily Record*, *The Bulletin*, *Glasgow Evening News*, the *Evening Times* and *The Citizen*.

On Wednesday, 5 May, the second day of the strike, the *Emergency Press* told its readers the country was quite calm, there were no scenes of disorder, government plans were working well and that in London thousands had walked to work. On Saturday, 8 May 1926, the fifth day of the stoppage, they reported there had been more rioting in Glasgow's East End, which they described as the city's 'Storm Centre'. They also got right up onto their high horses about a news-sheet the TUC was producing for the run of the strike called *The British Worker*.

> This paper announces that it is entirely worked by union men. It is thus clear that the strike in the printing trade is not a general strike, but only a strike against those newspapers of whose political opinion the T.U.C. do not approve.

The *Emergency Press* claimed that many in the printing trade had come out on strike 'with the deepest grief and reluctance'. They also carried a 'Notice to Citizens' from the Lord Provost of Glasgow and the Sheriff of Lanarkshire, issued on 7 May 1926:

> In the present emergency we earnestly recommend that law abiding citizens should refrain from congregating in the streets, and should avoid the main thoroughfares as much as possible. This would not only conduce to their own safety, but materially assist the police in the exercise of their duty.

There was a great sense of shared purpose among the strikers. Bill Cowe of Rutherglen found it inspiring:

> The strike was tremendously successful, the solidarity, the united determination of the working class. I've never seen it before or since, and as a young man it's always recorded in my memory as being the most outstanding example of how unity in action can bring a government to its knees.

John Wheatley agreed, describing the response to the strike call as 'magnificent and electrical':

> Highly respectable, middle-class railway clerks who had never struck on their own behalf had stood shoulder to shoulder with the grimy miner. Railwaymen and dockers brought their wages agreements and placed them on the altar of sacrifice. General transport workers stood still. Compositors, printers, and builders, with two or three times the income of a miner, rallied to the call. Millionaire newspaper magnates discovered that a 'fifth estate' had appeared in the realm.
>
> Everywhere among the strikers there was order, determination and confidence. It was a wonderful, unforgettable spectacle which put fresh hope and courage into the hearts of men whose lives had been devoted to the cause of working-class unity and intelligence.

And then came the betrayal. That's how thousands on the Left saw the actions of the TUC, which capitulated on Wednesday, 12 May. The miners stayed out until November, when they had to go back to work and agree to longer hours and less pay. The General Strike had totally failed to achieve its aims.

Strikers and their supporters were stunned and confused, unable to understand why the TUC had conceded defeat while the strike was still rock solid. John Wheatley called them cowards:

> Some days must elapse before we learn accurately all the cause of the dreadful debacle. But I have no doubt that when everything is straightened out cowardice will occupy a prominent place. The qualities which distinguish men in a drawing-room, a palace, or a debating society are of little use in a vital struggle. Smart quips and polished manners play little part amidst grim realities. From the first moment of the struggle, and indeed before it, prominent Labour leaders were whining and grovelling. The day before the general strike was declared we were told by one of the men who were going out to lead us, that defeat was certain.

Tom Johnston said he'd had his doubts about the strike but that once it had started, and with so many answering the call, the TUC should have had the courage to carry on 'until the Government had been compelled to throw the coalowners and their slave terms overboard'.

John S. Clarke dismissed the idea that what he called 'The Nine Days' Wonder' had been a revolution in the making, a sinister plot to bring down capitalism:

> Because Mrs. McNab, good soul, lost her rag at Brigton and fired a bag of pease meal at a car conductor in spats, it hardly follows that attacks upon Woolwich Arsenal were contemplated in East Ham with a view to procuring howitzers and machine guns.
>
> Baton charges by police are, in nine cases out of ten, the result of panic *in the police*. Many police, in Glasgow at any rate, were highly sympathetic to the strikers.

Clarke quoted some lines from Karl Marx all the same:

EFFORT

Let us do and dare our utmost,
Never from the strife recede,
Never live in dull inertia,

> So devoid of will and deed.
> Anything but calm submission
> To the yoke of toil and pain!
> Come what may then, hope and longing,
> Deed and daring still remain.

Forward had, of course, not broken the strike. In its first edition after it, on Saturday, 22 May 1926, it launched a ferocious attack on 'the blackleg press', listing those newspapers by name and ownership. Those included all those Outram- and Hedderwick-owned papers in Glasgow which had joined together with others to publish the *Emergency Press*.

In Dundee, Tom Johnston's accusing finger was pointed at the Thomson Press, owners of the *Dundee Advertiser*, the *Dundee Courier*, the *Weekly News* and the *Sunday Post*. He lashed out at the *Sunday Post*, condemning its 'sheer fatuity' in its story of a religious revival in Kilmarnock – those were still happening – when young children had solemnly told their parents they did not want to go to the sinful cinema any more: 'No, papa: I will not look at Charles Chaplin. I sin no more! Slow music!'

His solution for how to deal with the blackleg press was not only to boycott the papers themselves but to write to the companies which advertised in them to say you would not buy their products if they continued to do so. The bitterness was intense. One letter to the editor suggested that, while throughout history unsuccessful generals had been court-martialled, he did not want the TUC General Council to be treated in the same way: 'I think if they have any self-respect left they will fold up their cloaks and disappear silently into the night.'

Ramsay MacDonald tried to take some consolation from the solidarity of the working classes:

> But we must not be blind to the wonderful demonstration of working-class solidarity which we have seen. It has been a moving and heartening manifestation. It shows a single minded goodness and willingness to bear sacrifices which should put pride and thankfulness into our hearts. If the nation could only understand it, it would be proud that it possessed the spirit which made the demonstration possible, whatever it may think of the action itself.
>
> The general strike of 1926 will be a glowing point in the history of British Labour.

John Wheatley saw the solidarity but was bitter about the TUC:

> The workers have sustained a smashing reverse. It was not inflicted by their bosses due to their own weakness. It is a most astonishing result to a most magnificent effort. The struggle will surely rank as the greatest and most bungled strike in history.

The strike was followed by prosecutions for assault, breach of the peace and words and actions 'calculated to cause disaffection among the populace, contrary to the Emergency Regulations'. Fines and prison sentences were imposed, the latter with hard labour.

Many strikers had to apply to get their jobs back and give an undertaking they were not in any trade union and would not engage in any trade-union activity. This happened at Singer's in Clydebank and in many newspaper offices, including those papers owned by Outram's and Hedderwick's. In its first edition after the strike, on Saturday, 15 May 1926, the *Glasgow Herald* spelled it out, listing rates of pay and conditions, which included two weeks' paid holiday each year, 'funeral and sickness allowances':

> Owing to the action of certain Trade Unions in breaking agreements with us, to which they were parties, we can have no confidence that any contracts which might be entered into in future would be observed. As continuity of publication is essential in the interests of newspaper readers and advertisers, we are compelled to protect them and ourselves against any repetition of what has taken place on this occasion.
>
> We quite recognise the difficult position in which so many of our former employees found themselves, and desire to say that we have no unfriendly feelings towards them individually.

Applications from former employees would be considered as long as they had been received by nine o'clock that Saturday morning. He who pays the piper calls the tune.

Defiant as ever, Tom Johnston took some advertising space immediately after the end of the General Strike to promote his own newspaper and the cause of socialism:

SOCIALISM IS THE ONLY HOPE!

SOCIALISM—
WILL END POVERTY!
WILL ESTABLISH JUSTICE!
WILL ABOLISH WRONG!
WILL EXALT FREEDOM!

The way to get Socialism is to make Socialists.

The way to make Socialists is to push the sale of '**FORWARD**'

Let your slogan be **FORWARD**!

22

Ten Cents a Dance

*A low-class exotic from fourth-rate
saloons in the Argentine.*

It was years before people came to terms in any way with the shock, grief and sadness of the First World War. A generation of young women had lost their lovers. A generation of men who survived the nightmare had gazed into the abyss, seen how hideously far man's inhumanity to man could go. Perhaps the burden was too heavy to keep on carrying it.

The shift in mood came around 1925. Women cut their hair and their skirts short, dropped their waists and flattened their chests. Fashionable young men took to wearing soft, unstructured clothes, affecting a languid air to go with their floppy shirts and flannel trousers. In some circles there was a blurring of gender boundaries, as evidenced by the title of one of the hit songs of the time: 'Masculine Women, Feminine Men'.

It's not hard to see why some young men rejected the traditional role. That kind of masculinity was lying dead and broken in the green fields of France or, wounded in body and soul, shuffling like a sad ghost around the edges of other people's lives. Slamming the door on the nightmare, the generation which followed declared that life was all about having fun.

This was the Jazz Age, and the more its frantic gaiety horrified the older generation, the more the younger kicked up its heels and enjoyed it. 'Jazz' was used as an adjective. Put it in front of any noun and it meant modern, fashionable, just the ticket, right up to the minute. Deploying a creative crescendo of exclamation marks, an exasperated Helen Crawfurd had a go at it in 1921:

Today, we are living in the *jazz period*. We have jazz music, jazz dancing, jazz frocks, jazz furniture, jazz art, jazz politics, and Lloyd George the grand jazz master of Britain, like the trickster on the fairground . . .

If it is something capable of fulfilment – then for God's sake stop jazzing and get to work. Up Labour! Organise! organise!! organise!!!

She was on a hiding to nothing there, especially when it came to the dancing. Glasgow was famously dancing daft, as the *Evening News* told its readers in 1927, informing them that nowadays it had to be bright lights, swinging floors, palms and buffets and that '*thé dansant* is French for dancing interspersed with pastry':

Now Sauchiehall Street blossoms with dancing-palaces that vie in size with the greatest cinema-houses; incorporate features – garages, tea-rooms, lounges and club-rooms – out of the question for the theatres; and it looks as if more and more young people (and not so very young, either, some of them) are taking up evening dancing as their life's career.

Serious-minded socialists were not the only people who disapproved of this shocking frivolity. Free Kirk ministers and other puritans who had always nursed the suspicion that dancing was the vertical expression of a horizontal desire were absolutely appalled.

Fighting their corner, dancing teachers and owners of ballrooms went to great efforts to present dancing as respectable. They'd had their work cut out when the tango arrived in Glasgow in 1913. Fortunately, Mr James D. Macnaughton, president of the British Association of Teachers of Dancing, had a cunning plan. He staged a demonstration of tango dancing in the eminently respectable surroundings of the McLellan Galleries, in Glasgow's Sauchiehall Street. As the *Glasgow Herald* reported, during the evening he delivered a short talk which posed the provocative question 'Is the Tango suitable for the ballroom?'

. . . the public, having formed their opinions of the Tango from exaggerated performances at variety entertainments, Tango teas, and through press pictures, had only become acquainted with the objectionable side of the dance, and therefore there was little wonder that the Tango as thus shown to them had been objected to, and he heartily agreed with those who thus objected. He believed that the

Tango as commonly presented to the public was a low-class exotic from fourth-rate saloons in the Argentine. As such, it should be banned from the ballrooms.

Clever chap, Mr James D. Macnaughton. 'Fourth-rate saloons in the Argentine' was code for the brothels of Buenos Aires, where the tango began. Having met the major criticism head on – the tango was just too damn sexy – he reassured his audience that he and his fellow members of the British Association of Teachers of Dancing were working tirelessly to ensure good deportment and impeccable decorum in ballroom dancing.

Performed in the way these good people thought suitable, 'the tango rhythm was not only pleasing and fascinating but could be made as decorous and dignified as might be required'. After watching an exhibition of the dance, the *Glasgow Herald*'s reporter gave it cautious approval:

> It was certainly very different from some displays that have been witnessed in Glasgow and elsewhere. The dance gained much in gracefulness by the fact that the movements of all who took part in it were executed with uniformity to music of a strongly marked rhythm. And it did not appear to be difficult; quite suitable indeed for the ballroom provided it were danced correctly.

A second *Herald* reporter, dispatched to the new Alhambra Tango Teas, was distinctly unimpressed, finding it all rather dull, even if there had been 'an exciting scramble for admission':

> As to the dance itself, it would be futile to attempt a description. So far as one could gather from a first impression a great deal of the Art of the Tango – if there is any art in it – consists in the endeavour of the lady and the gentleman to come as near as possible to treading on each other's toes without actually doing so. Stepping alternatively 'fore and aft,' posturing and swaying, and 'ducking' the right knee until it touches the floor, varied by cross-limbed movements and some of the convolutions of ragtime, seem to be the principal movements of the dance.

So there, with a great big disapproving Presbyterian sniff. Dancing Glasgow couldn't have cared less, embracing the new dances and the music which went with them. Ragtime was wildly popular, 'Alexander's Ragtime Band' the big hit of 1912. The foxtrot reached Scotland in 1914. In her definitive *Oh, How We Danced!* Liz Casciani describes how well that went down:

> Of all the dances in the ballrooms, the Fox Trot seemed best suited to the times. The trotting movements and ragtime rhythm were new and different. Young men on leave from the War wanted to dance but had no time for formal instructions. Parents and girlfriends wanted to spend free time with them without the discipline of dancing lessons. The Fox Trot with its lack of formal steps was easy for everyone to pick up and they came along in droves to the ballrooms.

They danced on the ocean-going liners too. Glasgow's Louis Freeman ran an agency to supply the orchestra and the singers and became musical director for both the Anchor Line and the Donaldson Line. The musicians who worked on the ships were known as Louis Freeman's Navy.

Tom Johnston did his bit for the formal teaching of dance in 1911. Starting his political career by getting himself voted onto Kirkintilloch School Board, he was put in charge of the evening-class committee. Many of Kirky's young adults were not exactly bursting with enthusiasm to attend.

Hoping higher attendance would attract higher government grants which would allow a more attractive syllabus to be created, young Mr Johnston came up with the idea of starting dancing classes. There would be free entry to these for any students who regularly attended evening classes in the less enticing subjects: maths, sewing, English, mining and building construction. His idea proved hugely popular. They hired a band and a dancing instructor and the students formed a committee to make sure everything was conducted with that oh-so-important decorum:

> Indeed the order maintained was draconian, any exuberant being promptly and roughly conducted by a frog's march to the open air; the students' Committee took its duties very seriously. The experiment was a great success, and we had to limit the first dancing class to one hundred dancers.

Attendance at classes in the other subjects shot up:

Mothers sent letters of thanks in that they no longer feared for their daughters dancing at disreputable howffs; the ratepayers were saving money; further education was being promoted; we felt as if we were on top of the world.

Growing ever more ambitious, Johnston put on a boxing class. He and his friends did some discreet social work there: 'Contestants on the first evening who disclosed holes in their socks or ragged undergarments only came so circumstanced once.'

It was the boxing rather than the dancing which roused the ire of the local kirks:

Elders held meetings and we were denounced from pulpits with bell, book and candle; foremen in public works interviewed young apprentices and strongly 'advised' against attendance; letters showered upon the local press condemning our wickedness in teaching violence and bloodshed, and asking sarcastically when we were going to start breeding whippets, and teaching faro and roulette; clerical deputations waited upon members of the School Board, some of whom got windy, and the poor boxing (or physical culture) instructor, unable to stick it out, packed up and went off in disgust.

The most popular dance of the 1920s was, of course, the Charleston. Those who thought the young and the light-hearted were having far too much fun warned them no good would come of this shocking and vulgar dance. They would damage their ankles. The jerky movements might even lead to permanent paralysis. The Black Bottom left the killjoys speechless.

People continued to dance the tango, loving the smouldering passion of it, especially when you were in the close embrace of a handsome young man paid not to complain even if you did tread on his feet. Enter the gigolo, the archetypal lounge lizard. Most paid dancing partners were perfectly respectable professionals. It was a sought-after job in the 1920s and '30s, one way in which young working-class men and women with talent could dance their way out of poverty, although it was a hard slog. In Scotland it wasn't ten cents a dance but sixpence, of which the management of the dance hall or club kept fourpence.

In February 1927 Glasgow's *Evening News* reported on the boom in the dance trade, doubting it was going to be as short-lived as the enthusiasm for roller skating, as some people had thought. Some people had also thought the cinema was destined to be nothing more than a passing fad, and look how wrong they had been:

> The teaching of dancing, and the provision of facilities for dancing have become a lively and profitable industry, giving occupation to far more men and women than are employed in all the theatres, music-halls, and picture-houses put together. It may be that the craze for dancing (and the term is not extravagant) may sooner or later fade away as quickly as it began, and that the case of the roller-skating rink was a true analogy, but as yet there is not the slightest sign of it in Glasgow.

There's not much evidence from Scotland of the humiliating dance marathons depicted in the film *They Shoot Horses, Don't They?* However, there was a dark side to the happy feet, elegant evening suits, glittering gold and silver shoes and fringed dresses. In a well-choreographed sequence of events reminiscent of Hogarth's *Harlot's Progress*, dancing partners could find themselves coerced into prostitution.

Take an attractive young woman or man with dancing talent, give them a job doing something they love and a place to stay, buy them some nice clothes. A month or so down the line, demand to know how they're going to pay you back for all these pretty things. You could go to the police and press charges against them, your word against theirs, or they could agree to be booked out for private dancing lessons. That was the euphemism. The manager of the dance hall took one pound, the dancing partner ten shillings. It would take you an awfully long time to earn that the respectable way.

The biggest dancing-partner scandal of the 1930s in Scotland happened at Edinburgh's Kosmo Club, on Lothian Road, and those were the sums involved there. At the trial in December 1933, one witness was asked, 'As a man of the world, what did you think that this fee was paid for?' He offered the following reply:

> If young ladies stay in lodgings, and gentlemen take them home, there is the probability that they would say good-night at the door, but if they were in flats the gentlemen might be invited in for coffee, and there is no knowing what might happen.

Glasgow had acted to try to stop this covert prostitution in 1927, imposing a series of strict rules on the hiring of dancing partners which included their having to give details of what they were doing on their day off and not being allowed to sit a dance out with a paying customer. The city fathers were mocked for this as 'grandmotherly Glasgow'. The entertainments-licensing court at this time also banned smoking on stage at theatres and music halls unless it was necessary for the play. This seems less likely to have been a health measure than a precaution against a potential fire hazard. Cigarettes were still being advertised as good for your throat and your health, particularly recommended to people suffering from TB.

The *Glasgow Herald* defended the new rules for the hiring of dancing partners, albeit only very discreetly alluding to prostitution, not wanting to 'paint a lurid picture of the possibilities that are being guarded against'. The important thing was to make the dancing craze 'as happy, healthy, and enjoyably wholesome as may be'.

Using the pseudonym of 'Open Turn', one dancing partner wrote an indignant letter to the newspaper, defending the professionalism and respectability of her profession. It was good that booking-out had been done away with, but what on earth was wrong with sitting-out?:

> The average gentleman who may visit a dance hall without a partner cannot, and does not want to, dance every dance, and he appreciates the fact that he can have company between dances. To a stranger in the city the system is a perfect godsend. I talk from experience on this point, and there must be thousands of gentlemen who agree with me.

And, with or without dancing partners, under the glitter balls of the fashionable *palais de danse*, the bright lights of public halls, the gloom of disreputable howffs or at home in the kitchen to the strains of a dance band on the wireless, Glasgow kept right on dancing.

23

Sex, Socialism & Glasgow's First Birth Control Clinic

I never saw so many wives of comrades before.

O ne of the allegations used to discredit socialists was that they all believed in free love. If the revolution they were doing their best to bring about ever happened, everything would be nationalized, including women. Take a look at the lives of the Red Clydesiders and this claim quickly becomes risible.

Willie Gallacher described himself and the rest of them as 'tee-totallers and puritans'. Davie Kirkwood agreed: 'We were all Puritans. We were all abstainers. Most of us did not smoke.' James Maxton made up for them there. There was always a cigarette between his fingertips.

When it came to love and family, almost all the key male figures of Red Clydeside were devoted husbands and fathers who paid handsome tributes to their wives as friends and political comrades. Maxton remained a widower for 13 years after the death of his beloved Sissie. He was 50 when he married for the second time. Madeleine Glasier was a member of the ILP and worked with Maxton as a researcher. They had over ten happy years together until his death in 1946.

Helen Crawfurd agreed with free love in its literal sense, asking what other kind there could be. She believed it was wrong to associate sex with sin, describing making love with someone you loved and creating a child out of that love as something beautiful, clean and holy. She responded to those who accused socialists of believing in free love in the sense of promiscuous sexual intercourse by quoting Lenin. Klara Zetkin, one of the surviving leaders of Germany's Spartacist Revolution of 1918, had told the Soviet leader many revolutionary socialists in Germany believed sex was nothing more than an appetite to be satisfied. When you were thirsty, you drank a glass of water. When you were sexually attracted to someone, you had sex with them. No shame, no blame, no guilt.

Helen Crawfurd disagreed, believing there was an issue of gender equality here. Up until the sexual revolution of the 1960s and '70s, a woman could lose that most valuable of attributes, her reputation, for what nowadays no longer even raises an eyebrow. Living with a man to whom you weren't married was shocking. Having a baby out of wedlock was a disaster.

For men and women who had multiple sexual partners, there was also the threat of sexually transmitted diseases. Lenin too spelled this out, making it clear to Klara Zetkin that he disapproved of the German revolutionary socialists' attitude towards sex:

> I think this glass of water theory has made our young people mad, quite mad . . . I think this glass of water theory is completely un-Marxist, and moreover, anti-social . . . Of course, thirst must be satisfied. But will the normal man in normal circumstances lie down in the gutter and drink out of a puddle, or out of a glass with a rim greasy from many lips? . . . Drinking water is of course an individual affair. But in love two lives are concerned, and a third, a new life, arises. It is that which gives it its social interest, which gives rise to a duty towards the community.

Birth control was a highly contentious issue. In July 1920 American Margaret Sanger visited Glasgow to speak on the subject. Scotland enchanted her: the countryside, the people and the Glasgow sense of humour:

> Guy Aldred, who was in Scotland, had planned my schedule there, and I had three weeks of a Scottish summer – bluebells so thick in spots that the ground was azure, long twilights when the lavender heather faded the hills into purple.
>
> When I had been in Glasgow before, I had encountered only officials, but on this occasion I met the people in their homes and found them quite opposite to the stingy, tight-fisted, middle-class stereotype. They were hospitable, generous, mentally alert, just as witty as the Irish and in much the same way, which rather surprised me.

She was struck by how interested Scots of both genders were in hearing what she had to say:

> Fourth of July, Sunday, we had a noon meeting on the Glasgow Green. Nearly two thousand shipyard workers in caps and baggy corduroys stood close together listening in utter, dead stillness without cough or whisper. That evening I spoke in a hall under Socialist auspices, Guy Aldred acting as chairman. One old-timer said he had been a party member for eleven years, attending Sunday night lectures regularly, but never before had he been able to induce his wife to come: tonight he could not keep her at home. 'Look!' he cried in amazement. 'The women have crowded the men out of this hall. I never saw so many wives of comrades before.'

Margaret Sanger is a controversial figure, accused by her critics of advocating some of the worst excesses of eugenics, fiercely defended against those charges by her supporters. That her interest in birth control had a deeply personal and visceral basis cannot be doubted. She was the sixth of eleven children. Her mother gave birth to eighteen babies, seven of whom did not survive childhood.

Sanger is credited with having come up with the term 'birth control', although initially she advanced her ideas under the name of 'family limitation'. While she was touring Europe in 1920, her book of the same title was circulated by a fellow socialist and member of the Industrial Workers of the World, our old friends the Wobblies. That got her into trouble on her return to the States. It was illegal in both America and Britain to distribute literature promoting birth control.

Along with his partner, Rose Witcop, Guy Aldred, who organized Margaret Sanger's speaking engagements in Glasgow, was prosecuted in 1922 for publishing Margaret Sanger's *Family Limitation*, allegedly an obscene pamphlet. Aldred and Witcop are among the few characters in the story of Red Clydeside who advocated free love.

Originally from London, Aldred was an anarchist who lived for many years in Glasgow. As an angry young man, he thought romantic love between men and women was incompatible with his political views and any hope for equality between the sexes. In 1907 he published a pamphlet on *The Religion & Economics of Sex Oppression*. Although at this point he thought celibacy might be the only answer, he subsequently changed his mind.

Guy Aldred and Rose Witcop were married in front of a Glasgow sheriff in 1936 only to save her from being deported to her native Russia. By that time their relationship was over: 'We parted at the sheriff's chambers and each took a different way.'

There were some socialists who used free love to try to discredit birth control. Hiding behind a pseudonym, 'Nestorius' launched his attack – and he does sound like a man – in an article in *Forward* on 1 May 1926, just before the General Strike. He was responding to a letter to the editor from Dora Russell, wife of philosopher Bertrand Russell and one of Britain's most prominent campaigners for birth control.

Nestorius attacked Dora Russell for what she had written about free love. She was, of course, entitled to her views, but he thought that if the Labour Party ever adopted these as party policy the movement would be 'smashed to smithereens'. He was shocked by what she had written, that, for younger women, the war had made sexual relations more free and easy: 'Sex, even without children and without marriage, is to them a thing of dignity, beauty, and delight.'

For her part, Dora Russell was furious with Clydeside's Labour MPs for not having supported moves to allow municipal child welfare clinics to give advice on birth control. Labour MP Ernest Thurtle had brought a bill before Parliament in 1924 hoping to achieve this. First Labour minister of health in that first Labour government, John Wheatley told Thurtle in a debate in the House of Commons that he did not think public funds should be used to support such measures 'which are the subject of controversy'.

Dorothy Jewson, feminist and Labour MP, who later married Red Clydesider Campbell Stephen, MP for Camlachie, did not mince her words when she responded to John Wheatley:

> Is the Minister aware that many working-class women attending these welfare centres are unfit to bear children and to bring up healthy children, and the doctors know they are unfit, and yet they are unable to give this information, which any upper or middle-class woman can obtain from a private doctor; and will he consider the bearing of this on the question of abortion, which is so terribly on the increase in this country?

John Wheatley gave her a non-committal answer.

When Ernest Thurtle's bill was voted on, only one of the Clydeside Labour MPs went through the lobbies. Rosslyn Mitchell, now MP for

Paisley, voted against allowing child welfare clinics to give out birth control equipment and advice. The others abstained: James Maxton, Tom Johnston and all. *Forward* did carry regular adverts for birth control advice and supplies, to be bought by post from London.

The son-in-law of 1930s Labour leader George Lansbury, Ernest Thurtle also fought to abolish the death penalty in the British Army for soldiers found guilty of cowardice or desertion. Supporters of this measure included T.E. Lawrence, Lawrence of Arabia. Thurtle's proposals, which stopped any more men from being shot at dawn, became law under a Labour government in 1930.

The continuing failure of Red Clydeside's Labour MPs to support birth control provoked Dora Russell's letter to the *Forward* in 1926. Describing birth control as 'the most burning women's question of the day', she berated them for what she called their stupidity:

> Not one of them voted for Mr. Thurtle's Bill, or seems to realise that one subject with which it dealt is more serious and urgent to the average mother than even the housing on which so much good Scottish eloquence is expended. Countless downtrodden women of Clydeside who seem indifferent to politics can be stirred to active responsibility by an intelligent propaganda on Birth Control and creative motherhood. The shadow of threatened religious opposition blinds many Scottish members and organisers to the reality of possible support – great in numbers and passionate in belief – from these awakening women.

It was the highly respectable Govan housewife Mary Barbour of the 1915 rent strike who helped set up the first birth control clinic in Glasgow. She was its chairman. As 'patronesses', she had aristocratic support: the Countess of Strathmore, Lady Geddes and Lady Colquhoun of Luss.

Both men and women served on the committee of the Glasgow Women's Welfare and Advisory Clinic. It had its offices at 123 Montrose Street in Glasgow, tucked in behind the City Chambers, and its clinic south of the Clyde, at 51 Old Govan Road. A questionnaire filled out by attending physician Dr Isobel Sloan in November 1927 offers some fascinating details, not least of the industries which surrounded the clinic in 1920s Govan. They included shipbuilding and engineering works, docks, ropeworks, the Scottish Co-operative Wholesale Society, factories making jam, biscuits and pickles.

Another question asked who had started up the clinic and who was now organizing it. As with support for the suffragettes, once again the mining communities of Lanarkshire show themselves to have been ready to embrace change:

> Interest was aroused by a birth control campaign carried out mainly among the miners and workers in Lanarkshire in the Spring of 1926 followed by the initiation of the Birth Control Clinic, by an enthusiastic group of women. These agreed to follow the lines of the Walworth Clinic, London under the Society for the Provision of Birth Control Clinics.

The Govan clinic opened in August 1927 in what had previously been a shop. It was well kitted out, with three rooms and three cubicles, two gas fires and one radiator, various bits of medical paraphernalia 'and what Doctor requires'. Financial support came from a few trade unions, the Labour Party, the ILP and women's guilds attached to the Co-operative, including Dumbarton, Clydebank and St Rollox.

A separate list of those who had made donations includes Janie Allan, suffragette and socialist. Other contributors preferred to remain anonymous, perhaps because birth control remained such a contentious issue.

Although there were no official links, moral support and encouragement came from the child welfare clinics which had been set up in Glasgow. One of the doctors helping to run those was Dorothea Chalmers Smith, the suffragette who had been imprisoned in 1913 after the 'Halloween at the High Court' trial.

Dr Sloan noted that some probation officers were supporting the new birth control clinic 'and one of those a Roman Catholic'. She and the nurse who worked with her offered two sessions a week, one in the afternoon and one in the evening. They dispensed advice and supplies of the birth control methods available at the time, essentially Dutch caps, spermicides and condoms.

Some of the women being advised, all of whom had to be married, were suffering from the great scourge of TB. Their health would not allow them to bear another child. Others needed birth control for economic reasons, so they could have fewer children but look after them better.

Unemployment, wages not equal to the maintenance of the family already there, also lack of housing accommodation and generally the depression in industry specially felt in Glasgow and the Clyde area. With Birth Control Education, patients and mothers specially would be enabled to keep and raise the social condition of the family.

The researchers who asked Dr Sloan to fill out the questionnaire were keen to know if the clinic was 'getting information to the lower and less intelligent members of the working class as well as those of more foresight, initiative and intelligence', which would seem to bring us back to eugenics. One of the devices given out by the Govan birth control clinic was called the 'Prorace' cap, a rather uncomfortable name when we now know where eugenics went next.

In a telling reply to another question, Dr Sloan wrote that she had never been taught anything about contraceptive methods during her medical training or while she was doing her hospital residency. By 1934, the Govan clinic was advising that they could offer training to 'lady doctors'.

In 1927 Glasgow's libraries were offered a free set of a journal called *Birth Control News*. This was published by Marie Stopes's Society for Constructive Birth Control and Racial Progress, another uncomfortable name. John S. Clarke, socialist and lion-tamer, the man who'd taken in the banished Clyde shop stewards in 1916, was now a Glasgow councillor. Serving on the libraries' acquisitions committee, he and fellow councillor Kate Beaton, member with Helen Crawfurd and Agnes Dollan of the Women's Peace Crusade of the First World War, voted that the gift should be accepted. Two others voted against. One of them was Councillor Izett, who'd been on the side of the angels during the rent strike of 1915.

The argument blew up into a controversy, the issue debated by a meeting of the entire Corporation. Twenty-three councillors voted in favour of Glasgow's libraries stocking *Birth Control News*, sixty-two against, and Marie Stopes's gift was rejected. While all those 23 councillors who voted in favour were Labour, other Labour members voted against. Others again, like the Clydeside MPs in Parliament, tried not to come down on one side or the other. One of these was Patrick Dollan. He and his fellow socialist and suffragette wife, Agnes, were both born into large families. That they themselves had only one child may indicate where they actually stood on the issue of birth control.

Attitudes were changing, even if too many men in the Labour Party did not have the courage of their convictions. As J.J. Smyth wrote in *Labour in Glasgow, 1896–1936*, by 1930 the second Labour government 'quietly allowed clinics to provide information on contraception on health grounds but, as these could be interpreted quite widely, this was close to the demand for free advice for married women'.

That year also saw the establishment of the National Birth Control Association, which a few years later became the Family Planning Association. When the Glasgow Women's Welfare and Advisory Clinic published its annual report for 1934–35, nine years after it had been established, it felt there was still a long way to go before birth control would be accepted simply as a branch of public health provision.

This report listed three women they had helped at the Govan clinic. As it says itself, the facts require no further comment:

Mrs. X. Aged 34. Husband (unemployed), carter. 11 pregnancies. 5 children alive now. 4 born dead. Mother anaemic.

Mrs Y. Aged 33. Husband (unemployed), miner. 10 pregnancies. 7 children alive. Mother anaemic.

Mrs Z. Aged 39. Husband five years younger. 17 pregnancies. 16 children alive now.

These examples speak for themselves.

24

The Flag in the Wind

No man was more generously international in his outlook
and spirit, and yet to the very core of his
being he was a Scotsman of Scotsmen.

Home Rule for Scotland was on the political agenda before the ink had
dried on the Treaty of Union. Universally unpopular, the Union of
the Parliaments of 1707 which followed the Union of the Crowns of 1603
was contemplated only because Scotland was bankrupt. This financial
disaster was caused by the catastrophic Darien Adventure, a failed
attempt to establish a Scottish colony in Panama.

Scotland's precarious economic situation gave England the opportunity
to finally neutralize the threat its troublesome northern neighbour had
always posed. Bribes paid by the English commissioners whose job it
was to push the Union through persuaded the Scottish nobility to vote
their own country out of existence. These were the people Robert Burns
branded 'a parcel of rogues'.

Ordinary Scots were devastated by this betrayal, dismayed beyond
measure that their country was now to be swallowed up by England.
When the Treaty of Union was ratified on 1 May 1707, the bells of St
Giles' Cathedral in Edinburgh played an old Scottish air which caught
the despairing spirit of the moment: 'Why Am I So Sad on My Wedding
Day?'

There were some honourable exceptions within the parcel of rogues,
most notably Andrew Fletcher of Saltoun. Other members of Scotland's
gentry and aristocracy who spoke out against the Union were Lockhart
of Carnwath and Alexander Forbes, 4th Lord Pitsligo. Carnwath and
Lord Pitsligo were also Jacobites, supporters of the exiled House of
Stuart.

The longing to reclaim Scotland's lost nationhood was a powerful driver of the Jacobite risings of the first half of the eighteenth century. Most support for the Stuarts had little to do with religion or some mythic belief in their divine right to rule. What they offered was a focus for discontent and the possibility of change in a country a century and a half away from anything faintly resembling parliamentary democracy.

When Radical leaders James Baird, Andrew Hardie and James Wilson died for this ideal, one of the rallying cries was 'Scotland free or a desert!' When the long march towards democracy and universal suffrage really got under way after the Great Reform Act of 1832, it always went hand in hand with the cry of Home Rule for Scotland.

During the nineteenth century the burning question of Home Rule for Ireland made many ask why this was desirable for one of the Celtic nations of the British Isles and not the others. One of those who advocated 'Home Rule all round' was Liberal prime minister William Gladstone, the man who famously declared that his mission was to pacify Ireland.

The Gladstones were originally a Scottish family. The Prime Minister sat at times for a Scottish seat. This may have had some impact on his position, although the pamphlet he published in 1886 put the case of Home Rule for Ireland, Scotland and Wales on the basis of logic. He argued that the Union should be replaced by a federal Britain.

The idea was clearly in the air. It was also in 1886 that the Scottish Home Rule Association was formed. Keir Hardie was a supporter from the start, one of the SHRA's early vice presidents. As Ramsay MacDonald wrote in his foreword to William Stewart's biography of Hardie:

> No man was more generously international in his outlook and spirit, and yet to the very core of his being he was a Scotsman of Scotsmen, and it is not at all inappropriate that I came across him first of all at a meeting to demand Home Rule for Scotland.

MacDonald himself was for some years secretary of the London branch of the SHRA. Scottish miners' leader Robert Smillie also served as vice president, as did Cunninghame Graham. Don Roberto was a founding father of both the Labour Party and the Scottish National Party.

Founded some years after the SHRA, the ILP and the STUC shared its commitment to Home Rule for Scotland. Not all Scottish nationalists were political radicals but all political radicals were Scottish nationalists. Momentum built up, culminating in a Home Rule Bill being brought before the Westminster parliament in 1913. It might well have gone through if the First World War had not intervened.

The war itself gave a boost to Scottish nationalism. As H.J. Hanham puts it in his *Scottish Nationalism*, 'complaints about the dead hand of the Whitehall bureaucracy were an important element in Clydeside discontent'. In 1917 the STUC passed a resolution in support of a Scottish parliament:

> This Congress reaffirms its demand that the control of Scottish affairs should be placed in the hands of the Scottish people by the reinstitution of a Scots' Parliament, and regrets at this juncture the Scottish people should not be represented directly on the Imperial War Council.

In the aftermath of the First World War the Labour Party, of which the ILP was a more radical component, was also enthusiastic about Home Rule for Scotland:

> Now that the War is ended and an era of reconstruction begun, Scottish problems require the concentration of Scottish brains and machinery upon their solution.
>
> Your Committee is of the opinion that a determined effort should be made to secure Home Rule for Scotland in the first Session of Parliament, and that the question should be taken out of the hands of place-hunting lawyers and vote-catching politicians by the political and industrial efforts of the Labour Party in Scotland which should co-ordinate all its forces to this end, using any legitimate means, political and industrial, to secure the establishment of a Scottish Parliament upon a completely democratic basis.

On the Left, it was only communists like Willie Gallacher who rejected Home Rule for Scotland, calling instead for an international union of the working classes. John Maclean believed in a Scottish workers' republic, independent of England. Gallacher's and Maclean's profound disagreement on this point meant Maclean never joined the Communist Party of Great Britain.

ILP members continued to advocate Home Rule, often through the pages of the *Forward*. One of the paper's most loyal backers was Roland Muirhead, long-standing chairman of the SHRA. Tom Johnston described him as the 'Grand Old Man' of Scottish nationalism. On several occasions,

Muirhead rode to the rescue of the socialist newspaper:

> Time and again it looked as if our ship was heading for the bankruptcy
> rocks, but somehow we always escaped . . . A witty but rather cynical
> friend used to say he always knew when the *Forward* was in
> exceptionally deep water: it would then come out with a specially
> strong Home Rule issue: that would be preparatory to 'touching' Mr.
> Muirhead for a loan!

The victorious Labour MPs who got such a resounding send-off from St
Enoch Station in 1922 were all committed to Home Rule. Speaking at the
service of dedication held in St Andrew's Halls on the Sunday before they
left on the night mail for London, Govan MP Neil MacLean at first
addressed the still burning issue of rent. *The Bulletin* reported what he
said next:

> When they went to London Home Rule for Scotland would not be
> confined to the drawing-rooms of Brodick Castle. They would talk
> Home Rule in a way that several of these people did not realise. It did
> not mean a palace at one end of the glen and a ruined crofter's cottage
> at the other. It meant civilisation in Scotland, plenty and security for
> the Scottish people in the land of their birth.

Neil MacLean's 'drawing-rooms of Brodick Castle' is a reference to the
3rd Marquess of Bute, one of the aristocratic supporters of Home Rule.
There were several of those. In *Scottish Nationalism*, Hanham described
Bute as 'a Roman Catholic Tory philanthropist and antiquarian . . . outside
the realm of ordinary party politics. He was one of the first to evolve
something like a distinctive Catholic nationalist point of view.'

Yet the Marquess of Bute put Home Rule above his own traditionalist
and Conservative views, expressing his point of view in a letter to Lord
Rosebery way back in 1881:

> Allow me to say that I think there are many Tories like myself who
> would hail a more autonomous arrangement with deep pleasure. We
> would prefer the rule of our own countrymen, even if it were rather
> Radical, to the existing state of things.

Another aristocratic Home Ruler was the Honourable Ruaraidh Stuart

Erskine of Marr. His nationalism was rooted in the mysticism and mystery of Celtic Scotland and the Gaelic language. Despite having been born in Brighton and living for long periods of time in England and France as well as Scotland, he spoke Gaelic quite fluently.

As a Highlander, a Catholic, a royalist and a socialist stirred and excited by the Russian Revolution, Erskine of Marr's politics were something of a patchwork quilt. Communist Harry McShane described him as an old-fashioned Radical.

The focus always came back to Scotland. At the time of John Maclean's 1918 sedition trial, Erskine of Marr was critical of Maclean for not having fought the charges brought against him under the Defence of the Realm Act as not being valid in a Scottish court. The Clydeside Labour MPs of the 1920s took the argument to Westminster. Speaking in a debate on Home Rule in 1924, Tom Johnston delivered a typically passionate and romantic speech:

> Our historical and cultural traditions are different; our racial characteristics are different. The Celt has long memories, the Englishman forgets quickly. There are members on these Benches and on those Benches too who fight their electoral battles upon, say, the Battle of the Boyne. We have members on these Benches who fight them on the battle of Bannockburn. But the Englishman forgets quickly. We can never obliterate these national characteristics . . .

Johnston went on to cite Robert Louis Stevenson, Robert Burns and William Wallace, allowing Englishman Rudyard Kipling (slightly misquoting the poet) to sum up why you have to be a nationalist before you can be an internationalist:

> God gave all earth to men to love;
> But, because our hearts are small,
> Ordained for each, one spot should prove
> Beloved over all.

Despite having been known to say that the workers had no country, Davie Kirkwood said something very similar in the wake of the drama of the Zinoviev Letter:

> I take no orders from Rome or Moscow.

To the world I give my hand, but my heart
I give to my native land.

On one occasion Kirkwood objected to an English MP being in the chair of the Scottish Grand Committee. Sir Richard Barnet told him with some indignation that he was a direct descendant of King Robert the Bruce. Kirkwood bowed and apologized, saying, 'it would be a sin and a crime to torment a descendant of the victor at Bannockburn'.

In July 1924 Kirkwood brought forward a bill to return the Stone of Destiny from Westminster Abbey to Holyroodhouse in Edinburgh. The proposal went to a second reading, was co-sponsored by the Clydeside Labour MPs and garnered considerable support.

Kirkwood gave a typically eloquent speech arguing the moral case for the repatriation of the Stone of Scone, calling it a symbol of Scottish nationhood. He quoted the Bible and eminent historians. He spoke of William Wallace and Robert the Bruce. Telling the House that he stood before his fellow Members of Parliament 'representing an unconquered race', he also talked of the 'great spiritual, historical and sentimental bonds that bind together a race. When we seek bread and shelter for our people, we also demand roses.'

John MacCormick, one of the founders of what was to become the Scottish National Party, first joined the ILP when he became a student at Glasgow University in 1923. In his memoirs, *The Flag in the Wind*, from which this chapter has borrowed its title, he summed up the attitude of mind and spirit which inspired so many people at the time:

> Socialism in those days was not the doctrine of the State-planned economy which it has since become. The I.L.P. had inherited much of the old Radical tradition of Scotland and for the most part as a street-corner missionary I was expected not to expound the theories of Karl Marx but merely to give expression to the general sense of injustice and aspirations for a better way of life which were very natural feelings among the workers of Clydeside in the years between the wars.

'The general sense of injustice and aspirations for a better way of life': beautifully summed up. MacCormick wrote of how much, as a young speaker for the ILP, he enjoyed 'the almost religious atmosphere of enthusiasm in which we all worked'.

Enthusiasm for Home Rule within the Labour Party began to lessen.

There was a strong feeling that if Labour was to continue to make headway at Westminster it needed to do so as a British party, uniting Labour supporters from England, Wales and Scotland. The argument was again advanced that the workers have no country, as the STUC did when it officially withdrew its support for Home Rule in 1931: 'Workers should look upon themselves as workers, and not as Scotsmen or Englishmen. Let them be honest and get back to the ideals of international Socialism.'

Some kept the flame of self-determination burning. Two separate nationalist parties came together in 1934 to form the Scottish National Party. In 1948 John MacCormick and the Scottish Convention launched the Scottish Covenant at a ceremony at the Church of Scotland Assembly Hall on the Mound in Edinburgh. Two million people signed this pledge 'within the framework of the United Kingdom, to do everything in our power to secure for Scotland a Parliament with adequate legislative authority in Scottish affairs'.

John MacCormick was by no means the only person to make the journey from the ILP to the SNP. Another was John L. Kinloch, a man who wore the kilt each and every day of his long life. Knowledgeable as he was about Scottish history and traditions, Kinloch was also a visionary. Like Tom Johnston, he was an early advocate of hydroelectricity and other developments which would bring work and people back to Scotland's deserted glens.

Chief among these was a proposed new city and deep-water port at Loch Eriboll on Scotland's northern coast. The dolomite to be found in the surrounding rocks was to provide the abundant mineral wealth which would make this dream a reality.

In 1927, when Kinloch was a Labour Party candidate for Argyll, John MacCormick helped him campaign on Mull, 'addressing meetings in every *clachan*'. MacCormick noted that John L. was as keen on Home Rule as he was, as were their audiences. He also made a telling observation, which says as much about Labour and parliamentary politics as it does about John L. Kinloch, who had by then spent years putting the case for socialism and the Labour Party: 'But for his complete personal integrity and his ignorance of the art of wire-pulling he would by then have had a safe Labour seat in Parliament.'

There was a long road to be travelled for those who wanted Scotland once more to have control over her own affairs. On 11 September 1997, 60 per cent of Scotland's electorate voted in a referendum. By 75 per cent to 25 per cent, this demonstrated overwhelmingly that a Scottish parliament in Edinburgh was 'the expressed will of the Scottish people'.

On 12 May 1999, veteran MP and MSP Winnie Ewing opened the new Parliament at Holyrood in Edinburgh with these words: 'The Scottish Parliament, adjourned on the 25th day of March, seventeen hundred and seven, is hereby reconvened.'

In May 2011 the SNP under Alex Salmond swept to a stunning victory in the third election to the Scottish Parliament at Holyrood, securing an impressive overall majority of 69 seats out of a total of 129 and routing their political opponents. The Liberal Democrats won only five seats, Scottish Labour only thirty-seven. Tom Johnston might have had some advice for both those parties on the dangers of betraying the electorate or taking their votes for granted.

What he and his fellow Red Clydesiders would have thought of twenty-first-century Scottish politics and politicians we cannot know. We might hazard a guess that, internationalists as they all were, they would have shared the pride taken in the cultural diversity of the Scottish Parliament of 2011.

Honouring their own family origins, the new and returning MSPs took their oaths in English, some also in Scots, Gaelic, Doric, Italian and Urdu. Glasgow Labour MSP Hanzala Malik offered a prayer in Arabic. Humza Yousaf, newly elected SNP member from Glasgow, wore an elegant traditional Pakistani sherwani, to which he had added a bright splash of colour. Pinned to his right shoulder by a handsome silver brooch was a red plaid in Partick Thistle tartan.

Leading as it does to the likelihood of a referendum on Scottish independence, the sheer scale of the SNP landslide of 2011 took many commentators by surprise. Reaching for suitably dramatic metaphors, they told Scotland and the world that a seismic shift had taken place in Scottish politics. The BBC spoke of a political earthquake.

We've heard all this before. Back in 1922, when the first big group of Red Clydesiders was elected to the Westminster parliament, *The Bailie* wrote that 'there is a serious "fault" under our feet. Earthquakes are predicted.'

Plus ça change, plus c'est la même chose. Writing these words shortly after the event, it looks like we're once more living in interesting times.

25

Socialism, Self-improvement & Fun

Love learning, which is the food of the mind.

The ILP was always more than just a political party. Red Clydeside's socialists took an interest in all aspects of life, as *The Times* reported on 28 December 1922. In the wake of the Labour landslide in the November election, the newspaper had dispatched a correspondent north to find out how the political earthquake had happened. Unable to resist an amused curl of the lip at the fact that the ILPers were teetotallers to a man, the reporter acknowledged the socialists had worked hard for their victory:

I have been struck by the variety and extent of the propaganda. Even the stoniest ground has received its sowing. Socialist study circles, Socialist economic classes, Socialist musical festivals, Socialist athletic competitions, Socialist choirs, Socialist dramatic societies, Socialist plays – these are only a few of the devious ways in which they attempt to reach the unconverted. Then there are the Socialist Sunday Schools – a far more potent agency than the 'proletarian' Sunday Schools, with which they are not to be confused. Last, but not least, there are the Socialist newspapers, of which the *Forward* is the most important. From time to time free distribution of copies has taken place.

Socialist Sunday Schools were first established in London in the 1890s during a dockers' strike. Soup kitchens were set up to feed the strikers' children. Mary Gray came up with the idea of running classes for this captive audience, giving them the socialist analysis as to why they were poor and other people were not, and what might be done about that.

The idea caught on. By the beginning of the First World War, there were 200 Socialist Sunday Schools throughout Britain. They had their own version of the Ten Commandments:

1. Love your school-fellows, who will be your fellow-workmen in life.
2. Love learning, which is the food of the mind; be as grateful to your teacher as to your parents.
3. Make every day holy by good and useful deeds and kindly actions.
4. Honour good men, be courteous to all men, bow down to none.
5. Do not hate or speak evil of anyone; do not be revengeful, but stand up for your rights, and resist oppression.
6. Do not be cowardly; be a friend to the weak, and love justice.
7. Remember that all the good things of the earth are produced by labour; whoever enjoys them without working for them is stealing the bread of the workers.
8. Observe and think in order to discover the truth; do not believe what is contrary to reason; and never deceive yourself or others.
9. Do not think that he who loves his own country must hate other nations, or wish for war, which is a remnant of barbarism.
10. Look forward to the day when all men will be free citizens of one fatherland, and live together as brothers in peace and righteousness.

Glasgow ILP member and trade unionist Tom Anderson founded the South Side Socialist Sunday School in Glasgow in 1897. The children were taught about socialism, how to think for themselves and about working-class heroes and rebels. Songs helped get the message across.

Anderson later joined the Socialist Labour Party (SLP), the revolutionary group which ran much of the Singer Strike of 1911. The SLP set up proletarian schools and a proletarian college, where they taught economics, history, sexual science, drama and music. Anderson was principal of the college for 30 years, assisted at times by John Maclean and John S. Clarke, who wrote *The Young Worker's Book of Rebels*. Published by the Proletarian School at 550 Argyle Street, Glasgow in 1918, the first rebel it quoted was Spartacus.

Proletarian and Socialist Sunday Schools were anathema to some, the issue raised several times over the years in the House of Commons. In November 1920 the Conservative MP for Nottingham demanded there should be 'supervision over the Socialist Sunday schools of Glasgow and the industrial districts of the Clyde, the teachings of which are of an undisguisedly revolutionary character'. He was told no control could be exercised, as the Socialist Sunday Schools were outside the jurisdiction of the Scottish Education Department.

In the 1920s and '30s those who were appalled by the very existence of Socialist Sunday Schools tried to legislate against them. In 1927 a private member's bill got as far as a second reading. In 1933 Sir Reginald Craddock, MP for the Combined English Universities, tried again:

> I have often heard quoted, from Lenin's article in the publication called 'The Workers' Dreadnought,' these two sentences: 'Give us the child for eight years, and it will be a Bolshevik for ever.' 'Hundreds of thousands of teachers constitute an apparatus that must push our work forward.' It is no exaggeration to say that these two texts of Lenin are the inspiration of the anti-God campaigns which have, unfortunately, been introduced into this country. They are like the germs of some contagious disease, which may spread and destroy men's lives.

He based his information on the supposed iniquities of Socialist Sunday Schools on a lady of his acquaintance who had for years done charity work with disabled ex-servicemen: 'This work brings her into contact with working people, including some Communists. She keeps clear of all those things herself and is in no way a bigoted person.' Sounds like Sir Reginald himself didn't often come into contact with working people.

Exercising his cynical sense of humour, James Maxton told him the bill was never going to become law anyway:

> When a new member of Parliament comes here and draws a place in the ballot, well down the list, he goes to his Whips and consults them, as a child does his parents. They look down a long list and say, 'How can we find something that will not do anyone much harm, will give the people who are foolish enough to come on that particular Friday a pleasant entertainment, while the members of the Government can go down to the country or to the seaside?'

Maxton told the Duchess of Atholl, Scotland's first female MP, that he was surprised to see her supporting the proposals, 'although I have some doubts about my own rights in opposing it, because I notice she has taken care to exclude her own native land from the provisions of the Bill'.

Another MP asked Maxton, 'Has my honourable friend forgotten that

Scotland is still part of England?' Maxton asked him, 'Has my honourable and learned friend, who has a distinguished career at the English bar, forgotten that as far as legal matters are concerned he is not allowed to practise in Scotland?'

Although the ayes had it, the Seditious and Blasphemous Teaching of Children Bill never did become law. North and south of the border, Socialist Sunday Schools kept on going right into the 1930s.

There were plenty of educational opportunities for adults too. Although short-lived as an independent body, in existence for only five years, the Scottish Labour College founded by John Maclean in 1916 taught and influenced thousands. Evening classes on Marxism, economics and history were held in Glasgow, Aberdeen, Dundee and Edinburgh. With the same belief as Maclean in the power of education, Helen Crawfurd worked with him within the college.

Kinning Park Co-op put on Friday-evening lectures on subjects which included geography and post-war literature. Govan ILP put on winter lectures at seven o'clock on Sunday evenings. Glasgow University held extramural classes in Glasgow, Pollokshaws and Paisley. Their ten-week courses cost only one shilling and threepence and were free to unemployed women and men. Astronomy was popular, as was 'English Composition; Writing and Speaking'.

In Glasgow, the ILP put on regular Sunday lectures in the Pavilion and Metropole theatres, the venues chosen suggesting large audiences, and Saturday-afternoon classes on public speaking for women. In January 1926 a course of ten lessons cost two and six, half a crown: 'Come and prepare to spread the light when Summer days are fine.' The class books were Fred Henderson's *The Case for Socialism* and William Morris's *News from Nowhere*.

The same advert reminded ILPers of the carnival dance in the Central Halls in Bath Street. Socialists were allowed to have fun too. *Forward* carried adverts for pianos, fur coats and party frocks – bought at the Co-op, of course – engagement rings, bakers who would cater to 'picnics, excursions and outings of all kinds', tea rooms and restaurants, such as the King's Café and Granny Black's, and Socialist holiday camps.

One of those which regularly advertised was on the Norfolk coast, at Caister-on-Sea, near Great Yarmouth, open to both sexes from May to October. A week in a tent would cost you one guinea, a week indoors one pound five shillings. You could enjoy fine sea views, bracing air and lovely gardens: 'All surplus profits to the cause.'

Or you could go on excursions closer to home. One 'Catholic Socialist Notes' column advised, 'To all whom it may concern notice is given that the following Sunday will witness our annual descent on Gourock-on-the-sea. Pawn something and come.'

The sense of humour which runs through the *Forward* extended to its advertisers. In the first edition allowed to publish after Lloyd George's censorship of the paper of 1916, 'Tom Lloyd, "Himself", British and Best Tailor for Men, Argyle Street, Near Stockwell Street Corner', offered 'Uncensored News for Readers! The Greatest Tailoring Value Ever Offered in Glasgow!'

John S. Clarke's take on 'The Folk-Music Craze' in an article published in 1926 is funny but surprising. He didn't think much of Marjorie Kennedy-Fraser's newly published collection of Hebridean folk songs: 'It is simply marvellous, one might almost write miraculous, that an old lady can wander about the lone sheilings of the misty islands harvesting such a crop of folk melodies.' Nor did he much care for 'the negro singer, Paul Robeson,' dismissing the music of the man who was to be admired so much for his voice and the integrity of his politics as 'Three moans and a few howls.'

For socialists and everyone else who could afford the tickets, there was always plenty of entertainment on offer at Glasgow's many theatres, the Pavilion, the Metropole, the Empire, the Alhambra. In December 1915, at the King's Theatre, the D'Oyly Carte Opera were working hard to keep spirits up during the First World War. In one week, one night after another, lovers of light opera could see *The Yeomen of the Guard*, *Patience*, *The Pirates of Penzance*, *The Gondoliers*, *The Mikado* and *Iolanthe*. *The Bailie* was only a little sarcastic about Gilbert and Sullivan:

> If there was anything new to say we would say it, but there isn't. We welcome G. & S. as we do the song of the lark, the purr of the stream, and the laughter of girls. We grow young again under the influence of this essentially British opera, remembering first nights of their production away back in the 'eighties, and yet we do not envy those youngsters who are seeing these operas for the first time, for the reason that they grow better the oftener we see them.

More sombre entertainment was to be had on Monday, 13 December 1915 at St Andrew's Halls, when Mr Hilaire Belloc gave a talk with 'coloured lantern slides' on 'The New Development of the War'. Tickets went from five shillings down to one shilling. Those of an artistic turn of mind could view watercolours by an artist called W.B.E. Ranken. The proceeds of this show were being donated to 'Miss Fyfe's Belgian Relief Fund'.

During the First World War, the Glasgow Corporation Belgian Workroom had premises in North Portland Street, off George Street behind the City Chambers, and a central office in Bothwell Street. On behalf of the Belgian refugees, they gratefully received donations of clothes and shoes. Headed by the Lord Provost, the Corporation Belgian Committee was also 'pleased to receive offers to give Four or Five Days' Hospitality to Belgian Soldiers who are in the Trenches, and who, on getting leave of absence, are prevented from joining their Family Circle in the invaded parts of Belgium'.

One year-round and long-running attraction which cut across politics and social class was Hengler's Circus, a Glasgow institution which advertised in *Forward* and every other Glasgow newspaper. In February 1920 they were promoting the last three weeks of *The Sioux*. Playing every evening at half past seven and with matinees at half past two on Tuesdays, Wednesday and Saturdays, this offered a 'Sensational Water Spectacle'.

Dramatic water effects were Hengler's speciality, along with real live horses and riders performing 'feats of daring horsemanship'. At times there were elephants in the show and another favourite act was 'Duncan's Scotch Collies, Wonderful Canine Intelligence'. All of this went on at the Charing Cross end of Sauchiehall Street, in the lee of Glasgow School of Art, on the site later occupied by the ABC Cinema and which is now a music venue.

For years the *Forward*'s masthead carried an advert couched as a challenging question: 'Are YOU eating the ALLINSON Wholemeal BREAD?' Like healthy eating, the great outdoors was always popular, the benefits of fresh air and exercise another of the enthusiasms of the age. Running was particularly popular with young working-class men, many of them members of clubs like Garscube Harriers.

The Clarion Scouts were active in Glasgow and Clydeside. This group, where Patrick and Agnes Dollan first met, combined spreading the word about socialism with cycle rides and country rambles, often camping overnight or staying in their own hostels. By the 1890s, they had 120 clubs across Britain and an estimated 7,000 members.

Guy Aldred originally came to Glasgow because the Clarion Scouts invited him to speak at the Pavilion Theatre in 1912. He went down a storm, also addressing open-air meetings, including a rally held at the Charing Cross fountain.

Davie Kirkwood recalled in his memoirs that for many years he and John Wheatley made a point on Sundays of going out together for a walk in the country. People didn't only want to get out into the natural world, they needed to. It was a necessary counterbalance to the harsh and unnatural surroundings of the industrial world in which they worked.

For many working-class Scots their upbringing was both urban and rural. Industrial development having occurred where the resources were and without any checks on its sprawling growth, the coal bings and forges and shipyards were often no distance from the bluebell woods, the sparkling burns and the green and heather-clad hills. One woman who grew up as a girl in a tenement in Radnor Park in Clydebank remembered being sent up to buy eggs at a local farm at what is now the Boulevard dual carriageway which speeds Glaswegians to Helensburgh and Loch Lomond: 'The countryside was at the end of the street.'

Hillwalking and hiking could take you further afield. That walking in the country for pleasure was still considered a somewhat eccentric thing to do is demonstrated by the inverted commas in a report in *The Scotsman* in October 1933:

> An organised search for the Loch Ness monster by a party of Glasgow 'hikers' and ramblers took place yesterday, but it was unsuccessful. The monster was not seen. Wet, disagreeable weather prevailed, and the conditions were all against the possibility, a remote one at the best, of the monster making an appearance.
>
> The monster hunt created mild amusement in the district of Loch Ness-side, where it was known that there was not the slightest chance of the Glasgow party catching a glimpse of the monster. Local people exhibited no interest in the search, and wisely remained indoors. The stricter Sabbatarians regarded the Sunday search as an unwarranted intrusion.

So the 30 Glaswegians, all members of the Scottish Ramblers' Federation, returned home without a sighting, and Nessie remained undisturbed.

Founded in 1889 after correspondence in the *Glasgow Herald*, the Scottish Mountaineering Club was considered to be for those of a certain social status. Founded in 1930, the Creagh Dhu Club was made up of shipyard workers from Glasgow and Dundee. Their favourite stamping ground was the Arrochar Alps at the head of Loch Long.

The right to roam the hills and climb the mountains was hard won. This was even more the case in England and Wales, where a law of trespass applied and was often invoked against hikers and ramblers. The argument had been raging for 20 years and more when, in 1908, Scottish Liberal MP John Bryce argued that 'the people should not have this access to mountains on sufferance but as a right'. The following year, Bryce brought in his Access to Mountains (Scotland) Bill. This aimed to 'secure to the public the right of Access to Mountains and Moorland in Scotland'. It got to a second reading. In 1927, with characteristic directness, Davie Kirkwood told his fellow MPs, 'We said "Now" for the Access to Mountains Bill. Are we not going on with it?'

Twelve years later, in 1939, Kirkwood's fellow Clydeside Labour MP Campbell Stephen was still arguing for 'complete access to the mountains of Scotland and the moorlands of this country'.

After decades of lobbying, confrontation and direct action by the Ramblers' Association and others, the Countryside and Rights of Way (CRoW) Act of 2000 gave walkers in England and Wales a legal and much greater right of access to the countryside. What Scots often see as a time-honoured right to roam was finally enshrined in law in the Land Reform (Scotland) Act of 2003.

Everyone loved the Firth of Clyde, a sail doon the watter, from Craigendoran, Wemyss Bay or Largs to Kilcreggan, the Kyles of Bute, Millport or Brodick, on Arran. Or you could glide along the Forth and Clyde Canal from Speirs Wharf at Port Dundas, heading for the little resort of Craigmarloch, just beyond Kirkintilloch.

Dominated by the massive cooling towers of Pinkston Power Station and the tall chimney of the whisky distillery, the embarkation point was in the heart of dirty, smoky Glasgow but the crew of the excursion boats cleaned the cobbles of the quay thoroughly before the passengers got there. The fondly remembered *Gypsy Queen* and the *Fairy Queen* were the pleasure craft which plied this run.

At Stockingfield Junction the Port Dundas spur of the canal joined in with the main part and the boats had to move slowly to negotiate the turn. In a poignant reminder of the poverty in which so many Glaswegians lived, boys there would dive for coins the passengers threw into the canal.

At Craigmarloch there was a tea house called the Bungalow, an 18-hole putting green and swings for the children. Cooked by students from the Do School during their summer vacation, the Bungalow's menu never varied: Scotch broth, steak pie, pears and creamed rice, with ice creams to follow for those who had any room left.

The classes, lectures, clubs, hobbies and activities that people with not very much time and little spare cash took part in continue to impress, the sheer number and variety of them: cycling, hiking, dancing, photography, mending watches, sewing, knitting, playing in a band, putting on plays, stretching your body and your mind.

Men and women read widely. Many learned the poems of Burns, Byron, Shelley, Scott and others off by heart and, throughout their lives, delighted in reciting them aloud to admiring younger relatives. Alex McCulloch, uncle of the writer of this book, was one of them.

In the 1930s he worked as a shunter at the College Goods Yard, off Glasgow's High Street and on the site of the Old College, the original University of Glasgow. The railwaymen there like to joke that they were great scholars as they went every day to the College. Some lived up to that, forming a reading group. Among the books Alex McCulloch and his workmates discussed during their meal breaks were *Das Kapital* and *War and Peace*.

Poverty denied so many Clydesiders an education. They went to enormous efforts to get one for themselves, express their creativity and simply have fun.

26

The Hungry '30s

We don't just make ships here, we make men too.

D espite the Wall Street Crash of 1929, the keel of a new Cunarder was laid at John Brown's in Clydebank just before Christmas 1930. The first rivet was driven home by the shipyard manager in front of a crowd of cheering workers. As was traditional, the new liner had as yet no name. For the time being she would be known by her job number, and it was as 'the 534' that the ship which was to become the *Queen Mary* first became famous.

As the ship was built and began to grow, the skeleton of the 534 came to dominate Clydebank. Rising up like a spire over the tenement homes of the men who were building her, it made a pair with the Singer clock.

Disaster struck shortly before Christmas 1931. A year after the keel was laid, work on the 534 stopped. The slump which followed the crash had begun to bite and Cunard could no longer afford to keep building. Looming as she did over Clydebank, the unfinished and rusting hulk of the 534 became a potent symbol of the Depression.

It was two years before work resumed, two years during which thousands in Clydebank and elsewhere had no other option but to go on the dole, two years during which masculine pride took a battering and wives and mothers had an even tougher struggle than usual to make ten shillings do the work of a pound. That the skeleton of the 534 was so visible only added to the emotional as well as financial depression gripping the town.

One response to the mass unemployment of the 1930s was the hunger marches which took place throughout Britain. One of the Scottish organizers of these was Harry McShane, stalwart of the National Unemployed Workers' Movement (NUWM). The NUWM was established in 1921 and grew out of associations of demobbed sailors and soldiers. Those thrown out of work by the crash and the slump swelled its ranks.

The NUWM was dominated by members of the Communist Party, Harry McShane one of them. He took part in marches on London and, in the summer of 1933, along with John McGovern, a Glasgow Labour MP, led the Scottish Hunger March to Edinburgh.

A huge amount of planning went into the Scottish Hunger March of June 1933. Field kitchens were set up along the routes of the marchers converging on Edinburgh, donations of food and money to stock them gathered from trade unions and co-operative societies along the way. Bo'ness Co-op donated 600 'twopenny pies'.

The marchers came from Glasgow and Clydeside, Fife, Lanarkshire, Ayrshire, with a handful from Aberdeen. They were required to fill out and sign a recruiting form. Putting their name to this committed them to accepting 'strict discipline, as I realise that unless discipline is observed the greatest danger will arise for the marchers'. They also had to state they fully accepted the aims of the march and the five demands which were to be made of the government. *The Scotsman* listed those on Monday, 12 June 1933, the day after the marchers had reached Edinburgh:

1. Abolition of the means test.
2. An extra 1s. 6d. a week for each unemployed child and an extra 3s. 6d. a week for each adult unemployed and adult dependant.
3. The reduction of rents by 25 per cent.
4. The provision of relief work at Trade Union wages and under Trade Union conditions.
5. The repudiation of social service schemes and voluntary labour connected with them.

The Glasgow marchers set off from George Square on 9 June. Mainly men, there were some women in the ranks. It was a Friday afternoon and they were given a great send-off, with music playing and flags flying. They marched up out of Glasgow to Bishopbriggs and then on to Kilsyth. *The Scotsman* put the numbers of the Glasgow contingent at 600.

According to Harry McShane, at Kilsyth the Provost and the town councillors had found they had business elsewhere that Friday but the locals gave them a warm welcome, allowing them to spend the night in the local Salvation Army citadel. A meeting was held beforehand in the local park. Must have been quite an excitement on a long, light June evening in Kilsyth.

Along the route, people donated what money they could: 'Coppers, which could ill be spared, clinked into the boxes; women with tears in their eyes, wishing the men "good luck" and dropping their contributions into the collecting tins.' The next day was the longest of the march: 20 miles. McShane praised 'Comrade Heenan':

> . . . whose feet were in a terrible condition and who wrenched his ankle six miles from Corstorphine, but who obstinately refused even to consider giving up, and kept tramping doggedly on. How can one tell of the humour, the healthy, salty humour, that refused even to consider downheartedness even when tramping along at the end of a twenty-mile march through two hours of pelting rain?

The Glasgow marchers reached the arranged rendezvous at Corstorphine at four o'clock on the afternoon of Sunday, 11 June. Everybody cheered everyone else as they came in and there was a special cheer for the women. The field kitchens fed everyone and then they formed up behind their own bands and marched into Edinburgh:

> The Edinburgh workers sent out a strong contingent to meet us and march in with us. The streets were lined all the way into Edinburgh with sympathetic workers, tremendous enthusiasm prevailing.

The Scotsman confirms Harry McShane's description of the arrival and assembly at Corstorphine, the subsequent entry of the marchers into Edinburgh and the enthusiasm:

> Fife and drum bands accompanied them, and, as they entered Corstorphine, the marchers sang 'The International' and 'The Marseillaise' and other tunes. With the Ayrshire section was a one-legged man, who marched upon crutches.
>
> Only the Ayrshire section complained of indifferent treatment on the way. They had marched from Hamilton, and had to sleep in a stable. Huts and halls had been found for the other sections.
>
> The marchers were met outside Corstorphine by the Edinburgh contingent, which, like the other sections, contained members of the Young Communist League. Cards with various slogans were

particularly prominent among this section, which was headed by marchers in brown shirts and slouch hats, with red pompoms. When the two parties met cheers were raised, but a little further on these gave place to booing, as an armoured car containing soldiers passed the column.

A collection was taken en route from the large crowd which had gathered at the Corstorphine tram terminus and from sightseers and sympathisers who lined the streets of the city. As the marchers reached the city people were entering churches for the evening service, and the collectors took up their stands in the porches . . .

While the marchers were still on the road officialdom had agreed to meet a deputation on the Monday morning after they arrived in Edinburgh. This meeting was to take place at the offices of the Ministry of Labour, then located at 44 Drumsheugh Gardens. However, Sir Edward Collins, Secretary of State for Scotland, had not responded to requests that he should meet the marchers.

On the Sunday evening they headed for the Mound, where an open-air meeting was held. Harry McShane says 20,000 were there. *The Scotsman* puts it at 'several thousand'. Afterwards the marchers went on down to Leith, where they were given a meal in the ILP Hall in Bonnington Road. After a night in various hostels and halls, they formed up again the following morning and headed for Drumsheugh Gardens.

The deputation spent two hours in the Ministry of Labour offices, the rest of the marchers waiting outside. Secretary of State for Scotland Sir Edward Collins had remained in London and made it clear he had no intention of coming north to meet the marchers.

The deputation had some interesting demands. Although such a huge number of people were unemployed, the middle classes were still complaining about having to do their own housework. The marchers insisted that young women who were unemployed should not be forced into domestic service. Another suggestion was that new public-works schemes should be launched. These included the building of a road bridge over the Forth 'and a new arterial road through Glasgow'. The marchers also wanted more schools and 'better boots and books for the children of the unemployed'. They also protested against the trade embargo currently in force against the Soviet Union.

The Ministry of Labour officials told them all their points had been duly noted. Although the deputation didn't think much of that, its members withdrew and joined the rest of the marchers waiting outside in Drumsheugh Gardens. Their next move was to Parliament Square, where an impromptu outdoor cafeteria was set up, complete with those field kitchens and trestle tables. Harry McShane was very taken with the scene:

> The three camp-kitchens were soon belching forth large clouds of smoke. Gallons and gallons of tea were made, while boxes containing a large amount of food were unloaded. Some six or eight women assisted the Marchers' own cooks in preparing and serving the food.
>
> The unusual sight in this historical Square attracted large crowds of passers-by, and they seemed inclined to linger to watch the proceedings; but a large body of police arrived on the scene and kept them in motion.

The meal was simple: tea, a sausage roll and two slices of bread. Marchers sat down in Parliament Square to enjoy it in the bright June sunshine on the steps outside the entrance to St Giles' Cathedral and on the plinth around the monument to the Duke of Buccleuch. Harry McShane noted what a colourful lot they were 'with red flavours very much to the fore'. *The Scotsman* also commented on the profusion of red shirts and ribbons and one beret embroidered with a hammer and sickle.

Once they were fed and watered they marched down the Royal Mile, heading for Holyrood Park. The policeman at the gates of Holyroodhouse instructed them to wheel right. The marchers kept on going, taking a shortcut through the grounds of the palace. Harry McShane was beside himself with excitement, seeing huge political significance in this. In his pamphlet, *Three Days that Shook Edinburgh*, he waxed lyrical about the 'proletariat in their ragged clothes', walking into 'the most sacred precincts in Scotland'.

> The walls and grounds of the Royal Palace of Holyrood – that innermost sanctuary of all the Royal parasites in Scotland's history – echo the tramp of the first legions of the masses. The walls and grounds of Holyrood that heard the music of Rizzio, and Mary, Queen of Scots, heard the song of that murdered Irish leader, 'The Rebel Song', and then the thunderous battle cry of the world's workers, 'The Internationale.'

On Monday night the hunger marchers spent the night sleeping on the pavement in Princes Street. The police kept an eye on them but stood back and let them get on with it. Contradicting the 'you'll have had your tea' slur, many Edinburgers stopped by during the evening and gave the marchers cigarettes:

> The police . . . left the marchers to while the time away as they thought fit, contenting themselves with keeping the curious crowds on the move. This was not an easy task. The amazing spectacle was an unusual counter-attraction to the shops, and great patience and tact were demanded from the policemen to prevent serious congestion.
>
> From the police point of view matters were not improved when flute bands began to play and marchers took part in impromptu dances.
>
> One man was stretched out under a blanket, and had a white sheet laid across his forehead. A card on his chest informed passers-by that he was 'a victim of the means test.'
>
> The 'reveille' scene in the morning was remarkable. Men shaved with their mirrors supported on the railings of West Princes Street Gardens, and others washed and dried themselves at a fountain in the middle of the marchers' encampment.
>
> After a meal had been served in the middle of the day hundreds of banana skins were stuck onto the railing spikes, and remained there during the afternoon, forming a new decorative touch scarcely in harmony with the everyday dignity of the street.

Fortified by the bananas, the people who surely must already have had enough blisters on their feet spent Tuesday marching not once but twice through Edinburgh and the East Coast haar which had come down after the golden sunshine of the previous day.

Now estimated by *The Scotsman* at a thousand strong, it was midnight before they returned to Princes Street after a stravaig across North Bridge, South Bridge, Chambers Street, Candlemaker Row, the Grassmarket and through onto Lothian Road. Edinburgh came up trumps, having arranged from them all to spend the night in different halls around the city: 'It was stated that whether or not indoor accommodation had been found for the men last night, the women would have been accommodated indoors.'

On Wednesday morning breakfast was served on a piece of waste ground at Simon Square at the Pleasance. More bananas, in sandwiches this time, were washed down with tea. Meanwhile, McGovern and McShane called at the City Chambers, asking for help to transport the marchers home. Fine, said the Lord Provost and the police, but there's one condition: You have to promise not to come back and do it all again.

McGovern and McShane refused to give that commitment and for a while the situation grew tense. Edinburgh blinked first. Nineteen free buses were laid on to take the marchers home to wherever they had come from in the first place: Fife, Central Scotland, Glasgow and the West. Separate arrangements were made for the five marchers from Aberdeen. Maybe they got a ride home on the train:

> By half-past seven all the marchers had departed with the exception of one man from Glasgow, who for some reason or other refused to leave.
>
> As the buses passed through the town and along Princes Street, with red banners sticking out from the windows, the departing demonstrators cheered, shouted, and sang songs lustily, their exodus attracting as much attention as their stay in the city had done.

MP and marchers' leader John McGovern 'warmly congratulated the Edinburgh police on the way they had behaved in a difficult situation'.

The marchers' demands might not have been met but they had made their point and gathered lots of publicity and sympathy for their plight, although not from all quarters. Kicking men while they were down, Greenock Corporation decided hunger marchers from their town would have three days' dole money deducted for the time they had been away. Motherwell showed more compassion, leaving the benefit payments as they were.

Lord Provost Swan of Glasgow heard representations from Harry McShane and John McGovern on hardship experienced by the Glasgow hunger marchers. People had lost between six and sixteen shillings each when their unemployment benefit was docked. Significant sums of money for anyone in the 1930s, this was obviously a terrible financial blow for families surviving only on the dole.

The Lord Provost made up the full losses for the married men and asked McShane and McGovern to distribute money left over from this to the 'most deserving cases of single men. Mr McGovern thanked the Lord Provost for the interest he had taken in the matter, and for his generosity in meeting the situation so handsomely.'

Others among the unemployed tried different ways of improving their own situations. Smallholdings which came with a cottage and an acre of land where a man could grow vegetables to feed his family were built around the country. There are surviving groups of them near Kirkintilloch and on the hill above Inverkeithing in Fife.

The Scottish Allotments Scheme for the Unemployed, operating a joint committee with the Quakers, the Society of Friends, was willing to help people who wanted to grow their own produce or keep chickens. One young man who found his way to their Glasgow office in the summer of 1935 was 23-year-old Alex Craig of Old Monkland, whose first name was always pronounced *Alick*.

He had initially written to the enquiry bureau of a magazine called *The Smallholder, Poultry-Keeper and Gardener*. They sent him back a sympathetic and helpful typed reply:

> We are afraid, however, that there is no society which would help you financially to start a poultry farm, but we think that were you to get into touch with Sir A. Rose, Commissioner of Distressed Areas, he might possibly be able to help you. We understand that funds are to be available for cases such as yours, and we think that an application from you would be very favourably considered.

When he followed this up, he was contacted by the Scottish Allotments Scheme for the Unemployed and the West of Scotland Agricultural College, in Blythswood Square in Glasgow. Robert Hislop of the college sent a postcard saying he would 'be very pleased to see you at Coatbridge on Monday 2nd Sept. I shall be at the Cuparhead Plots in the forenoon and at Whifflets Plots in the afternoon.'

Practical advice and small loans were on offer. You had to show willing by already having a plot no smaller than a quarter of an acre and be at least in your second year of working it. Loans were interest free, with no repayment in the first year, half in the second and the remaining half in the third:

> The maximum amount of loan to each Plotholder will be £10. No cash advances will be made. Advances from the loan will be made by the

Committee by way of the purchase of goods, stock, plants, &c., as explained herein.

The Committee will be prepared to make advances to any approved Plotholder-borrower for the purchase of:-

Tools, Manures, Plants, Fruit Trees, Bushes, Poultry, Pigs, Bees, Goats, &c., and for the necessary equipment in connection with the management of these items.

Already keeping chickens and working a piece of ground near his home to help feed his widowed mother and brothers and sisters – he was one of eight surviving children – Alex Craig received a two-page letter from the Scottish Allotments Scheme giving him detailed advice on how he should look after the hens. They could offer him financial help to buy henhouses or more birds:

If you will first write out this in your own way mentioning any doubts or difficulties, it will assist me to do the best I can for you, as it is most pleasing to see a young man trying to do something for himself.

Years later, in the 1960s, Alex Craig met John L. Kinloch and came to share his passion for the dream of a new city and deep-water port at Loch Eriboll. Both men worked tirelessly on promoting 'Kinloch-Eriboll, a Pioneer City of the Scientific Age'.

Like the hunger marchers who wanted the government to start building a new road bridge over the Forth, Davie Kirkwood also believed the government ought to spend its way out of recession. As MP for Clydebank, he was doing his utmost to get work on the Cunarder restarted:

For more than two years, 534 had been engraved on my heart. In the morning I woke wondering if something could be done that day to bring the skeleton to life again. During the day I made myself a nuisance to all and sundry. They said I had a bee in ma bonnet. In the evening I would try to plan something new for the morrow.

Kirkwood's efforts did not go unnoticed. One evening in the lobby of the House of Commons, Conservative MP and society hostess Lady Astor came up to him and said the Prince of Wales was planning a visit to Scotland and wanted to speak to him about conditions on the Clyde.

Kirkwood at first refused, reluctant to have anything to do with the Playboy Prince.

Lady Astor persisted. When she sent him a formal invitation, he told her he had no evening clothes. She returned with the response that it was him the Prince wanted to talk to, not his clothes. He could wear a serge suit if he liked:

> There was a Robert Burns ring about that, man to man, Prince of the Realm and Engineer of the Forge – and behind it the thought of the great silent Cunarder. So I said: 'Then I'll go.'

Remembering the painting which shows the ploughman poet being lionized by Edinburgh society, Kirkwood thought of Burns again when he walked into an elegant first-floor dining room. He heard himself being announced and found Lady Astor and the Prince of Wales standing up and coming round the table to greet him. The Prince of Wales took him into the library of this grand house and asked him to give him the truth: What did the workers on the Clyde think about the current situation?

Kirkwood was an engineer to his fingertips and he had the soul of an engineer. He had been brought to meet the future Edward VIII in what he described as 'a beautiful motor-car, a masterpiece of the engineer's craft'. Now he told the Prince they were all living in momentous times when 'Man's ingenuity applied to nature has brought the age of plenty. But instead of plenty, we have reduction.'

There was, Kirkwood told the attentive Prince, an atmosphere of fear, and it was running right through society, 'so that those who are rich are curtailing expenditure'. There's a resonance with our own times in what he said next:

> It has become fashionable to be economical. It used to be fashionable to be lavish. Every one is afraid to spend, rich and poor. Those who have wages are afraid to spend them. They are banking their money instead of spending it.

And, Kirkwood went on, it wasn't only manual workers who were suffering. There were 2,000 qualified school teachers in Scotland who couldn't find work and the situation was similar in other professions. The Prince of Wales asked what was to be done. Kirkwood made his suggestion that the country should spend its way out of recession. Send the unemployed back to work and they would soon be able to start spending again, thus reviving the economy:

> Twenty minutes more passed in a friendly discussion. We were two British citizens talking about our land and our people. A man's a man for a' that. It was as if we were on a ship in a storm, when class and creed and caste are forgotten.

Whether the Prince of Wales exerted any influence or not, the government did decide to bale Cunard out. Work on the 534 started up again on the Tuesday after Easter Monday in April 1934, with a projected launch date for the new Cunarder of that September. On the first day back, the workforce was led through the gates of John Brown's by two kilted pipers and the streets of Clydebank were decorated with bunting.

A foreman rebuked a returning worker because his tools were rusty. The quick-fire repartee came right back at him: 'You should see my frying-pan.'

27

Pride of the Clyde: The Launch of the *Queen Mary*

Ten million rivets, sixty million hammer blows.

The *Queen Mary* was launched from Clydebank on Wednesday, 24 September 1934. All Glasgow's newspapers produced special souvenir supplements for the occasion. The *Daily Record*'s entire front cover was given over to the now iconic photograph of the bow of the ship, still known as the 534, stretching up towards the sky. By tradition, the name she would bear would be revealed only when it was pronounced by the Queen at the launch.

Queen Mary and King George V were joined there by their son Bertie. He had flown home from Paris for the occasion, staying the night at his home at Fort Belvedere 'before entraining for Glasgow'.

Selected guests were presented to Their Majesties and the Prince of Wales at the launch: the directors of John Brown's and Cunard's White Star Line; local dignitaries; six shipyard workers with fifty years' service apiece at John Brown's; and Clydebank's MP and tireless campaigner to get work started again on the 534, Davie Kirkwood.

He contributed an article to the *Daily Record*'s souvenir supplement entitled 'WHAT TO-DAY MEANS TO ME'. His words were wrapped around a poem specially written for the occasion by Poet Laureate John Masefield:

> For ages you were rock, far below light,
> Crushed, without shape, earth's unregarded bone.
> Then Man in all the marvel of his might
> Quarried you out and burned you from the stone.

Then, being pured to essence, you were nought
But weight and hardness, body without nerve;
Then Man, in all the marvel of his thought
Smithied you into form of leap and curve;

And took you, so, and bent you to his vast,
Intense great world of passionate design,
Curve after changing curving, braced and masst [*sic*]
To stand all tumult that can tumble brine.

Kirkwood's words were poetic too, and very personal. He recalled for the readers how he had cause to be grateful to John Brown's. In his youth, seeking work, he had tramped the 12 long miles from his home at Parkhead in the east of Glasgow and Brown's had taken him on. He was fiercely proud of the new liner, the largest ship that had ever been built, and of all the hard work put in by the men who had built the Cunarder:

As an engineer, I salute the architects and designers, builders and platers, riveters, caulkers, blacksmiths, joiners, carpenters, coppersmiths and plumbers. And with them the labourers. 'Unskilled,' they call them. None in a shipyard is unskilled and some of these labourers are as highly skilled as the craftsmen.

This is their Day, managers, draughtsmen, foremen, journeymen, apprentices and labourers, boilermakers, marine engineers, electricians and the rest.

It is everybody's Day. And how singularly British it all is. The Day, not of War, but of Peace. The Day of the Mercantile Marine.

The whole nation is built into this ship. Throne and Parliament, Commerce and Industry, Arts and Crafts, all feeling that they are moving onward as the 534 gangs doon the slip.

As the local MP, Kirkwood had a VIP ticket for the launch. Thousands heading for the Clyde from all over Britain had no ticket, and the touts were active. Anyone wanting to sell one could get £25 for it, a substantial sum back in 1934.

Writing about that in the *Daily Record*, Sir John Foster Fraser, 'the world-wide traveller – a journalist of unrivalled experience and great descriptive ability', also reported that the Queen was going to use a bottle of 'Empire wine' to launch the 534, which 'suggests Australian or South

African burgundy'. Some locals thought a good Scottish bottle of whisky would be more appropriate. One 'stiff-jawed engineer' told the worldwide traveller he thought the ship ought to be named *David Kirkwood*, although *Britannia* was the odds-on favourite.

Foster Fraser was indeed an excellent journalist, describing a conversation he'd had with 'a genial fellow primed with contrasts and bubbling with statistics'. He poked a little gentle fun at this avalanche of facts and figures but allowed his informant his pride in the Cunarder:

> 'Do you know,' he said, 'that if all the steel plates were laid end to end they would provide a path from London to Leicester?' No, I didn't know that.
>
> 'Or that there are ten million rivets, which means that hammers have delivered sixty million blows to drive them in?' I took his word for it.
>
> 'Has anybody told you that on one of the decks you could have three football pitches and that in the large lounge you could stack ten double-decked omnibuses?' I confessed nobody had imparted the information.

The local man told the celebrity journalist he should tell his English readers the Cunarder was taller than Nelson's Column in Trafalgar Square, with a promenade deck twice as long as the front of Buckingham Palace. That would 'make the Cockneys have respect for what we do on the Clyde':

> 'Man, 94 years ago the Cunard people built their first ship here; the "Britannia" it was called, and it could be stuck end-on in one of the funnels of 534 and be lost. Why, when she slips into the water to-morrow, there will be 26 drag chains weighing over 2350 tons, so she won't bump on the other side of the Clyde and knock Renfrew out of shape.
>
> 'There are steel cables as thick as your wrist and four anchors each weighing sixteen tons. Four thousand miles of electric cables, think of that.'
>
> I gasped that it was all very wonderful.
>
> 'Aye,' said he, 'nothing has been forgotten. You know, if anybody falls overboard the man on the bridge will just press a wee button and a whole bunch of life-belts will be catapulted at him. But come over here and I'll tell you some more. It's thirsty work talking.'

It took almost two years to fit the *Queen Mary* out with her beautiful art deco interiors and her luxurious cabins, saloons and restaurants. She also had her own chapel, cinema, theatre, libraries and tennis courts. Huge amounts of Clydeside craftsmanship and huge amounts of Clydeside pride went into all of that.

Artists and craftworkers from all over Britain made their contributions, from the specially designed crockery and silverware to the large-scale original paintings commissioned for the public spaces of this great ocean liner. One of the most famous pictures was Kenneth Shoesmith's *Madonna of the Atlantic*.

The *Queen Mary* left the Clyde in March 1936. It's estimated that as many as a million people lined the banks of the river to watch her go. One of the best views to be had was from Erskine, on the southern shore. Amateur film-maker James Blair stationed himself there and shot some unique colour footage of the ship as she steamed past. This can be viewed online today at the Scottish Screen Archive.

The emotions of those who had come out to bid the *Queen Mary* farewell from the river of her birth ran high and deep. Another contemporary observer summed up the overwhelming mixture of enormous pride and real sadness: 'She leaves a big gap in the landscape, and a hole in the hearts of thousands of Clydesiders.'

28

The Spanish Civil War

To fight by the side of the people of Spain.

The Spanish Civil War began in July 1936 and ended, finally, on 1 April 1939. It started with a rebellion launched from Spanish Morocco by General Francisco Franco against the democratically elected Republican government of Spain. While Britain, France and the US adopted a policy of non-intervention, Hitler's Germany and Mussolini's Italy weighed in on the side of the Fascists.

The Spanish Fascist forces styled themselves Nationalists, describing their rebellion as a crusade to save Spain from the socialist republic. Socialists, communists, anarchists and idealists in Europe, the United States and throughout the world found in this most vicious of civil wars a cause which set them alight. Thirty-five thousand people volunteered to defend Spain's democracy and the legitimate Republican government.

Those volunteers joined the *Brigadas Internacionales*, the International Brigades. Many were impelled to do so by the horror of the bombing of the small Basque town of Guernica in the spring of 1937. Nazi Germany and Fascist Italy were using Spain as a terrible training ground and dress rehearsal for the European war everyone feared was coming.

It was 26 April 1937 when the German Condor Legion bombed the market place in Guernica, raining death out of the sky. Commissioned by the Republican government, Pablo Picasso painted the masterpiece which forever remembers this event which so stunned the world. Wars were meant to be fought by soldiers on battlefields. In Guernica innocent civilians – men, women and children – had been slaughtered while peacefully going about their daily business.

What made Guernica even more shocking was that death had been delivered by aircraft. The Zeppelins of the First World War notwithstanding, up until Guernica planes had been seen as a shining symbol of the modern age, a magnificent example of the progress of the human race. After Guernica, it became chillingly clear that mankind could harness technological marvels to unspeakable evil, killing more people more effectively and with greater devastation than ever before.

Three thousand volunteers went from Britain to Spain to fight for the Republic, over five hundred of them from Scotland. Most of the Scottish volunteers were socialists and communists who'd seen plenty of action on the battlefield of politics. They went from Aberdeen, the coalfields of Fife, the shipyards of Glasgow, Dundee, Edinburgh and Inverness.

These people believed that if fascism wasn't fought in Spain it would sweep across Europe, crushing everything in its path. One contemporary poster from the Spanish government's Ministry of Propaganda shows a dead child lying under a sky full of planes, two numbered labels attached to her clothes. The caption reads, 'If you tolerate this, your children will be next.'

By January 1937 the *Glasgow Herald* was reporting that Nationalist forces were approaching Madrid. The Republican government had ordered civilians to leave the city and heavy fighting was raging around it. This is when Franco famously spoke about the fifth column he had within the city: covert supporters working in secret to bring about the Spanish capital's fall to the fascist forces.

As Madrid was poised to fall, British volunteers, members of the ILP, were setting off from Victoria Station, in London:

> Young men and girls sang the 'Internationale,' and a grey-haired woman wept silently on the Continental departure platform at Victoria Station, London, yesterday when 25 I.L.P. volunteers left on their way to join the Spanish Government forces.
>
> One voice of protest was heard above the farewells.
>
> 'It is suicide for all of you,' a young woman exclaimed. 'It is said that the volunteers have no dependants,' she said to a press reporter, 'but some of them have mothers who are pleading with them not to go.'

James Maxton's friend Bob Edwards was the captain of the ILP company, which numbered around 100 men in total. Their service in Spain began shortly after that departure from Victoria Station, when they served on the Aragon Front, near Zaragoza. Edwards remembered the bravery of the Spaniards with whom they fought:

> We spent much of our time training members of the Spanish Militia
> how to take cover and we were constantly trying to persuade them
> that to walk upright and bravely into an offensive was not necessarily
> the best method.

Author George Orwell joined this ILP contingent. Later, he was to write about his experiences in Spain in *Homage to Catalonia*. The Spanish Civil War attracted some famous volunteer combatants, writers and reporters: Orwell, Laurie Lee, Ernest Hemingway, legendary journalist Martha Gellhorn.

Meanwhile, James Maxton and John McGovern, who had led the Scottish Hunger March to Edinburgh in 1933, were trying to win hearts and minds at home. Lifelong pacifist though he had been, Maxton's standpoint on the Spanish Civil War was clear: this was a conflict between fascism and freedom and it had to be fought.

In August 1936 he had dispatched John McNair to Spain to see the situation on the ground. McNair and Maxton were old friends and comrades from their early days in the ILP. When McNair returned with the information Maxton initiated a fund-raising campaign for medical supplies and ambulances. People all over Scotland raised money for Spain.

Quite disparate groups of people sent medical help. The Scottish Ambulance Unit wanted to render assistance to both sides. One of its volunteers was Roddy MacFarquhar of Inverness. He is quoted in Daniel Gray's moving *Homage to Caledonia* on the horror of seeing a Spanish mother and her three children running for cover. As the young man watched, one of the children was hit by shrapnel.

Newly arrived in Spain though he was, experiencing war for the first time, MacFarquhar knew the little girl wasn't going to make it. It was a baptism of fire, yet when the unit returned to Spain for a second time, in January 1937, MacFarquhar went too, listed in the *Glasgow Herald*'s report of their departure from Glasgow:

> A crowd of several hundred persons gathered outside the Glasgow
> City Chambers on Saturday morning to see the reorganised Scottish
> ambulance unit leave to resume duties in Spain. The Lord Provost
> (Mr. John Stewart), in bidding the members of the unit farewell, said
> everyone knew the splendid work the unit had done previously.
> Taking on work of that kind in a country where civil war was being

carried on was a heroic act, but notwithstanding the danger, the unit felt that their work had been so much appreciated that they must go back.

Now Communist MP for Fife, Willie Gallacher travelled to Spain during the civil war. Some of the British volunteers of the ILP Battalion he went to see may well have been his own constituents:

> Around Easter, 1937, I paid a visit to Spain to see the lads of the British Battalion of the International Brigade. Going up the hillside towards the trenches with Fred Copeman, we could occasionally hear the dull boom of a trench mortar, but more often the eerie whistle of a rifle bullet overhead. Always I felt inclined to get my head down in my shoulders. 'I don't like that sound,' I said by way of apology.
>
> 'It's all right, Willie, as long as you can hear them . . . It's the ones you can't hear that do the damage.'

Afterwards, Gallacher made a speech to the lads and when he had finished everyone sang 'The Internationale' 'with a spirit that all the murderous savagery of fascism can never kill'.

Back in his hotel in Madrid, Willie Gallacher met Ellen Wilkinson, Eleanor Rathbone and the Duchess of Atholl. All three women were MPs. Ellen Wilkinson sat for Middlesbrough and then Jarrow, helping to organize the most famous hunger march of the 1930s. Eleanor Rathbone was an independent MP who lobbied successfully for the introduction of family allowances paid directly to mothers.

Willie Gallacher shared some of the journey home with them, writing that 'those three women gave an example of courage and endurance that was beyond all praise'. It's a handsome tribute, especially from a committed communist to the one woman in that group whose politics were the polar opposite of his.

Katharine Murray, Duchess of Atholl, was Scotland's first woman MP and the first woman to hold office in a Conservative government, spending five years as an under-secretary for education. One of those who saw that if fascism triumphed in Spain it would march all over Europe, she clashed with her party over the issue. They nicknamed her the Red Duchess as a result.

Many women volunteered to go to Spain, a few to fight, some to work as nurses in the corps which became known as the Red Nightingales, others to fight the battle for hearts and minds. The 'Bellshill Girl Anarchist' was one of those. Ethel McDonald was 25 years old when she went off to war with Jenny Patrick, who became the partner of Glasgow anarchist Guy Aldred after his relationship with Rose Witcop ended.

Although she joined the ILP in her teens, Ethel McDonald too became an anarchist and worked as Guy Aldred's secretary. In Spain she made broadcasts in English for the anarchist radio station in Barcelona, where she and her Scottish accent attracted attention. She stayed on in Spain alone after Jenny Patrick returned to Glasgow, as *The Biographical Dictionary of Scottish Women* relates:

> She visited anarchists in prison, helped others escape, and became known as the 'Scots Scarlet Pimpernel' and the 'Bellshill Girl Anarchist'. Imprisoned for several days herself, she spent further weeks in hiding, unable to exit Spain legally. Consular intervention got her out and she was welcomed back to Glasgow, telling the press: 'I went to Spain full of hopes and dreams . . . I return full of sadness, dulled by the tragedy I have seen.'

Whatever their politics, people in Britain were gripped by Spain's agony. Glasgow's newspapers overflowed with stories from the war. Writing in the *Glasgow Herald*'s women's page, Ann Adair got a whole column out of an 'encounter in the gown department' of an upmarket shop in London's Regent Street, when she met Inez, 'a daughter of Spain' employed there as a model, trying on dresses to demonstrate them to potential buyers. Ann Adair was contemplating buying an elegant blue dress:

> It was a lovely shade. The girl who showed it was lovely, too, a tall brunette with the slender figure and swaying gait of her kind. The saleswoman asked her some trifling question. As she answered it, she looked directly towards us, and it was then I saw her eyes. They were dark with misery, the eyes of one who had lain sleepless all through the night.

When the saleslady went off on some errand, the *Herald*'s correspondent started talking to the girl and found out that she was Spanish: 'Spain! So that was the explanation of her tragic mien.'

> On a sudden the professional mannequin was gone. In her place was

the Spanish patriot. She told me things I dare not set down on paper. She told me her promised husband had been wounded outside Madrid, that her mother, her young sisters had been obliged to flee their home, that they were now refugees in Portugal.

Both sides considered themselves to be Spanish patriots. There's no way of knowing which side the lady of Spain with the melancholic mien was on.

In late 1937 James Maxton went to Spain to see the situation for himself, an uncomfortable business for a man who was not in the best of health. He travelled by train from Paris to Toulouse and then by plane to Valencia, 'over the snowy peaks of the Pyrenees and I can't say I like the look of them from up above. The plane got oil and petrol and we got coffee . . .'

Tearing themselves apart, riven by bitter political divisions, the Republicans in Barcelona had begun fighting one another instead of the fascist enemy. Ideologically the ILP supported POUM, the anti-Stalinist Spanish Marxist Workers' Party, against the pro-Stalinist Spanish Communist Party. The vitriolic war of words and internecine strife between people who might have been thought to be on the same side reminded many ILPers in Spain of Glasgow. Presumably without the guns.

Four POUM members and some International Brigade volunteers had been imprisoned as spies. Despite not speaking any Spanish, Maxton managed to secure their release. One ILP member who didn't make it home from Spain was Bob Smillie. The grandson of the miners' leader of the same name, Bob Smillie junior did not die in battle but in mysterious circumstances while a prisoner in Valencia.

The Spanish Civil War ended in defeat for the Republicans and ushered in decades of dictatorship and social repression. One million died during the war and the brutal peace which followed. The psychological scars of the conflict sear Spain to this day.

When the volunteers from the International Brigades came home to Scotland, many found it hard to get a job. Roddy MacFarquhar was one of them. Having helped repatriate them, the Foreign Office wrote to all British members of the International Brigades asking them to kindly refund the £3.19.3d it had cost per head.

Many British and Scottish cities gave them a much warmer welcome. At railway stations and in city squares, 'The Internationale' and 'The Red

Flag' were sung. In December 1938 almost 100 Scottish members of the International Brigades came by bus from London to Glasgow and an official reception in the City Hall.

One of the speakers was John MacCormick of the Scottish National Party, author of *The Flag in the Wind*. He welcomed home those who had taken up arms in 'the fight for freedom without which there is no civilisation'. Hugh Roberton, conductor of the fondly remembered Glasgow Orpheus Choir, told the returning Scottish brigaders that he was proud of them.

In Kirkcaldy, a rugged stone commemorates the Scots who went from Fife and the Lothians to the International Brigades:

> Not to a fanfare of trumpets,
> Nor even the skirl o' the pipes
> Not for the off'r of a shilling,
> Nor to see their names up in lights.
> Their call was a cry of anguish,
> From the hearts of the people of Spain,
> Some paid with their lives it is true:
> Their sacrifice was not in vain.

In Glasgow, the Scots who fought by the side of the people of Spain are remembered on the banks of the Clyde by the dramatic statue of Dolores Ibárruri, 'La Pasionaria', and her ringing words of defiance: 'Better to die on your feet than live forever on your knees.'

The battle for Spain was lost. The battle for Europe had yet to be fought.

29

On the Eve of War: The Empire Exhibition of 1938

Let the spirit of the Exhibition live on!

Visitors to the Scottish Exhibition of 1911 strolled around Kelvingrove Park in Glasgow's West End under sunshine and blue skies. Those who went to the Empire Exhibition at Bellahouston Park on the city's South Side in 1938 weren't so lucky. There were grey skies and end-of-the-world downpours throughout that summer. The twelve million visitors didn't let the weather stop them from enjoying themselves.

Read up on the Empire Exhibition and you immediately get the sense of a much more democratic affair than the 1911 event. Glasgow had changed over the intervening years. Now that the Depression was at last beginning to recede into the past, a new generation of working-class men and women had grown up not only to hope for more out of life but to expect it.

Clydesiders were still standing up for themselves. There was a strike at Bellahouston at the end of February, when joiners building the place demanded higher wages. The plumbers on site came out in sympathy but the dispute was quickly resolved. Nobody wanted to hinder the birth of the exhibition. The world was coming to Glasgow.

What the millions of visitors saw was a celebration of all the British Empire had to offer, a showcase for Glasgow and Scotland and a celebration of the modern age. This was the era of streamlining, of the Mallard steam engine designed by Sir Nigel Gresley, of the Coronation-style Glasgow city tram.

Bellahouston's pavilions reflected this modernist aesthetic. One of them is still there today in the park. The *Palace of Art* was built to last, while the other pavilions were temporary structures, although no less impressive for that. Other than the two Scottish pavilions, rich blue to match the Saltire, the pavilions were painted in soft pastel shades. Also helping lighten the dull weather during the summer of the exhibition were the colourful paths which linked the pavilions. Those were made of red asphalt mixed with chips of white granite from Skye and pink granite from Banffshire.

There was one nod back to tradition. *An Clachan*, the Highland Village, had been one of the most popular exhibits of 1911, fondly remembered by so many. So it was recreated at Bellahouston, only bigger and better. It had traditional white-walled cottages from Skye and black houses from the Outer Isles and a burn with a bridge over it which flowed into a small replica of a sea loch.

Raise your eyes from the old stones of *An Clachan* and you saw a soaring and thrillingly tall tower. The Tower of Empire soon became Tait's Tower, named for the architect in overall charge of the design of the exhibition. One of the foremost architects of his generation and already famous as the architect of Sydney Harbour Bridge, people were proud to claim Paisley buddy Mr Tait as one of their own.

Three hundred feet high, placed at the highest point of Bellahouston Park and visible for miles around by day and by night, Tait's Tower soon became the symbol of the exhibition: tall, futuristic, reaching for the skies and the years to come. Also reaching for the skies was the acrobat known as 'the Stratosphere Girl'. She turned and tumbled at the top of a 200-foot-high pole, accompanied by the gasps of those watching her from below.

At the South African Village people could taste passion-fruit juice. More familiar refreshment was on offer at the Empire Tea Pavilion. The colourful saris of the Indian women who served the tea were much admired. This being Clydeside, there had to be a *Palace of Engineering*. The Australian Pavilion featured a kangaroo, led by a lead. Scotland's major churches each had a pavilion.

The concert hall was off Bellahouston Drive, close to the junction with Paisley Road West. Gracie Fields sang there and returned to the exhibition on a few private visits. On one of those, Our Gracie stood in front of the exhibition's Atlantic Restaurant and wowed the crowds with 'Sally', one of her most famous numbers.

Paul Robeson, who at that time was living in Britain, gave two concerts at the Bellahouston Concert Hall. Shamefully, he was refused accommodation at one Glasgow hotel because of his colour. Thousands of Clydesiders loved him for his voice, his humanity and his politics. He donated his entire fee for his first concert at Bellahouston to the Spanish Civil War Relief Fund.

At his second concert he sang 'Ol' Man River', 'Swing Low, Sweet Chariot', 'Curly-Headed Baby' and a few Scottish songs, including one in Gaelic. He delighted the rebels and revolutionaries in his audience with 'The Ballad of Joe Hill', the tribute to the Swedish–American union leader shot by firing squad for the murder he did not commit.

There was respite from the rain with a brief dry spell in August. The downpours began again in September, matching one of the year's biggest hit songs, 'September in the Rain'. While the crowds were enjoying themselves at Bellahouston, Britain was holding its collective breath. Look at one of the photographs of the picturesque ruined kirk of *An Clachan* and you'll see a man sitting on a stone bench with his gas mask in a carrying case slung over his shoulder.

In September 1938, while the Empire Exhibition continued to draw in the crowds, Britain's prime minister Neville Chamberlain was flying backwards and forwards to Germany to parley with Hitler. He made three separate visits there that month.

Hitler was determined to annexe the Sudetenland, the area in the west of Czechoslovakia populated by ethnic Germans. Chamberlain called for talks. One country could not simply march into another and take over a part of it. Besides which, the Nazi leader wanted more *Lebensraum* for the German people. He wasn't going to stop at the Sudetenland. Not present at the talks, Czechoslovakia's fate was decided by Germany, France, Britain and Italy.

As tension mounted, Britain hoped for the best but prepared for the worst. Defensive trenches were dug in towns and cities, plans for evacuating children from the industrial areas were drawn up and gas masks were issued to all. Children had their own special small ones, known as Mickey Mouse masks. Their mothers were advised to play a game with them every day so they got used to them.

There were masks which fitted over babies' prams but no masks for cats and dogs. When war broke out a year later, some pet owners made the heartbreaking decision to have their animals put to sleep rather than run the risk of them suffering in a gas attack.

Fear of air raids was high. Nobody could forget Guernica. In 1938 Spanish cities were still being bombed. Terror at the prospect of a gas attack went back to the trenches of the First World War. Everyone had seen the pitiful photographs of soldiers blinded by mustard gas, able to shuffle forward only because each had a hand laid on the shoulder of the comrade in front of him.

On the Clyde, the *Queen Elizabeth* was launched by the lady for whom she'd been named, the late Queen Mother. It was a low-key affair. This Cunarder was destined to spend her first years afloat painted in the drab colours of the Grey Funnel Line, the Royal Navy.

In Clydebank and Glasgow people tried to reassure themselves and each other that the Germans would never bomb the west of Scotland. It was too far away from Germany. Their planes couldn't carry sufficient fuel to make it. Pioneered by Scotsman Sir Robert Watson-Watt, radar was still in its infancy. How would the Germans ever be able to find the Clyde among all the other rivers, lochs and inlets of the West Coast?

There was a strange atmosphere, one of fear and gallows humour, a sense that the fight needed to come, that there had to be a showdown with Hitler. After his second meeting with the Nazi leader, Chamberlain made his famous speech: 'How horrible, fantastic, incredible it is that we should be digging trenches and trying on gas masks because of a quarrel in a faraway country between people of whom we know nothing.'

With the benefit of hindsight, the policy of Appeasement has been much criticized. Yet it's all too easy to forget how desperately Chamberlain and so many other Britons wanted to avoid another European war. Memories remained vivid of the last one, in which Chamberlain himself lost a brother in the trenches. Despite Spain, despite the rise of fascism, young people didn't want to believe there was going to be another war. That horror was something which belonged to their parents' generation.

At Munich on 29 September 1938, Chamberlain, French leader Daladier and Italy's dictator Mussolini met Hitler. Together they decided the Sudetenland would be incorporated into Hitler's Germany within the space of the next two weeks. Neville Chamberlain flew home with his now infamous piece of paper and a promise of peace in our time.

The tension of the long, wet summer exploded into acclaim for the Prime Minister. He was even nominated for the Nobel Peace Prize. When Chamberlain entered the House of Commons, only four MPs did not rise to their feet and applaud him. James Maxton was one of them.

When Maxton did stand up to contribute to the debate, he spoke of the ordinary people of Germany, allowed no voice under Nazi rule, and of his German socialist friends, some now in concentration camps, some now in exile. Maxton reluctantly congratulated the Prime Minister on what he had achieved but told him and the House that this was only a breathing space. Not everyone had the courage to look so clearly into the future.

The celebrations for the last night of the Empire Exhibition at Bellahouston Park in October 1938 were euphoric. They danced 'The Lambeth Walk' in the rain. They gazed open-mouthed at the sky as three aircraft staged a mock attack on Bellahouston Park. Caught in searchlights manned by the City of Glasgow Squadron of the RAF, the bandits were successfully driven off.

Then the lights went down and the vast crowd fell silent. Only Tait's Tower was lit up, standing out like a lighthouse in a dark ocean. The crowd sang 'God Save the King' and 'Auld Lang Syne'. The Union Jack on the tower was lowered and the lights began to fade. Once the darkness was complete, a voice rang out: 'Let the spirit of the Exhibition live on!'

It was over. The future beckoned. Whatever it might hold.

30

The Clydebank Blitz

Make for where the fires are greatest!

Some came from Beauvais in France, flying up the Irish Sea towards their target. Most travelled through the March night from Holland, northern Germany, Norway and Denmark. As they crossed over the Scottish coast near Edinburgh, people on the ground heard wave after wave of them pass above their heads. Every ten minutes there were more.

The drone of their engines could be heard as far south as Hull and as far north as Aberdeen. They were Heinkel 111s and Junker 88s. There were 236 of them and they were the German Luftwaffe, intent on dropping their deadly cargo on the shipyards, oil depots and munitions factories of Clydebank. The idea that the Germans would never be able to find the Clyde was proved horribly wrong on the devastating nights of 13 and 14 March 1941.

Clydesiders had watched the relentless bombing of London and other English cities over the winter of 1940 and shivered. The generation which lived through the Second World War came to have immense respect for the courage and resilience of Londoners, pounded by German bombers night after night for months on end.

The hideous whooping-banshee wail of the air-raid siren went off shortly after nine o'clock. It was a chilling sound but there had been a lot of false alarms and for a moment everyone thought this was just another one. In Singer's, turned over for the duration to the making of munitions, there was a daily sweepstake as to when the alarm would go off each night. It soon became clear this one was for real.

Those whose job it was to watch for such things had been pretty sure Clydebank was going to be bombed that night, first picking up the telltale signs of a German radio navigation beam and then spotting individual Luftwaffe reconnaissance flights. A decision was made not to alert the population. That might cause panic and a trek up into the Old Kilpatricks, the hills behind the town. Civil disorder might ensue. This was Red Clydeside.

One young woman whose father worked at John Brown's was already in bed and asleep in the family home close to the shipyard down on Dumbarton Road. Working long hours as a nurse, she was trying to catch up on her sleep. Wrenched from her much-needed rest, she demanded irritably that whoever was slamming those doors should kindly stop right now. Then she realized the banging doors were sticks of dropping bombs. The people who experienced the Clydebank Blitz use a distinctive word to describe the sound of death and destruction falling to earth. *Crump. Crump. Crump.* Like the footsteps of a malevolent giant, drawing nearer each time, the ground trembling with the impact.

Civilians headed for the shelters. Civil-defence volunteers made for the control centre in the basement of Clydebank's public library on Dumbarton Road. They'd just come back from it after weekly training. One ARP warden who'd already undressed reached for the trousers he'd laid over the back of a chair. There was a bomber's moon that night but inside a small house the darkness of the blackout was all-encompassing. The ARP warden slid both legs down the same trouser leg and promptly fell over. He swore comprehensively and started again.

The main squadron of Luftwaffe bombers was preceded by pathfinders. They dropped flares and then hundreds of incendiaries to light the way, bathing the town in an eerie greenish glow. One young woman who saw the flares float down thought they looked pretty, like fairy lights. Only later did she realize what a risk she'd taken by standing there and watching them.

Clydebank was soon to be ablaze with light. The timber yard at Singer's was hit, creating a huge bonfire. The distillery at Yoker went up, setting fire to the whisky, the sweet smell drifting over the town.

Up in Glasgow's maternity hospital at Rottenrow a junior nurse was told off for standing looking out of the windows. Criss-crossed though they were with brown parcel tape, an explosion some distance away could still shatter them into a thousand pieces. A nursing sister tried to reassure anxious mothers of newborn babies: 'Don't worry. It's Clydebank that's getting it.' One of the young mothers became distraught. She was from Clydebank.

Some bombs fell on the west end of Glasgow, one in Dudley Drive in Hyndland, others on Hillhead and Partick, another in Napiershall Street, off Great Western Road. An expectant mother living in a flat there took shelter in the crypt of a church at the top of Byres Road, in what is now the Òran Mór theatre.

That young woman's husband was working the night shift as a railway shunter in Rothesay Dock, at Clydebank. He and a workmate took shelter under a wagon, from where they squinted up at the night sky. In a surreal situation, the young man found himself thinking that the colours lighting up the sky were quite beautiful. The two men later discovered the wagon under which they had taken cover contained explosives.

When the workmate returned the next morning to the Holy City he found that his home no longer existed. The German bombers devastated the flat-roofed houses which had reminded the sailor of Jerusalem. Hundreds died here. Only yards away, the nearby cinema, always called 'the La Scala', survived the onslaught. People in Clydebank have talked ever since about how strange that was.

While the bombs were still dropping a nurse went to Radnor Park Church Hall, where casualties had been taken. ARP warden Mrs Hyslop was in charge there. Whether she was the same Mrs Hyslop of the Clydebank rent strikes is not clear. A young nurse appeared, saw there was no doctor and took an injured baby in an ambulance she had commandeered up to the Western Infirmary, in Glasgow. The Western's accident and emergency department was busy dealing with the local casualties of the raid. Plenty of qualified doctors were on duty, to the frustration of a group of medical students who were desperate to help.

When the young nurse appeared the students made the decision to head for Clydebank. As they were all unqualified, although only nine days away from their finals, the Western's medical superintendent refused to give them any medical supplies. They approached a nursing sister, Isabella MacDonald.

In his definitive *The Clydebank Blitz* I.M.M. MacPhail relates how Sister MacDonald immediately gave them what they needed: 'a comprehensive range of medical requisites, tied up in eight bedsheets like washerwoman's bundles'. The only thing she was not prepared to give them was morphine. The infirmary's senior medical officer had made it very clear that students could not be allowed to administer this.

Stopped by a policeman as they neared Clydebank because of the danger of unexploded bombs, they explained what they were about.

'Make for where the fires are greatest!' he told them. They made it to Radnor Park Church Hall, where a cry of relief ran round: 'The doctors have come! The doctors have come!'

They saved lives that night, tended to many of the wounded, although without the ability to use morphine to relieve terrible pain caused by terrible injuries. As a direct result of their experiences during the Clydebank Blitz, it was subsequently agreed that final-year medics would be allowed to give the drug to those injured in air raids.

Only seven houses in Clydebank were left undamaged by the Clydebank Blitz. How many people were killed or injured became a controversial issue. Although German bombing raids on British cities were reported during the war, those cities were often not named and the number of casualties tended to be played down for the sake of morale.

This could work both ways. Bombing raids on Liverpool, Clydebank and Greenock alike were sometimes reported only as having been 'on a northern port', giving people the sense that their own town's suffering had not been honoured. It was the same with the number of casualties. When told that 500 people had been killed in Clydebank, one member of the local Home Guard bitterly asked, 'Which street?'

More realistic estimates put the numbers who died in Glasgow and Clydebank during the Blitz of March 1941 at 1,200, with 1,100 seriously injured. In 1954 the Commonwealth War Graves Commission compiled a list of as many names as they could establish. The list was placed in the Roll of Honour at Westminster Abbey.

On the eerily quiet morning after the first night of the Clydebank Blitz, a man through from Arbroath selling fish from a van eventually found a working public phone in Glasgow and reassured his family that he was safe. He kept repeating the same words: 'It was terrible. It was terrible. It was terrible.' Over and over again, that was all he could say.

Animals had suffered too. Only a small proportion of them had been put to sleep because of their owners' fears of gas attacks. One of the most distressing sights in the aftermath of the Clydebank Blitz was that of dogs and cats which had lost their homes and their humans running around wild and beginning to form themselves into packs. They were rounded up within the next few days and, sadly, humanely put to sleep.

Many caged birds were luckier. As I.M.M. MacPhail put it in *The Clydebank Blitz*:

On the Friday and Saturday mornings of the raids a not uncommon sight was that of a homeless family with one of them in charge of a canary or a budgerigar in a cage, which remained with them wherever they went – to the Rest Centre in Clydebank, to the Rest Centre in the Vale of Leven or elsewhere.

The workers were heroes now. As the *Glasgow Herald* put it, 'Clydebuilt has hitherto applied to its ships. All that it implies in rugged strength and reliability in times of stress has been won by its people this past week.'

For weeks afterwards, the young woman who'd thought the flares were like fairy lights couldn't hold a cup and saucer without the two of them rattling together. Years later, speaking of the compensation paid out after the raids, she said in her best deadpan tones, 'You would never have guessed there had been that many pianos in Clydebank.'

Always the humour. Running through all these stories even in the darkest of times, this quicksilver vein of wit is the birthright of the people of Red Clydeside.

Legacy

M uch ink has been spilled in the debate over whether Red Clydeside ever brought Scotland close to revolution. Personally, I don't think so, certainly not in the sense of the convulsion which seized Russia in 1917. Different country, different history, different kind of people. Or maybe it's because Scottish mothers bring us all up to be too well-mannered. You can't have a polite revolution. Or a cheery one.

I find it sad that many historians who have written about Red Clydeside view it only in these terms. Since the revolution never happened, they disdainfully declare the whole thing to have been a failure. In addition to so often rendering a thrilling and passionate period of history boring, I also believe they're missing the point. Nor do I think it's fair to judge the early Red Clydesiders by the subsequent history and development of the Labour Party.

Red Clydeside did bring about a revolution, a sea change in thought, attitudes and expectations. The legacy is all around us, so much part of our daily lives we often hardly notice it, take it completely for granted. In 1922 James Maxton said that he and his fellow Clydeside Labour MPs wanted to abolish poverty. Although they may not have entirely succeeded in that, they did improve the lives of hundreds of thousands of their fellow citizens. Life for the majority in the Glasgow of 2011 is immeasurably better than it was in 1911: at home, in the workplace, in the health of men, women and children, in educational opportunity.

The Red Clydesiders inspired their fellow man and woman to expect more and demand more, for themselves, their children, their community and their country. They encouraged them always to ask *why* and to speak out whenever they saw something which wasn't fair. It's a simple principle but one which in Scotland runs bone-deep. You might call it rebel spirit.

In 1971, under the leadership of shop stewards of whom the most well known became Jimmy Reid and Jimmy Airlie, the workers at the Clydebank shipyard which had been John Brown's fought to keep their jobs and to keep shipbuilding on the Clyde. The late Jimmy Reid made a famous speech at the Upper Clyde Shipbuilders' work-in: 'There will be no hooliganism, there will be no vandalism, there will be no bevying' – cue dramatic pause – 'because the world is watching us.'

Responding as people did to the UCS war cry of 'the right to work', support came from throughout the UK and from some unexpected quarters. During the dispute, a florist delivered a bouquet of red roses addressed to Jimmy Reid at the yard. Checking the gift card, one of the shop stewards told the others it had only one word on it: 'Lenin'.

'Lenin's deid!' someone protested.

'No' the one who spells his name Lennon,' came the laconic reply. John and Yoko Lennon sent a generous cheque towards the UCS fighting fund along with their blood-red roses.

When Glasgow University's students chose him to be their rector a few years later, Jimmy Reid made another famous speech:

> The rat race is for rats. We're not rats. We're human beings. Reject the insidious pressures in society that would blunt your critical faculties to all that is happening around you, that would caution silence in the face of injustice lest you jeopardise your chances of promotion and self-advancement. That is how it starts, and before you know where you are, you're a fully paid up member of the rat-pack. The price is too high. It entails the loss of your dignity and human spirit. Or as Christ put it, 'What doth it profit a man if he gain the whole world and suffer the loss of his soul?'

Pure Red Clydeside. An instinctive and passionate sense of democracy, justice and fairness. The unshakeable belief that we all owe each other care and respect. Stirring words well chosen to put the message across. The conviction that the pen is mightier than the sword. The familiarity with the beauty and power of the language of the King James Bible. Jimmy Reid also quoted Robert Burns in his Glasgow University speech. Like a band at a demonstration, Burns always has to be there too.

Time and again while I was researching this book, I came across these same bright threads which link each generation of Scotland's people to those who came before them. Whether it was Davie Kirkwood or James Maxton, one man born into poverty, the other into comparative financial comfort, there's always that love of language, love of poetry, love of Scotland and the unshakeable conviction that this is a country more than able to run its own affairs.

James Maxton had something to say about revolution:

> The biggest mental revolution necessary is, I believe, the mental revolution which enables a man or woman to desire a social order in which no one will be better or worse off than himself or herself, a social order in which men and women do not get added prestige by the number of pounds they can show in their bank books, the numbers of superfluous rooms they have in their houses, or the number of spare suits of clothes they have.

Tom Johnston wrote an epitaph for James Maxton which could equally apply to himself, Helen Crawfurd, Mary Barbour and so many more of the Red Clydesiders:

> He played a forever memorable part in changing a public opinion which was complacent and acquiescent in face of needless suffering in the midst of plenty, to one that was resolutely determined upon fairer shares for all.

Warm and witty, kind-hearted and generous, interested in everything and everyone, the spirited men and women of Red Clydeside had one goal they set above all other things. It came before their own self-interest and self-advancement. Some sacrificed their liberty for it, some their health, some even their lives. Their aim was this: to create a fair and just society, one in which the children of the poor had as much right as the children of the rich to good health, happiness, education, creative expression and opportunity.

The world has changed. Politics has changed. We've all become deeply cynical about politicians. Political earthquakes or not, we all recognize the truth in the old saying that we Scots don't need enemies, we have each other.

Yet one thing does not change: the democratic spirit of the Scottish people, the belief that we're all Jock Tamson's bairns. Whatever our political views and the nuances within them, many of us still hold the ideals of the Red Clydesiders close to our hearts. It's what makes us who we are.

Select Bibliography

Bell, Thomas, *Pioneering Days*, Lawrence and Wishart, London, 1941

Brown, Gordon, *Maxton*, Mainstream Publishing, Edinburgh, 1986

Buchan, Alasdair, *The Right to Work: The Story of the Upper Clyde Confrontation*, Calder and Boyars, London, 1972

Canning, Audrey, 'Margaret Irwin – S.T.U.C. 100 Years', *Scottish Marxist Voice*, Issue 6, 1997

Casciani, Elizabeth, *Oh, How We Danced!*, Mercat Press, Edinburgh, 1994

Chalmers, A.K., *The Health of Glasgow, 1818–1925*, Glasgow Corporation, Glasgow, 1930

Crawfurd, Helen, Unpublished Memoir, Marx Memorial Library, London (copy held by Gallacher Memorial Library, Glasgow Caledonian University)

Damer, Seán, *Rent Strike!: The Clydebank Rent Struggles of the 1920s*, Clydebank Library, Glasgow, 1982

Gallacher, William, *The Chosen Few*, Lawrence and Wishart, London, 1940

Gallacher, William, *Revolt on the Clyde: An Autobiography*, Lawrence and Wishart, London, 1980

Glasgow Labour History Workshop, *The Singer Strike: Clydebank, 1911*, Clydebank District Libraries, 1989

Gray, Daniel, *Homage to Caledonia: Scotland and the Spanish Civil War*, Luath Press, Edinburgh, 2008

Hanham, H.J., *Scottish Nationalism*, Faber and Faber Ltd, London, 1969

Hood, John, *The History of Clydebank*, Parthenon Publishing/Clydebank District Council, Carnforth, 1988

Johnston, Thomas, *Our Scots Noble Families*, Forward Publishing Co. Ltd, Glasgow, 1909

Johnston, Thomas, *The History of the Working Classes in Scotland*, Forward Publishing Co. Ltd, Glasgow, 1922

Johnston, Thomas, *Memories*, Collins, London, 1952

Kenna, Rudolph, *Old Glasgow Shops*, Glasgow City Libraries & Archives, Glasgow, 1996

Kinchin, Perilla, *Tea and Taste: The Glasgow Tea Rooms 1875–1975*, White Cockade Publishing, Dorchester, 1991

Kinchin, Perilla, *Miss Cranston: Patron of Charles Rennie Mackintosh*, NMS-Publishing, Edinburgh, 1999

King, Elspeth, *The Scottish Women's Suffrage Movement*, People's Palace Museum, Glasgow Green, 1978

King, Elspeth, *The Hidden History of Glasgow's Women*, Mainstream Publishing, Edinburgh, 1993

Kirkwood, David, *My Life of Revolt*, Harrap & Co., London, 1935

Leneman, Leah, *The Scottish Suffragettes*, NMS-Publishing, Edinburgh, 2000

Lewenhak, Sheila, *Women and Trade Unions*, Ernest Benn, London, 1977

MacCormick, John, *The Flag in the Wind*, Birlinn, Edinburgh, 2008

Maclean, John, *Condemned from the Dock: John Maclean's speech from the dock 1918,* International Marxist Group, London, undated

McKean, Walker & Walker, *Central Glasgow: An Illustrated Architectural Guide (Limited Edition)*, The Rutland Press, Edinburgh, 1999

McKinlay, Alan, *Making Ships Making Men: Working for John Brown's – Between the Wars*, Clydebank District Libraries, Clydebank, 1991

McLean, Iain, *The Legend of Red Clydeside*, John Donald, Edinburgh, 1983

MacPhail, I.M.M., *The Clydebank Blitz*, Clydebank District Libraries, 1974

McShane, Harry (Introduction), *Glasgow 1919: The Story of the 40 Hours Strike*, Molendinar Press, Kirkintilloch, undated

McShane, Harry, *Three Days That Shook Edinburgh*, AK Press, Oakland, California, USA, 1994

Milton, Nan, *John Maclean*, Pluto Press, London, 1973

Muir, James Hamilton, *Glasgow in 1901*, White Cockade Publishing, Dorchester, 2001

Rowbotham, Sheila, *New World for Women: Stella Browne, Socialist*

Feminist, Pluto Press, London, 1977

Sanger, Margaret, *The Autobiography of Margaret Sanger*, Dover Publications, 2004

Smyth, J.J., *Labour in Glasgow, 1896–1936, Socialism, Suffrage, Sectarianism*, Tuckwell Press, East Linton, 2000

Stewart, William, *J. Keir Hardie: A Biography*, Cassell, London, 1921

Struthers, Sheila, *Old Clydebank*, Stenlake Publishing, Ayrshire, 2001

Young, James D., *The Very Bastards of Creation: Scottish International Radicalism 1707–1995: A Biographical Study*, Clydeside Press, Glasgow, 1996

Newspapers Consulted

The Bailie

The Bulletin

Daily Record

Evening News (Glasgow)

Evening Times

Forward

Glasgow Herald

The Scotsman

Online Resources

Glasgow Digital Library: gdl.cdlr.strath.ac.uk

Hansard Online: hansard.millbanksystems.com

National Library of Scotland: www.nls.uk

Oxford Dictionary of National Biography: www.oxforddnb.com

Scran: www.scran.ac.uk

Spartacus Educational: www.spartacus.schoolnet.co.uk

Index